The Paranoid Apocalypse

ELIE WIESEL CENTER FOR JUDAIC STUDIES SERIES
General Editor: Steven T. Katz

The Shtetl: New Evaluations
Edited by Steven T. Katz

The Paranoid Apocalypse:
A Hundred-Year Retrospective on The Protocols of the Elders of Zion
Edited by Richard Landes and Steven T. Katz

The Paranoid Apocalypse

A Hundred-Year Retrospective on
The Protocols of the Elders of Zion

EDITED BY
Richard Landes and Steven T. Katz

NEW YORK UNIVERSITY PRESS
New York and London

NEW YORK UNIVERSITY PRESS
New York and London
www.nyupress.org

References to Internet websites (URLs) were accurate at the time of writing.
Neither the author nor New York University Press is responsible for URLs
that may have expired or changed since the manuscript was prepared.

Library of Congress Cataloging-in-Publication Data

The paranoid apocalypse : a hundred-year retrospective on the
Protocols of the elders of Zion / edited by Richard Landes and Steven T. Katz.
p. cm. — (Elie Wiesel Center for Judaic Studies series)
Includes index.
ISBN 978-0-8147-4892-3 (cl : alk. paper)
ISBN 978-0-8147-4893-0 (ebook)
ISBN 978-0-8147-4945-6 (ebook)
1. Protocols of the wise men of Zion. 2. Antisemitism.
I. Landes, Richard Allen. II. Katz, Steven T., 1944–
DS145.P7P37   2011
305.892'4—dc22   2011028192

New York University Press books are printed on acid-free paper,
and their binding materials are chosen for strength and durability.
We strive to use environmentally responsible suppliers and materials
to the greatest extent possible in publishing our books.

Manufactured in the United States of America

10 9 8 7 6 5 4 3 2 1

Contents

Introduction

The Protocols *at the Dawn of the 21st Century*

RICHARD LANDES AND STEVEN T. KATZ

This volume of essays results from a conference held at the Elie Weisel Center for Jewish Studies at Boston University with the collaboration of the Center for Millennial Studies at Boston University a century after the publication of the *Protocols of the Elders of Zion*.

The *Protocols* stands out as both one of the most malicious forgeries in history—"an atrocity-producing narrative"—and the most widely distributed forgery in the world. Soon after publication, believers translated its "revelations" about an international Jewish conspiracy to enslave mankind into dozens of languages and spread the text from its Russian foyer to the rest of Europe, the Americas, and as far as Japan. At the height of its first wave of influence (1905–1945), it played a key role in inspiring and justifying the Nazi attempt at genocide of the Jews.

After the catastrophe wrought by a great and powerful nation seized by a genocidal paranoia in response to the conspiracy it perceived via the *Protocols*, those who vanquished it renounced and denounced the mad text. Modernity had won, and the broad public consensus held that "*Nie Wieder*" [Never Again] would we see either the "bloody tide" or the forged fantasies that fueled it. The *Protocols* quickly became a taboo subject in the West. Anyone who referred to it incurred the stigma of both ignorance and hate-mongering. Civil society, with its egalitarian rules, its scientific skepticism, and its high levels of tolerance for the "other," had won the battle against xenophobic paranoia. New, unthinkable institutions of international cooperation— the United Nations, the European Union—arose and survived in this new dispensation.

One might call this postwar attitude, embodied in Norman Cohn's path-breaking and disturbing study, *Warrant for Genocide*, the "modern" solution to the *Protocols*. "Positivist historiography," dedicated to find out "what really happened" (however the scientific chips about objective reality fall), condemned the *Protocols*, just as it condemned the forged evidence in the Dreyfus Affair. After the Nazis, the same "positivist" trials that, in 1923, had failed to quell belief in the *Protocols,* became normative. Sadder but wiser, the post-Holocaust world adopted the "modernist" position—the *Protocols* are a malevolent forgery, an "atrociously written piece of reactionary balderdash."[1] And, hand in hand with that conclusion, modernists held that anti-Semitism is a historically proven social and political toxin banished from legitimate discussion by political correctness.

This itself is part of a much broader consensus on the nature of the public sphere and what constitutes sane discourse in the period after the Holocaust. Human rights, respect for other people and cultures, self-criticism, historical accuracy all participate in a mild international experiment in transformative millennialism: the universal inauguration of civil society. People—Jews and Gentiles—who express astonishment at the return to prominence of the *Protocols* in our day represent the intellectual products of just such a paradigmatic approach to the public discussion in which the *Protocols* was understandably and justifiably banned.[2]

When Richard Landes first read the *Protocols*, while teaching at Columbia in 1985, he was part of this modern consensus. He was surprised by what he read. It turned out he had been hearing echoes of this text—what Stephen Bronner calls "analogs"—all the time, in particular from radicals at Berkeley, where he had spent the previous years arguing with them on Sproul Plaza about the Israelis in Lebanon. "The Jews control the media . . . the Jews control the markets [including the *oil* markets] . . . the Israelis are doing to the Palestinians what the Nazis did to them . . . Israel is part of a conspiracy with America to rule the world." An Iranian group even handed out a flier with excerpts from the *Protocols*. When he realized that the teachings of the *Protocols* were filtering back into political discourse, he suggested a scholarly edition, one that allowed informed citizens to become aware of the sources of such paranoid and demonizing rhetoric.

Then came his second surprise: Virtually everyone disagreed with him. As Fritz Stern, the senior professor in German history in the department, put it pithily, "You think you're inoculating people, but you're spreading the disease." That was 1985, when the *Protocols* seemed a dead letter to most, and keeping it quiet seemed like a good idea. They were halcyon days when Sartrian analysts figured that, with anti-Semitism nearly vanished from America, the Jews would soon follow.[3]

That was before the Internet, before Amazon.com, before everyone had access to the *Protocols*, not just from Iranian students' fliers at UCB or Louis

Farrakhan's bookstores but also from Walmart. That was before cable television and growing sophistication in movie-making in the Arab world produced serial programs bringing the *Protocols* to television screens around the world. And that was before, beginning in October 2000, the "New Anti-Semitism" in word and deed entered its global phase, allowing the virus that Fritz Stern had spoken of to spread far and wide, and before 9/11 triggered a wave of conspiracy theories that revived the *Protocols* in America, as Marc Levin suggests in his film, *The Protocols of the Elders of Zion*.[4] Its currency today—both as a text and as an analog, as a conspiratorial idea—in so many circles, right and left, high and low, red state, blue state, has to alarm anyone who keeps track of such things and understands the stakes. How can we understand this disturbing revival?

The chapters in this volume attempt to provide the reader with a range of information and analytic tools to understand four major questions:

1. What are the cultural origins of the *Protocols*?
2. What explains the *Protocols*' continued appeal?
3. Under what conditions does belief in the *Protocols* get activated and produce atrocities?
4. What, if anything, can be done to oppose the spread of belief in so dishonest and disastrous a libel?

Three major themes emerged from the conference in terms of the power exercised by the *Protocols*—(1) the psychological nature of paranoia in its appeal, (2) the problem of "truth" and the exegetical shiftiness that detaches the text from its empirical moorings as a forgery, and (3) the power of apocalyptic belief in "activating" the text as a social and political player. We present first two conceptual essays as introduction, then essays, primarily in historical order of topic.

Apocalyptic Conspiracy, Moral Failure, and the Crises of Modernity

We open this volume with two chapters that address this broader context on the one hand from the perspective of the historical *longue durée*, and on the other from a psychological one.

The first chapter (by Richard Landes) explores the way in which the *Protocols* takes up a very long and largely dominant strain of political thought, articulated by the ancient Athenians as "the law that those who can, do what they will, and those who cannot, suffer what they must." This represents the

Machiavellian position in fact rejected by the very text the *Protocols* plagiarized, the *Dialogue in Hell between Machiavelli and Montesquieu*. Eli Sagan, in a remarkable book on the origins and dangers of democracy, called this position the "paranoid imperative": *Rule or be ruled.*

This approach systematically projects the lust to dominate onto others, thereby justifying preemptive aggression: *Do onto others before they do onto you.* To understand both the logic and the appeal of the *Protocols*, one has to appreciate how profoundly consistent that projection is, how much it has shaped political relations both between elites and commoners and between states for millennia, during which "democracy" was a dirty word. Both Thrasymachus and Plato—"might makes right" and "justice is harmony"—at least agreed that democracy was a recipe for chaos and tyranny.

When one factors in the anxieties of freedom so lucidly analyzed by Erich Fromm more than a half-century ago,[5] one can understand how a modernity built on egalitarian slogans and democratic freedoms represents a terrifying anomaly to this "political philosophy" of *longue durée*. For people steeped in this tradition, taking away their right to dominate *must* be part of a larger plan to destroy them; democracy *must* be a prelude to slavery. No one can actually push democracy and its correlates—free press, legal equality of commoner and aristocrats, free markets—honestly. There must be a hidden agenda, and that agenda must be domination.

The Jew, in the *Protocols*, is, thus, necessarily a *demopath*—someone who uses and manipulates democratic values as a way to trap people for a despotic agenda, using the promise of democracy to enslave people. Only a dupe and a fool could sincerely support human freedom. The forgers of the text reason that the Jews can be neither. Behind every crusader for freedom and equality, warns the *Protocols*, lies a tyrant in waiting. And since both the French and the Russian revolutions rapidly turned from their egalitarian promises to dictatorial terror, the *Protocols* struck many an observer in the 1920s as prophetic. The *Protocols* was the demopath's Bible, and its publication ripped off modernity's beneficent mask to reveal its "true" malevolent agenda.

The more widespread modernity became, the more threatening the process appeared. And the more modernity has spread, the more globalization now penetrates into cultures the world over, the more hostility it provokes. By the early 20th century, a struggle of cosmic proportions emerged, most visibly among the humiliated and defeated Germans: This was an apocalyptic war in which "paranoid imperative" shifted from "rule or be ruled" to *exterminate or be exterminated.*[6]

Strozier's chapter explores from a psychological perspective "the links between paranoia and the apocalyptic and how and why that relates to violence." Rooted in a therapeutic practice that involved close contact with paranoids, he offers observations that take us inside the experience of people in the grip of such compelling beliefs.

> The paranoid lives in a world of heated exaggerations, one in which empathy has been leached out and one that lacks as well humor, creativity, and wisdom. The paranoid lives in a world of shame and humiliation, of suspiciousness, aggressivity, and dualisms that separate out all good from pure evil . . . grandiose and megalomaniacal and always has an apocalyptic view of history that contains within it a mythical sense of time. Many paranoids are very smart . . . paranoia focuses all of one's cognitive abilities in ways that can make one's schemes intellectually daunting—which is why I have always thought that paranoia is a pathology of choice for the gifted.

Apocalyptic intensity creates a self-enforcing cycle, throwing the paranoid into a projective feedback loop.

> The awful and disgusting evil other, who is created from within the self of the paranoid, serves as an objective correlative to stir desire and fantasy deep within the paranoid, who in turn strives to find relief by intensifying the imago of the evil other through more projection. The apocalyptic other is always objectified as the subjective self in this way, becoming in the process a ludicrous tangle of desire, power, and malice.

Strozier's paranoids experience a sense of fragmentation that closely resembles what some argue is the experience of modernity for many—what Sayid Qutb referred to as the "hideous schizophrenia" that the West insists on inflicting on the world.

> But to think in self terms, what we can surmise is that the paranoid's response to the *crisis of fragmentation* is a frantic attempt to stave off what he *inevitably experiences as the psychological equivalent of death* by constructing an alternate universe of *imagined dangers populated with projective imagoes of inner experience.* That new reality fills in for the old. The new reality is bursting with terror and is not a stable terrain—paranoia, like anxiety, spreads—but *at least this new world of malice is familiar.*

And, above all, the paranoid is a victim. Part of his megalomania of paranoia is believing that the entire world has nothing better to do with its time than scheme against him. And victimization justifies violence, what Strozier calls the "extraordinary sequence from victimization to violence."

> The paranoid intimately understands the secret world of evil he has created in his projective schemes. His rigid dualistic outlook further removes him from the malice as it loads him with virtue and righteousness. That other becomes, then, the embodiment of evil and not only can but must be dispensed with. In its more extreme cases, when fantasy turns to action, the paranoid feels more than simply an allowance to kill. It becomes an obligation. And, since in the paranoid world one acts on behalf of absolute righteousness, killing becomes healing, as Lifton wrote so eloquently about with the Nazis, or as Aum Shinrikyo, the apocalyptic Japanese cults in the early 1990s, sought in its wild schemes to carry out Armageddon.

Medieval Prologue: Cosmic Christian Anxiety and Global Modern Paranoia

Norman Cohn has laid out the medieval contributions to the *Protocols*, in particular the pervasive medieval Christian association of Jews with the devil and, by extension, of the Jews as forerunner and agents of the Antichrist. Jeffrey Woolf explores further elements in this medieval matrix in this volume, some directly linked to this diabolic Jew: the assumption of an undying hatred of Jews for Christians and the tendency to see the Jew not as person but as symbol. In particular, he focuses on the 12th- and 13th-century awakening of Christian thinkers to the development of Talmudic and (later) Qabbalistic thinking among Jews, which fed both their fears and their hatreds.

Here he finds an interesting paradox that sheds light on one of the major hermeneutic problems posed by belief in a patent forgery such as the *Protocols* (Hagemeister, Mehlman, Berlet). Both the Talmud and the Qabbalah are at once attacked as lies and scanned for proof of Christianity's truth: The selfsame text embodies both sacred and satanic "truth." The paradox embodies the deeply contradictory relationship of medieval Christians to Jews, a schizophrenic ambivalence that would only intensify under conditions of Jewish freedom in modern society. As Trachtenberg pointed out long ago, the demonization of Jews reached its height under *early modern* conditions, in the 16th and 17th centuries, when witchcraft paranoia struck so often, particularly in the modernizing regions of northern Europe, especially in Germany.

In the second chapter on the medieval origins of the *Protocols*, Johannes Heil explores the ways in which the anti-Semitism of medieval Christians produced narrative lines very similar to the conspiratorial one that lies at the base of the *Protocols* forgery. Heil starts with the the novel *Biarritz* (1886), the text that prefigures the shift in antidemocratic conspiracy theory from the evil Masons trying to enslave mankind (ca. 1800) to the evil Jews (ca. 1900). Here, in one of the chapters, we find out that, every hundred years, an international gathering of rabbis meets in the graveyard in Prague to advance their long and patient plan to enslave mankind. "'Eighteen centuries our enemies dominated—the new century will be Israel's century' the assembly concluded."[7] This chapter had a far greater impact than the eight-volume novel in which it was embedded and circulated widely as an independent tract. And it resembles closely the tale told by the mid-13th-century chronicler Matthew of Paris of the alleged enthusiasm with which Jews greeted the news of the Mongol hordes coming from the East in the 1230s.

Comparing modern and medieval versions of the cosmic conspiracy, Heil finds important similarities—secret meetings of an international elite, use of complex communications systems, a malevolent conspiracy to harm Christians and benefit Jews, cosmic/apocalyptic stakes. But he also finds two telling contrasts. In the medieval versions, the Jews have Christian allies who are essential to their success and they work, however maleficently, as part of a divine plan. In modern versions, the Jews (like the Promethean West) have broken free of a divine framework; they work alone, independently. In this desacralized tale, Jewish malevolence has survived the discarding of both the sacred and the satanic. Jews are no longer "messengers of the Antichrist" in any formal sense but agents of unnamable and unmitigated dread. Ironically, as modernity cast off the shackles of medieval theology, it retained avatars of medieval anti-Semitism and apocalypticism that, in the new, desacralized and technologically empowered setting, had still more explosive impact.

New Look at the Early Years: The Apocalyptic Matrix of Genesis and Launch

Despite the extensive medieval and religious prehistory to the *Protocols*, modern secular historians have paid little attention to the apocalyptic and religious dimensions of the book. Michael Hagenmeister's chapter here, however, highlights the role that the Russian Sergei Nilus played in framing the *Protocols* in a religious *and* apocalyptic discourse. Nilus, for a long time, was not a religious man, but eventually he

> succumbed to the apocalyptic mood that was that was taking hold of the country . . . join[ing] those victims of rapid modernization and secularization who identified the downfall of their own world with the end of the world in general.

Rising to prominence with his historical writings (both his own and epigraphic), Nilus had a broad antimodern reading public that relished "Doomsday scenarios" as the answer to revolution brought on by Jews and Freemasons—henchmen of the Antichrist. Indeed, as Nilus presented it, the text *was* an apocalypse, a revelation: Its publication *revealed* the workings of Paul's *katéchon* (the mystery of lawlessness), and the text sounded the alarm at the imminent appearance of Antichrist.

For Nilus, the "truth" of the text resided in its urgent and holy message. As he said to a skeptical Frenchman,

> Let us admit that the *Protocols* are a forgery. Cannot God make use of a forgery in order to illuminate the iniquity of what is about to occur? Cannot God, in response to our faith, transform the bones of a dog into the relics of a miracle? He can thus place into the mouth of a liar the annunciation of truth.[8]

At one level, this is what Plato might call a "noble lie" and a medieval cleric might call a "pious forgery." But this was an apocalyptic forgery—a crucial, cosmically salvific, lie.

Understanding that framework makes it easier to realize how, with the rebirth of "faith" in post-Soviet Russia, the *Protocols* is back, as well. In a passage, much of whose detail could be written about the Arab world, Hagemeister notes:

> In Russia today, there is a widespread belief in a conspiracy hatched by satanic forces and their earthly helpers. Through countless tracts and brochures, these eschatological, demonological, and anti-Jewish predictions— evolved over centuries—are being revived and propagated: expectations of the Antichrist, a Jew from the tribe of Dan who was born in Israel in 1962 and will become the false messiah of the Jews; rumors of the secret

construction of the future base of the Antichrist, the third Temple under the Al Aqsa Mosque, in Jerusalem; manifestations of the "Seal of the Antichrist" and the "Number of the Beast," which are believed to be printed in bar codes and on tax IDs; the appearance of demonic beings in the guise of aliens and unidentified flying objects; and, significantly, Jewish ritual murder of Christians.

Mehlman's argument takes us in a different direction, but one critical for understanding the epistemological stakes in the tale. Viewing the *Protocols* as the equivalent of a medieval "pious forgery," he examines the shifty and shifting boundaries between truth and lies, politics and philosophy, in Dreyfusard Paris. Indeed, Napoleon III's rule, with its strange combination of authoritarianism and revolutionary rhetoric, produced Joly's *Dialogue in Hell between Montesquieu and Machiavelli*, in which Machiavelli was a "stand-in" for the emperor. Ironically and appropriately, Joly sided with Montesquieu, whereas the conspiracists who plagiarized his work had their authors, the Jews, side with Machiavelli.

We end up in the twisting corridors of the Dreyfus Affair. Here, on the one hand, Charles Maurras could defend Lieutenant-Colonel Henry for forging evidence against Dreyfus for the sake of the truth about the Jewish peril—a "patriotic forgery" to match Nilus's pious one—and not only gain the support of so exceptional a poet as Paul Valéry but launch a stellar career at the head of the royalist *Action Française*. On the other hand, Marcel Proust, Dreyfusard and Jew, entertained the possibility that Lieutenant Colonel Picquart had forged the material accusing Esterhazy in order to achieve the higher "truth" of Dreyfus's innocence. Ultimately, one gets the impression that alongside the "intellectuals" ready to let the evidential chips fall where they may stood many highly intelligent men for whom forgery was a vehicle to truth.

From the very beginning, then, the status of the *Protocols* as a forgery, so critical to the modern consensus on the text, carried dubious weight. This helps to explain why the trials in which the *Protocols* was exposed to the evidence, most famously in 1923, had less traction than the book's opponents might have hoped for.[9] But when one adds to this general epistemological permissiveness the semiotic arousal of apocalyptic time, the combination becomes, for some at least, irresistibly toxic. The *Protocols*, in fact, gained traction in the "apocalyptic" period after World War I and the Great Influenza of 1918:

> Things fall apart; the centre cannot hold;
> Mere anarchy is loosed upon the world . . .
> Surely some revelation is at hand;
> Surely the Second Coming is at hand.

Yeats wrote *The Second Coming* in 1919 and published it in 1921 to an audience soon torn between the appeal of Marsden's approving translation of the *Protocols* in 1922 and Yeats's ironic lament: "The best lack conviction; while the worst are filled with passionate intensity." And, for "the worst," the *Protocols* was a most attractive revelation.

Paul Zawadski examines the role of the *Protocols* as part of that ominous new phenomenon that took shape in precisely these years: secular "political religions." He argues that the *Protocols* offers us a remarkable case study in the way that, under the secular pressures of modernity's skepticism, scientific rigor, and drive to separate church and state, religious beliefs reemerged in a new and different idiom. The *Protocols* appeared in the middle of the "1900 moment" (1880–1910), when "the general worldview was affected by the fall in influence of the great religions" and when that collapse of traditional religion created a devastating psychological void, in Weber's terms, "an iron cage."[10] In this sense, the *Protocols* as a mythical narrative participated in the "re-enchantment" of the world, not a regression from modernity but a response to it.

Zawadski quotes Cassirer's postwar reflections about the failure of prewar intellectuals (1946), which could equally describe those who, in the 1990s, thought the *Protocols* were dead and buried.

> We [intellectuals] have underestimated the power of myths. When we first heard about political myths, we found them to be so absurd, so ridiculous, and so crazy, that we had trouble taking them seriously.

And yet, for all their woes, early-20th-century observers who dismissed these allegedly "regressive forces" soon found themselves overwhelmed by forces of zealotry that made the coming decades the bloodiest time in recorded history. "Political" or "secular religions," it turns out, are "secular" millennial movements that promise salvation in the present, and, precisely because they are secular (no "God" will effect the necessary transformation), they are all the more active in bringing about the perfect society. Indeed, if more gentle approaches fail, zealots of secular religions will not hesitate to carve their imagined perfection out of the very body social if necessary.

And, at the heart of these ruthlessly coercive "secular religions" lay a new, a "modern" conspiracy theory.

> In a secularized world [conspiracy theories] claimed to make sense of the enigma of evil and more generally of everything that went wrong (crisis, revolutions, wars and natural catastrophes). One could ironically say that they brought the Devil back, only this time it was a human Devil. And he is not a character from a Boulgakov novel but the real-life prosecutor Vichinksi, who, during the Moscow trials, questioned Zelenski, one of the accused who was the head of the distribution network of consumer goods, in these terms: "Were there instances when members of your organisation who were in charge of stocking butter put crushed glass in the butter? . . . Were there instances when your co-workers, your criminal accomplices, plotted against the Soviet state and the Soviet people by spreading nails in the butter?" A scene of such absurdity would be laughably comic if we did not know that eighteen of the accused were immediately executed.[11]

Conspiracy theories negate the terrible tensions and the permanent and acute cognitive dissonance of modernity. They "recompos[e] a holistic vision of a social group that is homogeneous and in fusion, and yet that is threatened by the outside world." As a result, rather than see modern conspiracy theories, and in particular, the *Protocols*, as a regression to ancient religious beliefs, Zawadski argues that they arise from and answer the doubts and uncertainties of modernity, in modern, empirical (scientific) terms.

David Redles examines perhaps the most famous case of a "political" or "secular religion" in his chapter on the Nazis. He argues that the apocalyptic urgency and the absolute stakes of the *Protocols* appealed to precisely those Germans filled with passionate intensity who, embracing the text as "true," unleashed the "blood-dimmed tide" upon the world in the following decades. Hitler looked deep into the *Protocols* and discovered himself—what he wanted and how to get it. Hitler's attitude toward the *Protocols* reveals not a shrewd politician manipulating the masses but a profoundly religious mind struggling with apocalyptic gnosis:

> Hitler and his inner circle believed that world history was essentially the struggle of . . . two chosen races, one Aryan, chosen of God, and one Jewish, chosen of Satan. These two races were locked in mortal combat, with a final reckoning imminent. In this scenario, "the Jew" became an abstract and symbolic Evil Other whose extermination was essential for ultimate

salvation. Once again, this was not simply rhetoric designed solely for audience effect but a believed vision of a coming eschatological battle that could have only one end possible: extermination of either the Aryans or the Jews. The *Protocols* was taken to be a revelation of the Jews' attempt to take over the world in fulfillment of the covenant. The Nazis then extended this myth to include the notion that, once the covenant was fulfilled, the Jews would attempt to exterminate the Gentiles. Only a counterextermination of Jews could prevent this apocalypse. While exactly how this apocalyptic scenario would play out was unknown to Hitler and his inner circle, the belief that it would occur in their lifetimes was absolutely an article of faith. Germany, and the world for that matter, had arrived at an eschatological turning point. It was a time of apocalypse or salvation in a millennial Third Reich. In this way, an imaginary enemy, involved in an imaginary world conspiracy as revealed in the imaginary *Protocols*, led to a very real genocide.

Postwar Protocols: *Non-Western Variants*

However thoroughly banned from the public sphere in the West, the text continued both to survive at the margins of Western culture and to thrive outside the West. In particular, during the 1970s—a time when Zionism had been declared "racism," and the PLO had an honored place in the United Nations led by the ex-Nazi Kurt Waldheim—the *Protocols* was translated into virtually every major language in the world and distributed worldwide from Turtle Bay.

Goodman's chapter on Japan traces the long-standing presence of the text there, its natural alliance with a number of both Christian and Buddhist millenarian traditions, and the political—often imperial—schemes it helped inspire among its "believers." He then examines in more detail its heyday in the 1980s via the writings of a Christian preacher, Uno Masami. By assuring Japanese that he could help them understand the world and Japan, he wrote huge bestsellers, and the *Protocols* got a respectful, even enthusiastic look in mainstream, even academic circles.

And yet, he notes, despite the text's popularity, it did not necessarily translate into the atrocities characteristic of the Nazis; on the contrary, in some cases it led to alliances with the Jews, efforts to bring them to Japan so that Japan could benefit from their intellectual and cultural resources. (This is not infrequently the reason that many world leaders today consult with international Jewish agencies.) In part, Goodman's chapter illustrates the point made by Bronner that not all believers in the *Protocols* take it as a "warrant for genocide" against the Jews. On the other hand, however, in the one fairly clear case of Aum Shinrikyo, a group that first emerged in the *Protocols*-saturated atmosphere of the 1980s and did indeed commit terrorist atrocities on the principle of "destroying the world in order to save it," we find the telltale conjunction of *Protocols* and apocalyptic paranoia.

If Japanese culture managed, however, to integrate the *Protocols* into a mainstream public discussion without necessarily melting down into toxic conspiracism the way Japan's wartime allies, the Germans, did, the same cannot be said about the Arab world, the other major adopter of this text in the postwar world. Marcus and Crook's chapter documents a public sphere that offers an almost mirror image of the Western one. Conspiracism, as Dan Pipes pointed out in his 1998 study, is coin of the realm. Or, as Thomas Friedman quipped in the third of his "Mideast Rules to Live By": *"If you can't explain something to Middle Easterners with a conspiracy theory, then don't try to explain it at all—they won't believe it.*[12] In this cultural sphere, exacerbated ferociously by contact with the "real" Zionists who so humiliated the Arabs in 1948 and 1967, the text penetrates from the top down, embraced by rulers, religious figures, academics, journalists alike . . . red meat for "the Street."

Nowhere do we find stronger examples combining acceptance and action of this "atrocity-provoking narrative" than in the Palestinian Authority (1994–?). Marcus's study makes it clear that the consequences of this belief for political actions are both consistent and devastating for any possible coexistence with Jews.

The Palestinian Authority successfully used the *Protocols* libel, together with other hate propaganda, to transform the killing of Jews from immoral murder into legitimate self-defense and even a service to humanity. The overwhelming Palestinian popular support for the suicide terror war against Israeli civilians and the transformation of the murderers of Jews into Palestinian heroes and role models for children can be seen as proof of the complete success of the Palestinian Authority's policy of demonizing Jews and Israelis. This revival of the *Protocols* libel was for the Palestinian Authority an important component, as it gave academic support and "authentic" authorization to the intrinsically evil depiction of Jews and Israelis that was so important to the PA, and it made for Palestinians fighting and killing Jews a natural response.

When the dust settles, it may well be that historians will identify belief in the *Protocols* as one of the major poisons that made the "Oslo Peace Process" a failure.

And, since the outbreak of the "Al Aqsa Intifada," in late 2000, as Marcus further points out, the belief in the *Protocols* has joined up with apocalyptic Muslim beliefs—in particular the Hadith of the "Rocks and the Trees"[13]—to produce genocidal urges unrivaled since the Nazis. Indeed, German priests and ministers during the Nazi period, unlike Palestinian imams, never openly espoused genocide from the pulpit.[14]

Postmodern Protocols: *The Return of the Repressed*

The consistent and tragic conjunction of belief in the *Protocols*, a sense of apocalyptic urgency, and the genocidal urges that we see in the Nazis, Aum Shinrikyo, and the Palestinian Authority become all the more problematic as we move further into the 21st century. Here we find the *Protocols* not only reactivated within the mainstream of one of the largest religious movements on the planet—Islam—but reentering the Western public sphere from both secular and religious sources.

Above all, we reencounter the epistemological problem: The modernist bulwark against the *Protocols* depends on a commitment to some idea of "objective" reality. We reject the *Protocols* as a legitimate narrative in part because it is a documented forgery but also because we have documented that this forgery has led people to do abominable things. Revisionism, however, can undermine all kinds of "objective truths," something that, Jeffrey Mehlman's piece reminds us, happened at the highest levels of cultural discourse in Dreyfusard France. However sophisticated one gets, the chips don't all fall neatly along the lines of the modernist narrative. And, as soon as one opens up the definition of reality, one finds oneself faced with "higher truths"—narratives, myths, legends, conspiracy theories.

Michael Barkun's chapter on UFOs and the *Protocols*, in which beings from outer space "reveal" the fact that the Zionist conspiracy reaches into the worlds beyond ours, may seem like the comic relief of this collection. And it certainly provides examples to smile at. But it gets at one of our epistemological vulnerabilities. Having discarded the modernist grand narrative, we discover that elaborate fantasy narratives can adopt the *Protocols* without even bothering to address the critical issue of forgery. They *assume* the conspiracy and move on to tell their tale.

In response to criticism for fomenting genocidal hatreds, the UFOlogists using the *Protocols* plead innocent. They distinguish between "true" and "false" Jews. On the contrary, they insist (much as did Nilus) that they do not hold innocent Jews guilty for the sins of the "Elders," who victimize Jews every bit as much as they victimize Gentiles. (Post–World War II believers in the *Protocols* explain the Holocaust by asserting that the "Elders" willingly sacrificed six million Jews in order to get sovereignty in Israel, the next phase of the *plan*.) Such believers protest that they actually want to *save* the Jews from their fate at the hands of these evil men. Thus, in one deft move, they avoid the accusation of malevolence and reassert the supersessionism of their narrative. The good Jew is one who denounces the "Elders" among his people.

These narratives allow the return of the *Protocols*, among other ways, by leveraging their status as "stigmatized knowledge." Resistance to modern or Western hegemony (however one conceives of it) can take the form of privileging precisely that *gnosis* that the hegemon stigmatizes: The powerful banish it *because* it is true. Notes Barkun, "the *Protocols* is compelling because it has been rejected, not in spite of it."

As a result, a collection of discredited and fantastic ideas gains mutual affirmation—that the *Protocols* is true, that on their way to Earth are spaceships peopled with "Ascended Masters" carrying directions from Atlantis for the next evolutionary leap in humanity. Together, they make a compelling narrative attractive to far more people than "modern" intellectuals imagine.[15] And we can expect patterns among the UFOlogists similar to those that characterized Henry Ford (who also did not think himself an anti-Semite): "ignorance, unpredictable absurdity, utter conviction, and naiveté."[16]

Moreover, not all UFOlogy is explicit about the *Protocols*. Much of the discourse uses *analogs*—the oral (improvised) performances of the written text, with or without specifically identifying the evil Elders of Zion. Conspiracism permeates the discourse. Barkun ends with the paradox that defines our postmodern dilemma:

> [T]he inability to convince that audience [of believers in the *Protocols*] hinges not so much on the intensity of its anti-Semitism (although that may certainly be a factor) as on the *Protocols'* stigmatization, leading to the paradox that discrediting them is precisely the characteristic that makes them attractive and that the more convincing our arguments, the less their power to persuade.

But since, as Barkun deftly analyzes, these narratives "draw the *Protocols* into a formidable modern religious tradition, Theosophy and its offshoots," we can unfortunately glimpse a terrain that resembles the world of the Thule Society of Ariosophists in post–World War I Germany whence sprung Nazism, discussed by Redles. These are not problems we can safely disregard.

While Barkun takes us on a magical mystery tour of the marginal world of UFOlogy, Deborah Lipstadt begins her chapter in the world of mass marketing at Walmart. Here, in 2004, the *Protocols* appeared on the shelves, and the Walmart management's response to the uproar was that it had not "seen a clear and convincing version" of the argument that the *Protocols* were a fake. It cited Henry Ford and "certain Russians" to suggest that the book was not only valid but that we need it to understand current affairs. Lipstadt expresses the rightful indignation of the sane scholar as she laments that "statements by scholars and serious historical research were being given the same weight as the claims of anti-Semites." Welcome to the 21st century.

Lipstadt examines the history of the *Protocols* in America, from Henry Ford and Father Coughlin in the 1920s and 1930s to the anticommunism of the 1950s—when a reluctant J. Edgar Hoover had to assign precious resources to examine the validity of the text, so often did some anticommunists invoke it—to Louis Farrakhan's Nation of Islam, starting in the 1970s and continuing into the present. Her study illustrates how the *Protocols* is a constant if largely marginal presence on the American scene. Together with Berlet's analysis of the parallel history of Masonic and Jewish conspiracy theory in U.S. history, her essay serves as excellent preparation for Berlet's analysis of the *Protocols* in the United States at the turn of the third millennium.

Here we find the "usual suspects"—Christian Identity, Nation of Islam, neo-Nazis—but also some new and troubling ones in "New Age" circles and on the "left." Indeed, just as the right-wing popularity of the *Protocols* forced Hoover to investigate, so, notes Berlet:

> anti-Semitic conspiracism has become such a problem on the political left that the international progressive magazine *New Internationalist* published a special issue on Judeophobia, including a refutation of the *Protocols*.

And, just as Jeffrey Mehlman picks his way through a 19th-century France in which the boundaries between "left" and "right" were transgressed by semiotically promiscuous seekers, so does Berlet present us with a world of constantly shifting boundaries rendered all the more porous by a shared conspiracist metanarrative that permits people "to take conspiracy allegations rooted in the *Protocols*, sanitize the anti-Semitic references, and peddle the resulting analogs to the political left." Berlet's extensive and thickly textured analysis of the currents at work in American political discourse deserves close attention. We ignore these players at our peril because, their moment come, they can end up becoming foreign policy experts, as happened with Hitler.

Berlet's analysis also opens up a window on one of the most disturbing directions in recent politics—the wildly self-contradictory alliance of progressive pacifists and war-mongering jihadis in the same "peace protests" against the war in Iraq in the winter and spring of 2003. There, side by side with pacifists, one found marchers parading pictures of Saddam Hussein and Yassir Arafat and wearing headbands saying "Death to the Jews."[17] In part, this had been set in motion in 1991, when George H. W. Bush's remark about a "New World Order" set off apocalyptic alarm bells the world over. The American protests against the first American Gulf War fostered an alliance between *Protocols* conspiracists and leftists dedicated to fighting "American/Western hegemony."

> It is unclear how much of this [alliance] was latent anti-Semitism among leftists and how much was picked up from the right-wing groups using the Gulf War to recruit from the left, but this period opened up new vistas for right-left synergy, especially around anti-Semitic conspiracy theories.

But, still more important, Berlet explores the impact that apocalyptic beliefs can have on *Protocols*-inspired conspiracism in triggering murderous scapegoating. Apocalyptic beliefs dualize all human interactions into good and evil forces. In Berlet's words, they "transmogrify"

> contemporary sociopolitical or socioreligious forces . . . into absolute contrast categories embodying moral, eschatological, and cosmic polarities upon which hinge the millennial destiny of humankind.

Citing other students of millennialism, including R. J. Lifton and Damian Thompson, Berlet suggests that, when Hofstadter wrote of the "paranoid style," he actually meant the "apocalyptic style." He then traces the career of the "Heroic Gnostic" who gains a following and, using scapegoating of the apocalyptic enemy as his major rhetorical trope, launches a movement that moves from the margins to the center. Like Hitler with his "Nationalsozialismus," the Gnostic hero moves back and forth from right to left, from authoritarian to egalitarian, with ease, making sure at every step to foment violent hatred. The *Protocols* is nothing if not protean.

Assessments: The Protocols, the New Anti-Semitism, and the Jews

What to do? How can sane people, Jews and non-Jews, respond to beliefs that defy the very rules of discourse and nonetheless get traction? Berlet, at the end of his chapter, makes clear the necessity of engagement:

> Nonetheless, the spread of conspiracy theories across a society is perilous to ignore because scapegoating and conspiracist allegations are toxic to democratic civil society and are tools used by cynical demagogic leaders to mobilize a bigoted mass base. There is no reason for intellectuals to feel smug and superior. History demonstrates that conspiracism cuts across political, social, economic, and intellectual boundaries. We need to teach each generation about the dangers of apocalyptic dualism, demonization, scapegoating, and conspiracism. The forgery of the *Protocols* needs to be a centerpiece of such a curriculum. We must never forget that tragic apocalypticism merged with aggressive dualism and demonization can create social movements that use conspiracist scapegoating to justify genocide as a final solution.

On the other hand, Deborah Lipstadt urges caution in carrying out the task:

> Even as we are alert to the *Protocols* and to the conspiracy theories they spawn, we must be careful not to become our own worst enemies by aggrandizing the potential of that threat—thereby creating a self-fulfilling prophecy, giving this century-old forgery an importance and publicity it would otherwise not get. In short, let us—for possibly all the right reasons—not do for the *Protocols* what the American Jewish community did for the Mel Gibson's *Passion of the Christ*.

Stephen Bronner extends Lipstadt's warning from a matter of practical tactics to one of moral strategy. We must, above all, he argues, not allow fears of the *Protocols* in the 21st century to blind us to the differences between the text's role in our day and its role a century ago on the one hand, and not allow our fears of anti-Semitism to silence responsible self-criticism, in particular that of Jews criticizing aspects of Israeli policy, on the other. A rigorous critique of Israel, he argues, is not only legitimate, but necessary.

The very creation of Israel has fundamentally changed the situation. No clear moral thinking about the *Protocols* can take place if we do not "admit that Jews are no longer in the ghetto or an oppressed minority." Thus, Bronner suggests, one cannot compare the "real victims" of *Protocols*-inspired genocidal paranoia to Israeli Jews, who can now defend themselves. In particular, he is concerned with the misuse of accusations of anti-Semitism in the context of the Israeli-Palestinian conflict. This practice, he holds, impairs a real, potentially fruitful dialogue between the two antagonists in the conflict.

Richard Landes warns against the possibility that, in an effort to avoid the Scylla of a tribal "Israel, right or wrong," one can fall into the Charybdis of "Palestinians right or wrong." Indeed one can end up adopting *Protocols*-inspired Palestinian narratives about their own innocence and Israel's guilt in place of the discarded Zionist "myths." As a result, by adopting a postcolonial language of Israeli imperialism and antidemocracy, one can end up feeding the paranoid fantasies of Arabs who believe that the two stripes on Israel's flag represent the stretch of their imperial ambitions to rule from the Nile to the Euphrates.

Landes argues, on the contrary, that a careful analysis of the way the paranoid apocalyptic themes found in the *Protocols* operate in Palestinian and, more broadly, in Arab-Muslim culture suggests that the scrupulous, often rhetorically inflated self-criticism that some Jewish "progressives" engage in—Israel is imperialist, colonialist, racist, fascist—has a noxious dual impact. First, rather than encouraging dialogue, it fuels hatreds by confirming the paranoid fantasies on the other side. Second, it produces an epistemological crisis among outside observers who do not know how to factor in both Jewish tendencies toward self-criticism and Arab tendencies toward scapegoating in assessing the information they receive about what has happened.

"Those who are merciful to the cruel will end up being cruel to the merciful," commented the rabbis in the 2nd century. "The best lack conviction, while the worst are full of passionate intensity," wrote Yeats in 1921. When paranoid intensity meets misplaced mercy, the results can be terrifying.

Indeed, the spread of paranoid conspiracy theory and *Protocols*-inspired anti-Semitism has arguably done terrible things to both European and Arab culture in our young century. While some argue that "it's not so bad," some argue that we live in a dynamic like that of the 1930s, when well-meaning progressives placated remorseless imperialists (who accused the Jews of imperial plots), in the hope of bringing "peace in our time." In the 1930s, that appeasement failed spectacularly. Whether or not this is the 1930s and, if it is, no matter where we are in the apocalyptic curve of totalitarian violence, we now have another chance to deal with a waxing wave of *Protocols*-lubricated anti-Semitism. Can we—can modern culture—do better? Can we choose life this time *before* tens, even hundreds of millions have drowned in that blood-dimmed tide?

1. Norman Cohn, *Warrant for Genocide: The Myth of the Jewish World Conspiracy and the Protocols of the Elders of Zion* (New York: Harper and Row, 1967), 74.

2. For a fascinating analysis of the illusion of "Reason's triumph," see Lee Harris, *The Suicide of Reason* (New York: Basic Books, 2007).

3. See Alan Dershowitz, *The Vanishing American Jew* (New York: Touchstone, 1997).

4. Marc Levin, *The Protocols of the Elders of Zion*, http://www.independentfilm.com/ films/protocols-of-zion-marc-levin.shtml. See also Richard Landes, "Jews as Contested Ground in Post-Modern Conspiracy Theory," *Jewish Political Studies Review* 19, nos. 3-4 (2007): 9–34.

5. Erich Fromm, *Escape from Freedom* (New York: Rinehart, 1941).

6. See David Redles in this volume.

7. Sir John Retcliffe [Hermann Goedsche], *Biarritz. Historisch-politischer Roman in acht Bänden*, Bd.1, Berlin 1905, 130ff.

8. Quoted by Jeffrey Mehlman in this volume.

9. For the most recent study of these trials, see Haddasah Ben-Itto, *The Lie That Wouldn't Die—The Protocols of the Elders of Zion* (London: Valentine Mitchell, 2005).

10. Arthur Mitzman, *The Iron Cage: An Historical Interpretation of Max Weber* (New York: Transaction, 1984).

11. H.Carrère d'Encausse, *Staline, l'ordre par la terreur* (Paris: Flammarion, 1979), 58.

12. Daniel Pipes, *The Hidden Hand: Middle East Fears of Conspiracy* (New York: St. Martin's Press, 1996).

13. "The Hour [of Judgment] will not arrive until the Muslims fight the Jews, and the Muslims will slaughter them, until the Jew will hide behind the rocks and the trees. The rocks and the trees will say: 'O Muslim, O Servant of God—there is a Jew behind me, come and kill him!'" Hadith related by Abu Haraira (603–681), one of the most quoted reciters of Hadith. One should note that, although there are a number of classical versions in which Jews are not mentioned, modern apocalyptic literature cites only the versions mentioning the Jews: David Cook, *Contemporary Muslim Apocalyptic Literature* (Syracuse: Syracuse University Press, 2005), 36.

14. For the extensive examples of Palestinian (and other Arab) groups preaching genocide against the Jews, see PMW (www.pmw.org.il) and MEMRI (www.memri.org).]

15. On UFOs, see Richard Landes, *Heaven on Earth: The Varieties of the Millennial Experience* (New York: Oxford University Press, 2011), ch. 13.

16. Stephen Watts, cited in Lipstadt in this volume.

17. See Nick Cohen, *What's Left? How Liberals Lost Their Way* (London: Fourth Estate, 2007).

PART I

Conceptual Prelude

On Paranoid Politics and Apocalyptic Violence

The Melian Dialogue, the *Protocols*, and the Paranoid Imperative

RICHARD LANDES

Like most Americans Jews, in 1985 I had never read the *Protocols*. I had, however, read Norman Cohn's *Warrant for Genocide*, and so, at the end of a year's worth of teaching "Political and Moral Philosophy" at Columbia, I decided to give it to my students in the week dedicated to totalitarianism. I was in for something of a surprise.

Most people, myself included, think of the international conspiracy "revealed" by the *Protocols* as one in which the Jews manipulate capital markets to create chaos and take over the world. And, in one sense, this is both true and historically relevant. The Nazis were only the most virulent group to believe that the great crash of 1929 and the ensuing worldwide Depression was the work of the Jews. The more fundamental issue raised by the *Protocols*, however, struck me with peculiar force in the context of this course on political philosophy. The opening volley spoke in a voice I'd become familiar with over the year's readings:

> It must be noted that men with bad instincts are more in number than the good, and therefore the best results in governing them are attained by violence and terror, and not by academic discussions. Every man aims at power, everyone would like to become a dictator if only he could, and rare indeed are the men who would not be willing to sacrifice the welfare of all for the sake of securing their own welfare.
>
> What has restrained the beasts of prey who are called men? What has served for their guidance hitherto?
>
> In the beginnings of the structure of society, they were subjected to brutal and blind force; after words—to Law, which is the same force, only disguised. I draw the conclusion that by the law of nature right lies in force.[1]

This is hardly a Jewish voice. Indeed, both the Bible and the rabbinical corpus spend much of the time exploring precisely how to discipline power, to render it less adversary. For both man and God, *gvurah*—manly strength—represented self-control: "Who is the Gibor [man of strength]? He who conquers his own drives."[2] The very notion of *voluntarily* taking on "the yoke of the kingdom of heaven" represents the opposite view: Man can learn to control himself from abusing power to his own advantage, even if no one can "perfect" so difficult a task.[3]

My reading in political thought that year convinced me that much of the thrust driving toward democracy in the West came from this biblical tradition.[4] And one of the odder anomalies I noticed was the degree to which the political scientists, heirs to a tradition of political thought with much stronger elements of the *dominating imperative*—Greek, Roman, medieval Christian—ignored this biblical dimension when looking for the roots of modern democratic thought.[5]

In any case, the voice of the *Elders* was not a recognizably Jewish voice. But it was familiar. Indeed it was a common voice, even a cacophony of voices. It was Socrates' foe in book II of the *Republic*, Thrasymachus arguing "might makes right."[6] It was the Athenians' to the Melians according to Thucydides.[7] It was *libido dominandi*, invoked favorably by the Romans and, even as he deplored it, accepted by Augustine as an immutable dimension of political life.[8] It was the voice of Carolingian lords and clergymen as they hewed their way through tribal Europe; it was the voice of the German aristocracy in the century before the Peasants' War of 1524, when they argued that private warfare—that is, their rampages—were good for public peace because it "pruned back" the troublesome peasantry.[9] It was the voice of Machiavelli in his advice to *The Prince*. It was the voice of Bismarck. In a more civil form, it has a school in modern academies called "realism."

Prepared by Cohn's remark about "atrociously written . . . reactionary balderdash," I had expected a stupid and outlandish text addressed to idiots. Instead, I found a familiar voice, one that, with few exceptions, dominated premodern political discourse—one that was neither stupid nor inarticulate. And its reproach to the "idealists," who spoke of such fair and just principles as equality before the law and freedom for all, was to accuse them of using democratic language in order to gain power so that they could do to others what they complained about others doing to them. Nietzsche made the same point in *Genealogy of Morals* about moralists like Tertullian (and, behind him, all egalitarian millennialists) who excoriate the powerful: People parade their weakness and dream cruelly of the day when the meek shall rule the powerful.[10]

Eli Sagan lays out many of these issues in his meditation on the origins of democracy, *The Honey and the Hemlock*. There he labels this notion of "rule or be ruled" the *paranoid imperative*, based as it is on a projection of bad faith that then justifies . . . *demands* acts of protective bad faith.[11] Indeed, as the Athenians explained to the Melians:

> Of the gods we believe, and of men we know, that by a necessary law of their nature they rule wherever they can. And it is not as if we were the first to make this law, or to act upon it when made: we found it existing before us, and shall leave it to exist for ever after us; all we do is to make use of it, knowing that you and everybody else, having the same power as we have, would do the same as we do.[12]

In other words, "we do unto you before you do unto us."

Notes Charles Strozier, in this volume:

> The paranoid knows the evil other because he is his own creation. When asked to describe that other, a look of horror will come over the face of a paranoid that comes from a place of secret awareness. It is really very striking. Sometimes, indeed often, he will tilt his head slightly, jut his chin, perhaps turn somewhat sideways to look askance, and smirk with a knowing smile that can become a terrifying and haughty laugh.

The paranoid is a Gnostic; he has secret knowledge about the world that the masses do not. He knows that *anyone who is somebody* wants to dominate the world.

According to Sagan, this paranoid axiom of political life has dominated political action for the vast period of human polities—from the Neolithic revolution ten thousand years ago to the past two centuries—and must be overcome in order to attempt that experiment in freedom called democracy.[13] Indeed, political scientists of a more practical bent object to calling this axiom paranoid; it is, rather, according to the "Realist School," rational. (As a result of this, I refer in subsequent discussion to the principle of *rule or be ruled* as the *dominating imperative* and reserve *paranoid imperative* for times when, under conditions of apocalyptic conspiracism, it shifts to "exterminate or be exterminated.")

Which brings us back to the *Protocols* and Norman Cohn's dramatic title, *Warrant for Genocide*.[14] While on one level, it is "atrociously written . . . reactionary balderdash," the *Protocols* is actually a reasonably sophisticated text that works entirely from the main axioms of premodern political philosophy.

Starting with the *dominating imperative*, one derives a number of further corollaries and proofs. If all men—more specifically, all political men—are ruled by *libido dominandi*, then any notion of a democracy/constitutional government/liberal experiment in self-rule that hopes to create order by freeing commoners and counting on them to act morally (to prefer self-control to dominion over another) is doomed to failure. This, by the way is even, to some extent, Plato's position: *Democracy* is a formula for chaos; it cannot work.[15] It is the fundamental aristocratic argument: The *demos* cannot be trusted with power, and only when imposed from above with force—as the Jews in the *Protocols* say, "with violence and terror"—can there be any hope for order. Such a system may be oppressive, but at least it promises stability . . . order.[16]

One can shrewdly conclude that if democracy is a recipe for anarchy, then people who support and encourage democracy cannot possibly do so in order to create democracy. They must have an ulterior motive. What might that motive be? What else than the conquest of everyone else and their subjection to slavery! The *dominating imperative* constitutes not only the default mode but the inescapable mode. All interactions are a struggle for power.

But, unlike Nietzsche's "healthy" blond beast who openly rejoices in his dominion, the [Jewish] agents of this world conquest operate secretly, by manipulation. More specifically, they are *demopaths*: They use democracy to destroy democracy. They use the values inherent in democratic cultures— equality before the law, freedom of conscience and of expression, fairness to the weak—to lull people into taking steps that will ensure their own downfall.

Here, the *Protocols* lays out the plan: Since "we" Jews are weak and cannot confront or fight the "gentile aristocracy," who are too strong for us and know what we are up to, we must convince the Gentile commoners to rise up against them and overthrow them. Then, once these fools have been duped into ridding themselves of their only natural defenders, their iron-fisted aristocracy, the Jews will unleash the chaos that inevitably accompanies democracy—market crashes, revolutions, and massive convulsions. And, once in power, they will make the previous regime seem mild indeed. QED.

Again, this may not be how Jews think, but it is precisely how the people who composed the text thought. For them, the very notion that one might sincerely espouse democratic emotions *cannot be*: Any democrat is, by definition, a liar and a demopath. Thus, the *Protocols* is a "pious forgery" that, like the Donation of Constantine, merely supplied the written form of something that is anyway "true," indeed, crucially, "salvifically" true.[17]

The irony here is that the "higher truth" the text embodies is not about the Jews but about this particularly powerful strand of Gentile political thought.

In some senses, its author(s), men from an international aristocracy increasingly alarmed at the advances of liberal constitutional governments over the course of the 19th century, produced a classic work of cognitive egocentrism: The Jews thought as they did. Those who embrace the dominating imperative as a political axiom assume others do, as well.

(No better incident illustrates this point than the first visit of the Japanese delegation to Hebrew University in 1978. They brought as their gift—crucial and carefully thought out in a gift culture—a beautifully bound translation of the *Protocols* into Japanese. This was so perfect a story, so deeply cutting and dark a joke, it seems like a perfect candidate for urban legend. But it is not.)[18]

To people who adopt the dominating imperative, the advent of modernity could not represent a sincere experiment in freedom. It had to be a trap. The aristocracy's loss of arbitrary powers, forbidden by egalitarian lawgivers who instituted the "slave morality" of *isonomia* / "equality before the law," was a prelude not to everyone's renunciation of arbitrary power but to a still greater imposition of tyranny. Shorn of aristocratic privilege, watching meritocratic upstarts undermine their old-boy network, increasingly threatened by the advances of commoners' freedoms (including freedom of the press and freedom to assemble), feeling the world of wealth shake beneath their plodding legs, those from the *ancien régime* who persisted in their belief in the dominating imperative could not tolerate this world turned upside-down.

In a sense, the *Protocols* expresses their understanding of the anomalous present. Democracy is a prelude to horror. Someone is secretly planning its overthrow. Who else, but a people smart enough to con Gentile commoners into overthrowing their own aristocracies? Even some pathetic aristocrats become "infected with the idea of freedom, SO-CALLED LIBERALISM, and, for the sake of an idea, are willing to yield some of their power." Hence, free press, free thinking, Darwin, and Nietzsche are all pawns of the Jewish conspiracy. "Jews must know what we know," reasons the conspiracist, "and they must be planning what we would plan were we in their position."[19]

If this psychological projection underlies the composition of the *Protocols* and appealed to some of its readership, the prophetic nature of the text, the extraordinary accuracy of its predictive powers over the early decades of the 20th century, provided it with a much wider and more frightened audience. Above all, it was disturbingly accurate in its reading of egalitarian ideologues.

Whenever the egalitarian zealots managed to pull off a revolution, whether in France in 1789 or in Russia in 1917, no sooner did they acquire power than they turned to terror to rule. All the fair promises that lured the commoners to support the leadership ended in mob rule and bloodthirsty demagogues. Given that the *Protocols* came out little more than a decade before the Russian Revolution and that by the time Marsden translated it into English, in 1922, the Bolsheviks had begun their purges and mass arrests, the work seemed utterly prophetic.

The text addressed a particularly painful aspect of modernity's horrors: the lonely terror of the disciple of the *dominating imperative* in a culture where liberalism is triumphant. It spoke directly to him in his own language, and even if it gave him a terrible sense of danger—which he felt anyway—it also gave him two more things: a clearly defined enemy—the Jews—and permission to wipe that enemy out. Part of the *frisson* of the *Protocols* is the chance to hear how Jews, these people who think they are God's moral gift to mankind, think behind closed doors. It offers the voyeur a glimpse behind the curtain at the manipulators who terrify with their strange and hostile glances.

And what do these people say behind closed doors? Not only do they believe in "might makes right" but they express it as a scientific truth and justify it. In the first protocol, they address moral objections: "Should anyone of a liberal mind say that such reflections as the above are immoral, I would put the following questions. . . ." And the argument is classic Athenian self-defense: "It has been a law long before us, and will be long after us, that those who can, do what they will; and those who cannot, suffer what they must." The reader of/believer in the *Protocols*, then, even as he can hate the Jews for wishing what he wishes, can thank them for justifying what he wishes.

Hitler's reaction, in the recounting of Hermann Rauschning, embodies every aspect of this analysis:

> We must beat the Jew with his own weapon. I saw that the moment I read the book . . . down to the veriest detail I found the *Protocols* immensely instructive [on such topics as] political intrigue, the technique of conspiracy, revolutionary subversion, prevarication, deception, organization.[20]

As he plotted his own war of conquest to enslave the world's races, he projected precisely that intention on the Jews. "In reading . . . *the Protocols*, one has the feeling that one is reading descriptions of Hitler's own . . . plans. Page after page, all one needs to do is substitute the words 'Hitler will . . .' whenever the *Protocols* say 'the Jews [*sic*] will . . . .'"[21]

And the same phenomenon repeats in the 21st century among the most zealous believers in the *Protocols*, the Islamists who plan to do what they accuse the Jews of doing. Here a Turkish Muslim working for the imposition of Sharia on Turkey outlines the plan of action:

You must move in the arteries of the system, without anyone noticing your existence, until you reach all the power centers . . . until the conditions are ripe, they [Muslim followers] must continue like this. If they do something prematurely, the world will crush our heads, and Muslims will suffer everywhere, like in the tragedies in Algeria, like in 1982 [in] Syria [Hama] . . . like in the yearly disasters and tragedies in Egypt. The time is not yet right. You must wait for the time when you are complete, and conditions are ripe, until we can shoulder the entire world and carry it. . . . You must wait until such time as you have gotten all the state power, until you have brought to your side all the power of the constitutional institutions in Turkey. . . . Until that time, any step taken would be too early—like breaking an egg without waiting the full 40 days for it to hatch. It would be like killing the chick inside. The work to be done is [in] confronting the world. Now, I have expressed my feelings and thoughts to you all—in confidence . . . trusting your loyalty and sensitivity to secrecy. I know that when you leave here—[just] as you discard your empty juice boxes, you must discard the thoughts and feelings expressed here.[22]

It sounds precisely like what the *Protocols* imagined—long, slow, patient infiltration, using democracy to gain power, biding one's time until the proper moment to strike, the need for secrecy lest people who, were they to learn of the plans, would immediately and effectively terminate the conspiracy. *The Project*, a Muslim Brotherhood plan to bring Europe under Sharia rule first uncovered in Switzerland in 2001, resembles the *Protocols* so strikingly that readers—especially Jewish readers, who know how terrible it is to be accused of such awful plans—initially recoiled at even entertaining the possibility that such things are true.[23]

Activating the Atrocity-Producing Narrative: From Paranoid to Apocalyptic

The leap from believing in a worldwide conspiracy to striking out against it constitutes an enormous step—what in millennial studies one would call moving from passive to active apocalyptic. As Daniel Pipes pointed out in *The Hidden Hand*, conspiracy theory often acts as a depressant:

Imagining conspiracies of malicious, omnipotent adversaries can induce a profound sense of hopelessness. After all, how can an enemy so shrewd, so powerful, and so vast be challenged? At the same time, how can one negotiate or compromise with such an implacable and evil force?[24]

What inspires people to fight back against their demons? How does the *dominating imperative* become the *exterminating imperative*? And how does such a virulent strain move from the margins to the center of a society, drawing increasing numbers into the vortex of its mad logic?

Here we approach a largely uncharted terrain to which this book hopes to make a contribution: *the dynamics of apocalyptic rage at the violations of modernity*. For reasons that deserve close attention, modernity challenges traditional gender roles, in particular demanding levels of restraint from alpha males that seem to many like emasculation.[25]

> All of these modern changes entailed profound challenges to conventional assumptions about self, gender, and society that, insofar as they seemed to erode traditional bases of male authority, were frequently interpreted as assaults on virility itself.[26]

If a culture defines manhood as that which one acquires by killing another man, then a capitalist culture (in which, as Schumpeter pointed out generations ago, one can be a man without killing another) and civil society (in which killing, indeed, any kind of violence, is heavily circumscribed), deny men their virility. And, of course, Jewish men, so successful in "modern" meritocratic conditions, were, almost by definition, effeminate:

> Few acknowledge that [the Dreyfus Affair's anti-Semitism] was also coextensive with the traditional assumption that Jewish men . . . were bookish, sedentary beings, whose weakness, cowardice, and effeminacy rendered them unfit for military service.[27]

The demands of modernity strike many a "traditional" culture as asphyxiating, emasculating, and infuriating. Current Muslim apocalyptic writers consider the modern West already permanently humiliated by the Jews:

> Thus the Jewish slap on the faces of the Christians continues, who apparently enjoy and allow this sort of humiliation and attack, and give them their other cheek so that the Jew can continue to slap the Christians—just as we see—ruling them in Europe through the Masons who dig the grave of Western civilization through corruption and promiscuity. The Crusader West continues like a whore who is screwed sadistically, and does not

derive any pleasure from the act until after she is struck and humiliated, even by her pimps—the Jews in Christian Europe. Soon they will be under the rubble as a result of the Jewish conspiracy.[28]

And, if shame and humiliation are fates worth than death, then staving off such an unbearable death becomes a consuming obsession.

Thus, the more widespread modernity, the more threatening the process. In 1800, when democratic revolutions were just beginning to take root and prosper, most of democracy's enemies believed that it was a Masonic plot. After a hundred years of Jewish "freedom," their extraordinary success in so many "modern" professional fields convinced anxious observers by 1900 that the Masons were mere pawns of the real schemers, the Jews.[29] And the more modernity has spread, the more globalization penetrates into cultures the world over, the more what Bronner calls modernity's "losers" feel suffocated. What had been a potentially manageable enemy in the early 19th century—after all, the Restoration had triumphed over the Revolution in 1815—became, by the early 20th century, a struggle of cosmic proportions, an apocalyptic conflict defined by the radically dualistic version of the "paranoid imperative"—*exterminate or be exterminated.*

The path from passive to active apocalyptic, from complaining about the conspiracy to fighting it openly, goes hand in hand with the movement of the discourse from the margins of a culture to the center: The more people openly express their belief in the conspiracy, the more empowered the leaders feel. As the movement gains momentum, things once inconceivable, in particular, fighting back against such vast powers, become possible. What the manly soul longs for suddenly becomes a viable option. Humiliation calls for revenge, cosmic humiliation for cosmic revenge, and the collective strength of a mob can become formidable when mobilized by a ruthless leader (e.g., one who really does hold the attitudes attributed to the Elders of Zion).

We need to study the paths that an active paranoid vision can take from the margins to the center—analogs, apocalyptic narrative frames, new media of communication conveying scapegoating hatreds, mob psychology of strength-in-panic, failure of the guardians of a sane public order to respond to dishonest and atrocity-provoking narratives. Only then can we identify those places where conspiracist paranoia joins up with what Erich Fromm called the "sadistic craving for power," and interprets the *Protocols* as salvific call to fight back—a "redemptive anti-Semitism," a "warrant for genocide."[30]

1. *Protocols of the Elders of Zion* (Boston: Small, Maynard, 1920), 11.

2. "Who is strong? He who conquers his evil inclination, as it is said: 'Better is one slow to anger than a strong man, and one who rules over his spirit than a conqueror of a city' (Proverbs [at latest, 3rd century b.c.e.] 16:32)." *Ethics of the Fathers* [ca. 200 c.e.], 4.4.1.

3. This notion of the Yoke of the Kingdom of Heaven permeates all three monotheistic traditions, albeit in different ways. For a survey of the biblical literature and its relationship to early Christianity, see J. C. O'Neill, "The Kingdom of God," *Novum Testamentum* 35:2 (1993): 130–141; the very term "Islam" means *submission* to Allah's will.

4. See a brief outline in Richard Landes, "The Biblical Origins of Democracy: Equality before the Law, the Dignity of Manual Labor, and Literacy for Commoners," *Tikkun Magazine* 3 (1998); a more developed argument is made in Landes, *Heaven on Earth: The Varieties of the Millennial Experience* (New York: Oxford University Press, 2011), 229–40.

5. See the reflections of Yoram Hazony in his "Forward" to Aaron Wildavsky's *Moses as Political Leader* (Jerusalem: Shalem Center, 2005), ix–xxi.

6. "Justice is the advantage of the stronger" (338c); "Injustice, if it is on a large enough scale, is stronger, freer, and more masterly than justice" (344c), Plato, *The Republic*, Book I.

7. "Right, as the world goes, is only in question between equals in power, while the strong do what they can and the weak suffer what they must." Thucydides, *Peloponnesian War*, Book V, ch. 17.

8. For a good selection of quotes, see Sabine MacCormick, "Sin, Citizenship, and the Salvation of Souls: The Impact of Christian Priorities on Late-Roman and Post-Roman Societies," *Comparative Studies in Society and History* 39:4 (October 1997): 646–647.

9. "The Social Use of Private War: Some Late Medieval Views Reviewed," *Tel Aviver Jahrbuch für deutsche Geschichte: Zur Sozial- und Begriffsgeschichte des Mittelalters* 27 (1993): 253–274.

10. Friedrich Nietzsche, *Genealogy of Morals*, Essay I, 13–17; ed. Walter Kaufmann (New York: Vintage Books, 1989), 44–56.

11. Eli Sagan, *The Honey and the Hemlock: Democracy and Paranoia in Ancient Athens and Modern America* (Princeton: Princeton University Press, 1991).

12. Thucydides, *Peloponnesian War*, Book V, ch. 17; tr. Rex Warner (New York: Penguin Books, 1954), 400–408.

13. For additional analysis of this postneolithic dimension of politics, see John Kautsky, *The Politics of Aristocratic Empires* (Chapel Hill: University of North Carolina Press, 1982); John A. Hall, *Powers and Liberties: The Causes and Consequences of the Rise of the West* (Berkeley: University of California Press, 1990); Ernest Gellner, *Plough, Sword, and Book: The Structure of Human History* (Chicago: University of Chicago Press, 1989).

14. Norman Cohn, *Warrant for Genocide: The Myth of the Jewish World Conspiracy and the Protocols of the Elders of Zion* (New York: Serif, 1996).

15. Irving M. Zeitlin, *Plato's Vision: The Classical Origins of Social and Political Thought* (Englewood Cliffs, NJ: Prentice Hall, 1993); the most relentless attack on Plato's politics comes from Karl Popper, who attacks him not for his criticism of democracy so much as for his failure to even mention the key democratic principle, *isonomia* (equality before the law): *The Open Society and Its Enemies: Plato* (Princeton: Princeton University Press, 1971).

16. For an excellent sociological study of the effects of this thinking, see John Kautsky, *The Politics of Aristocratic Empires* (Piscataway, NJ: Transaction, 1997).

17. Jeffrey Woolf in this volume; on the salvific quality of Nazi anti-Semitism, see Saul Friedlander, *Nazi Germany and the Jews* (New York: HarperCollins, 1997), 1:72–112; Landes, *Heaven on Earth*, ch. 12.

18. Confirmed to me in conversation and e-mail by Menahem Milson, head of the Institute of Asian and African Studies at the time, who received the gift from the delegation.

19. This is a significant factor in the outcry of Muslims about Jewish infiltration of the media. They assume that Jews will use their positions to advance their people's cause, whereas, as in the case of the *New York Times* during the Holocaust, they actually do the opposite: Laurel Leff, *Buried by the Times: The Holocaust and America's Most Important Newspaper* (Cambridge: Cambridge University Press, 2005).

20. Hermann Rauschning, *The Voice of Destruction* (New York: Putnam, 1940), 238–241, cited in Robert Waite, *The Psychopathic God: Adolf Hitler* (New York: Da Capo Press, 1993), 118–119. Some historians would minimize the reliability of Rauschning's remarks, noting that he was too dependent by 1940 on playing the ex-Nazi for the West. Why and how he would come up with this particular formulation and how that would help his case in the West, however, needs explication. As both Waite (note 21) and Redles (in this volume, ch. 9) both note, this quote matches Hitler's mindset quite closely.

21. Waite, *Psychopathic God*, 119.

22. The sermon can be viewed and heard at Youtube.com, http://www.youtube.com/watch?v=oNi3Z3qZ7Z4&mode=related&search; the translation is at MEMRI, http://memri.org/bin/latestnews.cgi?ID=IA37507#_ednref4.

23. On the "Project," see the text and analysis by Sylvain Besson, *La conquête de l'Occident: Le projet secret des Islamistes* (Paris: Seuil, 2005).

24. See Daniel Pipes, *The Hidden Hand: Middle East Fears of Conspiracy* (New York: St. Martin's Press, 1996), 225–226, for the personality profile of conspiracy theorists.

25. Zygmunt Bauman, *The Holocaust and Modernity* (Ithaca, NY: Cornell University Press, 1989); Robert Nye, *Masculinity and Male Codes of Honor in Modern France* (Berkeley: University of California Press, 1993); Christopher Forth, *The Dreyfus Affair and the Crisis of French Manhood* (Baltimore: Johns Hopkins University Press, 2004).

26. Forth, *Crisis of French Manhood*, 7.

27. Ibid., 18.

28. Cited in David Cook, *Contemporary Muslim Apocalyptic Literature* (Syracuse: Syracuse University Press, 2005), 220, n. 7.

29. The first sign of this shift came with the 1868 text *Biarritz*, by Hermann Gödsche; by widespread consensus, however, the final decades of the 20th century mark the key phase. See Mehlman's article in this volume. See also Steven L. Pease, *The Golden Age of Jewish Achievement: The Compendium of a Culture, a People, and Their Stunning Performance* (Sonoma, CA: Deucalion Press, 2009).

30. Erich Fromm, *Escape from Freedom* (1941; New York: Henry Holt, 1968), 246; on "redemptive anti-Semitism," see n. 17.

3

The Apocalyptic Other

On Paranoia and Violence

CHARLES B. STROZIER

The *Protocols* is a text that operates at several historical and psychological levels simultaneously. Most important, it is a malevolent expression of anti-Semitic rage. Jews in this text become cunning monsters scheming to take over the world. At this level, the *Protocols* fit into a long tradition of hatred against Europe's designated victim, though the text should be privileged for its role in helping to shape Nazi justification for policies that led to the Holocaust. Read today, however, the *Protocols* is so banal that one wonders how it captured the imagination of so many readers. The answer to that question lies in locating the text historically at a particular moment of crisis in late-19th and early-20th-century Europe, which as we know now was about to explode in a paroxysm of violence that hardly resolved the intense national struggles of the day and in its failure generated mass movements of great evil, another huge war, and the Holocaust.

But one must also consider another important dimension of that fin-de-siècle moment for understanding the *Protocols*. It was a time of intellectual ferment about so-called scientific racism. Serious thinkers worried seriously about issues of race and difference that many sought to locate within new scientific paradigms that emerged in the 19th century, especially after Darwin. The problem, of course, is that the location of what they called racial difference in the late 19th century, which even the most narrow-minded would recognize as cultural differences today, got caught up a century ago in the fanatical hatreds of the new anti-Semitism. The *Protocols*, a basically foolish text on the level of some of the conspiracy theories about 9/11 that are currently being bandied about that I bet few really read at the time, came to serve as proof of Jewish malevolence and racial separateness and of Jews as the source of evil in the world that in some mysterious way caused the suffering of decent Christians.

But, in another sense, the *Protocols* operates at a mythic level. The text transcends its portrait of the Jews, or, perhaps more accurately, its portrait of Jews connects with themes of paranoia and the apocalyptic in the self that frame a broader understanding of the malevolent other. And it is at this level that the *Protocols* is an integral part of the general problem of fundamentalism and the apocalyptic in the contemporary world. What I am personally most interested in are the links between paranoia and the apocalyptic and how and why that relates to violence. I will begin with paranoia, which I would say is a potential in the self that can readily be actualized in historical moments of crisis; conversely, historical crisis can readily evoke paranoia in the self. It is synergistic. There is always some paranoia in the self, which David Terman of the Chicago Psychoanalytic Institute has suggested recently fits into a pattern of a "paranoid gestalt."[1] The range and depth of what we see now in the world suggests a larger historical crisis we only dimly understand. I think this sensitivity to the historical moment underlay the approach Richard Hofstadter wisely took a half-century ago in his essay on the paranoid style in American politics, even though he used different language, and explains why his essay has justly been so enormously influential.[2] Within psychiatry, there is a mostly irrelevant literature on paranoia that is concerned with the choice of appropriate drugs for treatment. The more psychological literature, especially within psychoanalysis, got off to a bad start with Freud's 1910 explanation of its basis in repressed homosexuality[3] and continues in the margins, since few psychoanalytic psychotherapists actually treat paranoids, for the simple reason that they respond very badly to the prolonged experience of inquiry into motivations. Jerrold Post has written about narcissism and paranoia;[4] VamikVolkan has been concerned with what he calls the "second skin" of nationalism;[5] Joseph Berke and his colleagues have put together a valuable collection of essays on paranoia (*Even Paranoids Have Enemies*);[6] Robert Jay Lifton, as always, is excellent on the subject but a lone voice and somewhat idiosyncratic;[7] and I have written one book and edited several others relating to the subject[8] and am the convener of a study group in New York on the psychology of fundamentalism that connects with the study of paranoia, along with some other analysts. But for such a vital subject that is so important if we are to understand contemporary violence, we are left with a surprisingly thin literature that tells us anything.

In what follows, the reader should keep in mind that the apocalyptic dimension of fundamentalism and paranoia do not necessarily overlap. But, to analyze systematically the relationship of fundamentalism and apocalypticism to violence, we must begin with paranoia. Certain things are clear. The paranoid lives in a world of heated exaggerations, one in which empathy has been leached out and one that lacks as well humor, creativity, and wisdom.[9]

The paranoid lives in a world of shame and humiliation, of suspiciousness, aggressivity, and dualisms that separate out all good from pure evil. The paranoid is grandiose and megalomaniacal and always has an apocalyptic view of history that contains within it a mythical sense of time. Many paranoids are very smart, and I have long felt that paranoia may be the pathology of choice for the gifted. There is no question paranoia focuses all of one's cognitive abilities in ways that can make one's schemes intellectually daunting, which is why I have always thought that paranoia is a pathology of the gifted. Some have noted that a heightened degree of suspiciousness bordering on mild paranoia can be adaptive in situations of real chronic danger, as many African Americans experience in the ghettos of American cities or as Palestinians feel about their lives in the West Bank or in Gaza. To talk of "adaptive paranoia" in this way, however, is tricky; such talk often emerges with a political agenda in mind, that is, a desire to clarify the identity of the evil persecutor. Such formulations also usually fail to recognize the serious deformations in the self that come with any degree of paranoia. For its sufferers relinquish much to its pathology. In paranoia, everything is intense and of the moment, and time is forever running out. Paranoiacs' understanding of history is truly diseased. Great forces are arrayed against the paranoid; in fact, virtually the workings of the cosmos are aligned to punish and persecute the victim. One is helpless and beaten down, but this keen sense of victimization and what can be seen as negative grandiosity—no one has suffered as much as I have in the face of this persecution—readily turns positive in its most malignant and psychotic form—I am actually greater than my tormenter, I am the creator, I am Napoleon, I am Jesus, and so on. The conspiracies that abound in the world in the mind of the paranoid are not just isolated events that affect him but are actually the very motive force of history. There is nothing of consequence to understand in the world except how these large conspiracies work, which explains why paranoia is so totally self-absorbing.

Furthermore, the instrument of the conspiracies and the source of dread is a large figure, or a conglomeration of figures or forces of dark mystery, which psychological observers have always agreed is a projection of one's own inner sense of evil.[10] What makes psychotherapeutic treatment of paranoids so difficult is that the therapist usually becomes rather quickly established as the persecutor in the mind of the patient. But, for our purposes, it is worth noting that these subjective images of evil that are rooted in trauma become distilled and institutionalized into collective imagoes and designated victims—Jews for Europeans over many centuries, Westerners now for Islamists in the Middle East (the "Zionists and Crusaders" in the discourse of Osama bin

Laden), blacks and Jews for American radical racists—that in turn intensify the paranoid potential in the self. Such imagoes may exist in very different ways for different individuals and even groups. They are, however, imbedded in the collective self (which I do not mean in any technical sense), capable of assuming virulent form in moments of historical and social crisis.

This experience of the apocalyptic other, in other words, grows out of confused and ambivalent but deeply personal knowledge. What gets established is a kind of paranoid projective feedback loop. The awful and disgusting evil other, who is created from within the self of the paranoid, serves as an objective correlative to stir desire and fantasy deep within the paranoid, who in turn strives to find relief by intensifying the imago of the evil other through more projection. The apocalyptic other is always objectified as the subjective self in this way, becoming in the process a ludicrous tangle of desire, power, and malice.

Hofstadter, for example, made an astute observation about the pedantry that always makes a mockery of paranoid attempts to describe the conspiracy he faces.[11] In the literature of those who deny the Holocaust, for example, one finds that some of these tomes have literally thousands of footnotes and other academic trappings, which unconsciously imitate the best of Jewish learning. Timothy McVeigh, in his letters to upstate New York newspapers after his return from the Gulf War but before he embarked on his murderous project, talked vaguely of understanding the big picture that no one else could see or understand, but his letters read like those of the intellectuals he seems to mock.[12] The paranoid knows the evil other because he is his own creation. When he is asked to describe that other, the face of the paranoid takes on a look of horror that comes from a place of secret awareness. It is really very striking. Sometimes, indeed often, he will tilt his head slightly, jut his chin, perhaps turn somewhat sideways to look askance, and smirk with a knowing smile that can become a terrifying and haughty laugh.

The paranoid is a haunted soul. While Freud got the homosexual issue wrong, his most profound insight into the psychology of paranoia was its restitutional character. The actual psychological illness and collapse into paranoia is rooted in some deep and abiding trauma that is almost always beyond the reach of a clinician to unpack in any meaningful way because paranoids are usually so resistant to psychotherapeutic investigation. But to think in terms of the self, what we can surmise is that the paranoid's response to the crisis of fragmentation is a frantic attempt to stave off what he inevitably experiences as the psychological equivalent of death by constructing an alternate universe of imagined dangers populated with projective imagoes of inner experience. That new reality fills in for the old. The new reality is bursting with terror and is not a stable terrain—paranoia, like anxiety, spreads—but at least this new world of malice is familiar. It cannot be taken away, and if one can just understand it properly, maybe, maybe it won't cause more misery and torment.

I cannot stress enough the suffering that lies beneath the often angry, arrogant, and superficially confident exteriors of a paranoid person. I have encountered it often in my clinical practice but usually fleetingly, for the reasons I have mentioned, but for the past two years I actually have had a fully paranoid and often florid psychotic patient in my practice. Treating her has been quite a journey, as she has often been close to suicide, but of late she is actually improving enough to get to the gym and venture out into the world. Harriett is a seventy-three-year-old woman whose neighbors send poison gas in through the air vent, whose colleagues in her local Greenwich Village AA meeting are conspiring to turn her into a "lesbian, drug-addicted slut," and who can barely recover during the night from the pains in her neck from the tasers that are used against her. Her landlord sneaks in at night to do unspeakable things to her sexually, and once she woke up with a large, growling German shepherd in her bed. She once described to me how Karl Rove was engineering her suffering, and the question she kept asking is why he would care about someone so insignificant. In my treatment of Harriett, I decided to take a risk and from the outset regarded her paranoid ideation as absolutely real. Those ideas are, of course, real psychologically, so it is not as though I am being dishonest in a core sense with this troubled patient, but it was a risky stratagem that stretched the limits of my own empathy and forced me into something of a performative mode to talk with her, for example, in a convincing way about her landlord or Karl Rove. But what often is so painful it brings tears to my eyes is to hear Harriett talk about the tormentors in her immediate life and feel how much she suffers *and* seeks in her wild fantasies for explanations that are completely crazy and far-fetched. The world makes absolutely no sense for Harriet. All she really knows is that she suffers.

There is, however, visible rage that surfaces in Harriett's experience. She reports in therapy that in her apartment she often starts yelling at those who torment her, those malevolent figures who are listening in either at the door or via a microphone in the fan or outside her window. Sometimes, she throws things out of frustration and anger. She would kill, she says, though such violent fantasies usually get turned on herself, reducing her to despair and suicidal ideation, and she collapses on the floor in tears. The most important point for our purposes here is that Harriett experiences her fantasies of violence, however fleeting in her case, as ethically justifiable, given what she feels she has been forced to endure. In her experience, the feelings of extreme victimization so embedded in the template of paranoia turn to fantasies of killing her oppressors.

One must dwell on this extraordinary sequence from victimization to violence. The paranoid intimately understands the secret world of evil he has created in his projective schemes. His rigid dualistic outlook further removes him from the malice as it loads him with virtue and righteousness. That other becomes, then, the embodiment of evil and not only can but must be dispensed with. In its more extreme cases, when fantasy turns to action, the paranoid feels more than simply an allowance to kill. It becomes an obligation. And, since in the paranoid world one acts on behalf of absolute righteousness, killing becomes healing, as Lifton wrote so eloquently about with the Nazis, or as Aum Shinrikyo, the apocalyptic Japanese cults in the early 1990s, sought in its wild schemes to carry out Armageddon.[13]

The violence of the paranoid always exists as a potential in fantasy and as such can be turned into action, depending on the moment. Violence is intrinsic to paranoia, even, I feel, ontological within it, at least in fantasy. Such violence is often described as counterphobic, that is, the feeling that "I must strike out at the evil other before it attacks me." Such violence, even in fantasy, is experienced by the paranoid, in other words, as self-protective. But, given the rigid dualistic world that the paranoid inhabits, to act against the perceived tormentor in the name of self-protection is to become a savior. Violence heals and redeems. The evil of the world threatens our very existence. The paranoid becomes himself the vehicle of salvation and redemption, which is why, I think, paranoia plays such an important role in religious fundamentalism and the apocalyptic.

The model I am proposing for understanding the psychological dimensions of the fundamentalist mindset might be conceptualized as a number of overlapping circles that includes but is by no means limited to paranoia and the apocalyptic. In its deeper meanings, paranoia is inevitably apocalyptic (though the converse is not necessarily true). The spaces turn back on themselves, and, in quite a startling way, a clinical investigation of paranoia finds us squarely located in the world of the apocalyptic, which in turn lies at the heart of contemporary religious fundamentalism that we so urgently need to understand. Then again, perhaps the model is more like the mortuary chambers of an Egyptian pharaoh. The mummified body is in one chamber, the preserved heart in another. Long and winding pathways dug into the bedrock often hundreds of feet below the ground open to rooms with food and wine to feed the soul for eternity. All is one yet separate and discreet, the inner secrets of the imposing pyramidal structure that dominates the landscape.

In any event, it is clear that paranoia contains within it the apocalyptic, which is itself a hugely complicated subject. For one thing, apocalyptic ideas are rampant in the culture and by no means restricted to religious fundamentalism. Everywhere there are images of Armageddon and the end, from Homer Simpson, who works fitfully for the local nuclear plant, to Schwarzenegger's *The Terminator*, to the banal *Left Behind* series.[14] Sometimes, a genius like Don DeLillo explores apocalyptic themes in ways that bring new meaning to old forms. In *White Noise* (1991), for example, a professor of "Hitler Studies" moves through traumatic history to nuclear threat, and in *Mao II* (1992) the narrator links the cultic frenzy of the Moonies with immersion and death in the Beirut terrorism of the 1980s. Some of our most perceptive contemporary philosophers are equally drawn to the power of the apocalyptic. How can they not notice it, since it defines the most terrifying and yet sublime levels of contemporary existence? It is not surprising that a new shelf of books on 9/11 appeared in 2002, filled by Jacques Derrida (*The Work of Mourning*), Paul Virilio (*Ground Zero*), and Giovanna Borradori (*Philosophy in a Time of Terror*), among many others.[15]

The powerful idea of totalistic redemption is not without its element of hope. Our own successful 19th-century experience of abolitionism would have been inconceivable without its apocalyptic undertow.[16] In Christian theology, people as diverse as Daniel Berrigan and Liberation Theologians such as Allan Boesak, Elisabeth Schussler Fiorenza, and Pablo Richard read the Book of Revelation as a call for the oppressed to overthrow the world in their own image.[17] Lois Ann Lorentzen, in turn, describes the apocalyptic nature of the environmental activism of Earth First![18]and, one could add, that of PETA and the very interesting and hopeful movement of antiglobalists among young people all over the globe. Even on the wacky edges of this movement, among the millions of those who either feel they have been abducted by UFOs or have faith in the truth of the phenomenon, the feeling among many, as the late John Mack of Harvard described it, is that alien beings outside our familiar Cartesian world are attempting to save us from our path of destruction toward collective death.[19] Finally, people such as the German theologian Jurgen Moltmann, in *The Theology of Hope*, argues for a renewal of Christian eschatology in his read of Revelation, and Catherine Keller, a theologian at Drew University, argues passionately, in *Apocalypse Now and Then* and in many subsequent essays, that Revelation is a text of hope, filled with dark and ominous images, especially directed against women, but that the wild and poetic flux of end-time images must be yoked toward our salvation.[20]

But nor can we ignore the malevolent power of the apocalyptic and its role in the creation of "atrocity-producing narratives."[21] Personally, I am impressed (and appalled) at the Revelation images of blood running up to the bridles of the horses, of seals opening to death, of trumpets blowing violence, and of vials pouring forth destruction in three great sequences of sevens, each linked forward and backward at the endpoints of destruction. Revelation is a story of biblical genocide, with God acting, in the words of James Jones, as a "Divine terrorist."[22] The text is presented as a dream, which is why John writes it in the past tense, and it moves quite logically from the release of great violence at the hands of an angry God to final redemption in chapters 19 through 22. Revelation is also a survivor narrative, for the text proves simultaneously the death and torment of the other and the salvation and redemption of the elect. There are, of course, many survivor narratives, and some can become paradigmatic of the hopeful for all time. But in the apocalyptic the survivor narrative gets corrupted and turned into violence as it gets totalized, or turned into an absolute story of redemption.

I would say, sadly, that we also must understand that the destruction of the apocalyptic other, even if the agency is switched from man to God as in Revelation, is subjectively experienced by those who become violent as serving the highest of purposes. Endism, or the location of self in some future narrative, as I called it in 1994, is highly motivated. Dispensing of the other in collective ways, something we call genocide, grows out of an intensely felt idealistic and moral commitment to make the world better.[23] People commit individual violence for all kinds of idiosyncratic reasons, but it is the deeply idealistic goal of changing history, of correcting it, of purifying it racially and ethnically, that leads to genocide. And, for the most part, those who carry out exterminatory projects feel they are acting on behalf of a messianic goal or on behalf of God's end-time purposes in the world or with some variation of these motivations.

Finally, and most generally, the endist narrative also is not one thing but has itself evolved historically, from the Egyptian *Book of the Dead* in the 13th century b.c.e., to the early Zoroastrians some six centuries later, to the later biblical prophets, including Daniel (ca. 200), to John of Patmos in 95 s.c., and to Joachim of Fiore (1135–1202) in the Middle Ages, but in no way more importantly than in our recent historical discovery of the ultimate power of destruction with nuclear weapons and, increasingly, with biological agents. In fact, nuclear and other ultimate weapons have changed us psychologically in ways we are just beginning to understand. We don't need God anymore, as we have since the beginning of culture, to carry out the end. The agency shifts. Ultimate power of destruction is now in human hands. It changes our world of desire. Nuclear and other ultimate weapons are, of course, dangerous in and of themselves in the hands of wild, apocalyptic groups below the level of the state, such as Aum Shinrikyo, or in the hands of new, religious terrorists like Osama bin Laden, but the more important and subtle psychological point is that the very presence of nuclear weapons in the world evokes the existence of murderous cults and new terrorism, indeed, of fundamentalism itself. Robert Jay Lifton defines "nuclearism" as the "worship" of nuclear weapons for the power of God that they possess. As Lifton put it in 1979: "The ultimate contemporary deformation is a condition we may call *nuclearism*, the passionate embrace of nuclear weapons as a solution to death anxiety and a way of restoring a lost sense of immortality. Nuclearism is a secular religion, a total ideology in which 'grace' and even 'salvation'—the mastery of death and evil—are achieved through the power of a new technological deity."[24]

Nuclear weapons represent the religion of our age. They define our politics and values and most of all set forth the end-time narrative by which we live. Failed states such as North Korea yearn for and acquire the weapons, as do problematic regimes such as the government of Iran. Most informed observers believe that if Osama bin Laden had had access to a nuclear weapon before 9/11 and the operational ability to use it, he would have placed one or more on the planes that struck New York and Washington, DC; he also obtained a *fatwa* (a ruling on a point of Islamic law that is given by a recognized authority) from a radical cleric in 2003 to allow for the use of such weapons in the future.[25] Does he imagine wiping out New York City or ending human history? Such a question in his case is almost certainly hypothetical but may not remain entirely fantastical for other figures in future decades. But we must also remember our own deep and obsessive involvement with nuclear weapons. We joined with the Soviet Union for a half-century in an exterminatory project over ideology that at several points nearly brought about the end of history. We have pulled back from that brink, but now proliferation to other states and probably in the future to terrorist groups has made the world even more unstable. Yet, we cling to the weapons and their power. As others, we worship them in our own peculiar way. It is no longer, if it ever was, an issue of freedom or democracy. Nuclear and other ultimate weapons and all they mean call forth human desire to possess that power, to own it, to make it our own, to reverse the divine sequence, to make ourselves gods.

By this extraordinary psychohistorical turn of events, the apocalyptic other transforms personal suffering into a collective worship of nuclear weapons. It is a dangerous sequence. Paranoia is hardly new in human experience, and it probably emerged countless thousands of years ago in the self as adaptive (e.g., fear of snakes). But paranoia in the contemporary era has perhaps long outlived its useful adaptive meanings. Paranoia, as I have tried to make clear, is inherently apocalyptic, and its tendency to construct the other in these terms opens the self to violent fantasies and, sometimes, action. In a world of rising and often raging fundamentalisms, there emerges a dangerous potential nexus of paranoia and strong faith that embraces nuclear weapons. We can guard against such dangers only by first becoming acutely aware of their dynamics.

NOTES

1. David M. Terman, "Fundamentalism and the Paranoid Gestalt," in *The Fundamentalist Mindset: Psychological Perspectives on Religion, Violence, and History*, ed. Charles B. Strozier, David M. Terman, James W. Jones, and Katharine A. Boyd (New York: Oxford University Press, 2010).

2. Richard Hofstadter, "The Paranoid Style in American Politics," in *The Paranoid Style, and Other Essays*, ed. Hofstadter (Chicago: University of Chicago Press, 1964).

3. Sigmund Freud, "Psycho-analytic Notes on An Autobiographical Account of A Case of Paranoia (Dementia Paranoides)," in *The Standard Edition of the Complete Psychoanalytical Works of Sigmund Freud*, ed. James Strachey, 23 vols. (London: Hogarth Press, 1958), 12:3–84.

4. Jerrold Post, *The Psychological Evaluation of Political Leaders, with profiles of Saddam Hussein and Bill Clinton* (Lansing: University of Michigan Press, 2003); Post, with Barry Schneider, *Know Thy Enemy: Profiles of Adversary Leaders and their Strategic Cultures* (Air Force Counter Proliferation Center, 2003); and Post, *Leaders and Their Followers in a Dangerous World: The Psychology of Political Behavior* (Ithaca, NY: Cornell University Press, 2004).

5. Vamik Volkan, *Bloodlines: From Ethnic Pride to Ethnic Terrorism* (Boulder, CO: Westview Press, 1999) and *Killing in the Name of Identity: A Study of Bloody Conflicts* (Baltimore: Pitchstone, 2006).

6. Joseph H. Berke, Stella Pierides, Andrea Sabbadini, and Stanley Schneider, *Even Paranoids Have Enemies: New Perspectives on Paranoia and Persecution* (New York: Routledge, 1998). Note as well some interesting materials in Robert S. Robbins and Jerrold Post, *Political Paranoia: The Psychopolitics of Hatred* (New Haven: Yale University Press, 1997).

7. Robert Jay Lifton, *The Broken Connection: On Death and the Continuity of Life* (New York: Basic Books, 1979), is Lifton's most theoretical book, but there is much of great interest on fundamentalism, violence, and paranoia in what is now an opus of twenty-six volumes.

8. Charles B. Strozier, *Apocalypse: On the Psychology of Fundamentalism in America* (New York: Beacon Press, 1995); Strozier and Michael Flynn, *The Year 2000: Essays on the End* (New York: New York University Press, 1997); Strozier and Flynn, *Trauma and Self* (Plymouth, UK: Rowman and Littlefield, 1996); and Strozier and Flynn, *Genocide, War, and Human Survival* (Plymouth, UK: Rowman and Littlefield, 1996).

9. Heinz Kohut, "Forms and Transformations of Narcissism," in *The Search for the Self: Selected Writings of Heinz Kohut: 1950–1978*, ed. Paul H. Ornstein, 4 vols. (1968; New York: International Universities Press, 1978), 1:427–460. Note also my biography of Kohut, *Heinz Kohut: The Making of a Psychoanalyst* (New York: Farrar, Straus andGiroux, 2001).

10. One anonymous reader of this essay strongly suggested that I use the Jungian term "shadow" in this context. I would prefer not to employ a Jungian term, however, for it would imply a construct that, however useful in some contexts, suggests an entire theoretical apparatus that I am not comfortable adopting.

11. Hofstadter, "The Paranoid Style," 35–37.

12. Charles B. Strozier, "Apocalyptic Violence and the Politics of Waco," in *The Year 2000: Essays on the End*, ed. Charles B. Strozier and Michael Flynn (New York: New York University Press), 97–111.

13. Robert Jay Lifton, *The Nazi Doctors: Medical Killing and the Psychology of Genocide* (New York: Basic Books, 1985) and *Destroying the World to Save It: Aum Shinrikyo, Apocalyptic Violence, and the New Global Terrorism* (New York: Metropolitan Books, 1999).

14. Tim LaHaye and Jerry B. Jenkins, *Left Behind: A Novel of the Earth's Last Days* (1996); *Tribulation Force: The Continuing Force of Those Left Behind* (1997); *Nicolae: The Rise of Antichrist* (1998); *Soul Harvest: The World Takes Sides* (1999); *Apollyon: The Destroyer Is Released* (1999); *Assassins: Assignment: Jerusalem, Target: Antichrist* (2000); *The Indwelling: The Beast Takes Possession* (2001); *The Mark: The Beast Rules the World; Desecration* (2001); *Antichrist Takes the Throne* (2001); *Glorious Appearing: The End of Days* (2004); *Armageddon* (2004), all from Carol Stream, IL: Tyndale House. Note Glenn Shuck, *Marks of the Beast: The Left Behind Novels and the Struggle for Evangelical Identity* (New York: New York University Press, 2004), and James W. Jones, "Eternal Warfare: Violence on the Mind of American Apocalyptic Christianity," in *The Fundamentalist Mindset: Psychological Perspectives on Religion, Violence, and History*, ed. Charles B. Strozier, David M. Terman, James W. Jones, and Katharine Boyd (New York: Oxford University Press, 2010), 91–103.

15. Jacques Derrida, Pascale-Anne Brault, and Michael Naas, *The Work of Mourning* (Chicago: University of Chicago Press, 2003); Paul Virilio and Chris Turner, *Ground Zero* (London: Verso, 2005); Giovanna Borradori, *Philosophy in a Time of Terror: Dialogues with Jurgen Habermas and Jacques Derrida* (Chicago: University of Chicago Press, 2004).

16. See my chapter, "The History of American Endism," in *Apocalypse: On the Psychology of Fundamentalism in America*, ed. Charles B. Strozier (New York: Beacon Press, 1995), 167–193.

17. Catherine Keller, *Apocalypse Now and Then* (Boston: Beacon Press, 1997), xi–xiv.

18. Lois Ann Lorentzen, "Phallic Millennialism and Radical Environmentalism: The Apocalyptic Vision of Earth First!," in *The Year 2000: Essays on the End*, ed. Charles B. Strozier and Michael Flynn (New York: New York University Press), 144–153.

19. John Mack, *Abduction: Human Encounters with Aliens* (New York: Ballantine Books, 1995).

20. Jurgen Moltmann, *The Theology of Hope: On the Ground and the Implications of a Christian Eschatology* (Kitchener, ON: Fortress Press, 1993); Keller, *Apocalypse Now and Then*.

21. Robert Jay Lifton, *Home From the War: Learning from Vietnam Veterans* (Boston: Beacon Press, 1973), 65.

22. James W. Jones, "Eternal Warfare: Violence on the Mind of American Apocalyptic Christianity," in *The Fundamentalist Mindset: Psychological Perspectives on Religion, Violence, and History*, ed. Charles B. Strozier, David M. Terman, James W. Jones, and Katharine A. Boyd (New York: Oxford University Press, 2010).

23. Robert Jay Lifton, *Thought Reform and the Psychology of Totalism: A Study of 'Brainwashing' in China* (New York: Norton, 1961), 433–437, talks of the "dispensing of existence" as central to what he calls "thought reform."

24. Lifton, *The Broken Connection*, 369.

25. Michael Scheuer, the author of *Imperial Hubris: Why the West Is Losing the War on Terrorism* (Dulles, VA.: Potomac Books, 2004), revealed later in the year that he published his book the quite remarkable *fatwa* that bin Laden had sought from a radical Saudi sheik after 9/11. Scheuer had been the senior intelligence analyst at the CIA in the late 1990s. He headed the secret group of analysts following bin Laden then and for several years after 9/11. Shortly after his resignation from the CIA, he appeared on *60 Minutes*, the CBS news program, on November 14, 2004. In that show, Scheuer said two things about bin Laden and nuclear weapons. One is that he confirmed how serious had been the efforts of bin Laden before 9/11 to acquire weapons of mass destruction, In the period after 9/11, in part responding to criticisms from some in the Muslim world regarding the killing of Muslim civilians, bin Laden then sought a *fatwa* from Hamid bin Fahd in May 2003 that would allow their use. In the *fatwa*, Fahd specifically allowed for the use of nuclear weapons against Americans.

PART II

Medieval Prologue

Cosmic Christian Anxiety and

Global Modern Paranoia

4

The Devil's Hoofs

The Medieval Roots of The Protocols of the Elders of Zion

JEFFREY R. WOOLF

The late Professor Walter K. Ferguson concludes his classic study, *The Renaissance in Historical Perspective: Five Centuries of Interpretation*,[1] with a chapter entitled "The Revolt of the Medievalists," which might better have been termed "The Revenge of the Medievalists." In it, Ferguson describes how 20th-century medievalists (starting with Charles Homer Hastings) sought to redress the balance of historical interpretation as far as the European Renaissance[2] was concerned. Rather than marking the birth of the firstborn son of modern Europe, as Jakob Burckhardt would have had it,[3] the Renaissance (assuming that there was one) was the child of High and Late Medieval culture and would have been impossible without the latter's intellectual, cultural, and technological achievements and advances. The medievalists' revolt against the primacy of the "Renaissance," begun by Haskins and company, added crucial dimensions of understanding and appreciation for the high degree of continuity and the significance of the discontinuities that obtain between medieval and modern Western culture.

From many, perhaps from most, perspectives, *The Protocols of the Elders of Zion* is a modern creation, just as anti-Semitism and, indeed, Auschwitz are the rightful, though bastard, children of modernity. It is modern in its *sitz-im-leben*. It is modern in the power-hungry nature and goals that it ascribes to the Jews. Certainly, it is modern in the issues and phobias that possessed its authors and readers. It is, thus, quite legitimate that a significant number of the more recent studies engendered by the *Protocols* address questions such as the sources used by the authors in its creation and the enigma of its continued attraction, power, and impact. While traditional Christian anti-Judaism does receive proper mention in these discussions, many scholars, and certainly more popular writers, seem to underplay its role, either because they assume that its nature and function are self-evident or because they are loath to touch it.[4]

Of course, there are a number of central studies that do give due weight to the heavy contribution of medieval anti-Judaism to the creation of the work (dare we call it that?). Chief among these, of course, is Norman Cohn's *Warrant for Genocide*.[5] As is well known, Cohn's central thesis in that work is that the image of the Jew in *The Protocols of the Elders of Zion* is primarily a modern version and expression of the traditional Christian image of the Jew as either the Devil's apprentice or, more typically, Satan incarnate. In this, he was following the line of argument first developed by Cecil Roth[6] and later expanded by Joshua Trachtenberg in *The Devil and the Jews*,[7] with fine tuning by Robert Bonfil and Jeremy Cohen, in the context of their respective analyses of Raymundus Martini's polemical masterpiece, *Pugio Fidei Adversus Mauros et Judaeos*.

Still and all, while fully acknowledging the accuracy of this contention, I suggest that a considerable amount of work remains to be done in reconstructing the processes by which medieval themes were developed into the shape that they occupy in the *Protocols*, and in anti-Semitic discourse generally. Such an enterprise is valuable both per se, as an inquiry into the history of ideas, and because it will give us an insight into how modern anti-Semitism both modifies and continues medieval anti-Judaism.

The points to be considered in this connection are really of two different types. The first is topical. The text of the *Protocols* is rife with assumptions about the Jews that can often be traced back to the earliest days of Christianity but that attained their full expression and form in the High and Late Middle Ages, whence they were transmitted to the modern world. Among these, in addition to an adumbration of the identity of the Jew with Satan, are his alleged unflagging hatred for Christians and Christianity, his desire for vengeance against Christians, Jewish carnality and materialism, and so on.

The second point is, in my opinion, of even greater importance. The effectiveness of the *Protocols* is partly attributable to the tendency to think symbolically and typologically. In the Middle Ages, the individual Jew was perceived to be little more than than the embodiment of the "Theological Jew," whose contours were cultivated by Paul, the Church Fathers, and their successors. Similarly, the *Elders of Zion* provides the so-called real Jew of the modern era for authors and readers of the *Protocols*. Typological perception of reality and the assumption that "what you see is not really what you get" were hallmarks of medieval culture and society (indeed, of most traditional societies), as has been so effectively proven by Le Goff, Mâle, and Gurevitch.[8]

The propensity to do so continued into the modern world and found its tangible expression in the *Protocols* and in the Nazi cinematic masterpiece

Der Ewige Jude. I suggest that taking the measure of the medieval modes of processing reality will provide needed insight into the power of the *Protocols* in the century just concluded and currently in the Muslim world, as pointed out by Itamar Markus in this volume. (As an aside, I would like to suggest, following an insight derived from Jean Baudrillard's essay *America*, that the Internet and electronic culture have created a new type of illiteracy and revived [or reinforced] a penchant for symbolic and typological thinking in contemporary culture. In light of Richard Landes's efforts regarding *Pallywood and Al Durah*, this development does not bode well for our topic.)[9]

Here I would like to focus upon one theme whose appearance in the *Protocols* both continues and modifies a central theme and dilemma of medieval anti-Judaism: anxiety and ambivalence about the depth of Jewish knowledge and fear of a global Jewish conspiracy. The way in which Christianity resolved these dilemmas over time—the projection of their own insecurities—gives us insight into both the psychological dynamics of the fantasy, and to whom it appeals with its "higher truth."

On several occasions, the author(s) of the *Protocols* has the speaker boast of the fact that he possesses secret knowledge that allows for world domination (13) or that the social sciences were foisted upon the Christian world by the Jews in order to sow dissension and to undermine morality (9–10).

The idea that the Jews possess a secret lore is intimately connected with the question of the attitude of the Church first to the Talmud and rabbinic literature and later to Jewish mysticism, or Qabbalah.[10] Until the 12th century, Western Christendom was largely ignorant of the fact that contemporary Judaism no longer literally reflected biblical norms but had developed into rabbinic or Talmudic Judaism. When it did discover this, it came as something of a shock, since, as Jeremy Cohen has shown,[11] the Augustinian theory of the Jews as witness to the advent of Christianity had been predicated upon Judaism being frozen in a biblical mode, that is, the Judaism that Jesus had ostensibly transformed, spiritualized, and superseded.

In the early 13th century, under the aegis of Raymond da Peñaforte, the Dominican (and later the Franciscan) order developed a two-tiered response, an inherently contradictory attitude toward the Talmud. On one hand, the Talmud was to be excoriated and placed on trial as a blasphemous, heretical, and dangerous document and physically destroyed. The Talmud was deemed to be heretical because it presumed to complement divine revelation through the Oral Law. It was dangerous because, through largely tendentious, though (I am fairly convinced) sincere, interpretations of passages throughout rabbinic literature, the Talmud seemed to embody and dictate behavior that expressed the unflagging hatred of the Jews for non-Jews, Christianity, and its founder. This approach tallies well with the rise of anti-Jewish sentiment and violence that began with the First Crusade. Furthermore, it fits in with the growing perception that the Jews posed a physical threat to Christians (blood libels) and were also a spiritual menace, on the assumption that Jews are responsible for whatever heresies might imperil the soul of Europe's Christians.

Simultaneously, the self-same Talmud (along with the rest of rabbinic literature) was interpreted as a *Testimonium Adventum Christi*. Out of a profound conviction of the self-evident truth of Christianity, the friars strove to demonstrate that the rabbis of the Talmud, who lived in the days of Jesus and the earliest Christians, must have known the truth but, in their perverse obstinance, refused to acknowledge that which they knew to be true. Nevertheless, in anticipation of the Freudian slip, they averred that the rabbis had strewn their writings with formulations from which the basic truths of Christianity could be demonstrated.

The first interpretation was unveiled at the so-called Disputation of Paris, in 1240, in which the Talmud was put on trial and convicted. Two years later, twenty-four cartloads of Talmudic manuscripts were publicly burned on the site of the Hôtel de Vosges. The second tack was effectively launched two decades later, in the Barcelona Disputation of 1263, which pitted R. Moses Nahmanides against the apostate Paulus Christianus. One hundred sixty years later, the anti-Pope Benedict XIII staged a two-and-a-half year spectacle at Tortosa and San Matteo in 1413–1414.

Both approaches continued to be used interchangeably throughout the Middle Ages and into the modern era. I would like to stress the word "interchangeably" because, paradoxically, this two-pronged offensive is inherently self-contradictory. After all, how can the same Talmud both blaspheme against and testify to the truth of Christianity?[12] How can the same literature require both destruction and preservation (not to mention dissemination)?

The usual answer to this is that the Jew is the ally of Satan, or the Devil incarnate.[13] Just as Satan knows the truth but tries to destroy it and its adherents, so do the Jews. No matter which role the Talmud filled, then, the secret lore of the Jews was a diabolic creation—with, in the hands of Christian exegetes, redeeming features.

At this juncture, it is worth noting that the exact same two-sided approach developed regarding Jewish mystical literature. As is well known, Giovanni Pico della Mirandola and his teacher Marsilio Ficino noticed the affinity between Zoharic Qabbalah and neo-Platonism. They propagated the idea, in terms that were typical of Renaissance Italian humanism, that Qabbalah represented a secret lore that confirmed the truths of Christianity, especially the concept of a triune godhead.

Significantly, the clearest formulation of this position may be found in *De Arte Cabalistical*, by Johannes Reuchlin. Reuchlin firmly believed that the writings of the ancient rabbis, among whom he included the author of the mystical tract the *Zohar*, possessed and withheld precious testimony and proof of the truth of Christianity, proof that must be elicited and propagated among Christians and employed in the interest of converting the Jews. Indeed, this contention formed the backbone of his defense of the Talmud (*Augenspiegel*), in response to the charges of blasphemy and heresy leveled against it by Johannes Pfefferkorn in 1509, that is, that the Talmud is referred to as Tradition, or Qabbalah, and that Qabbalah testifies to the truth of Christianity.[14]

Reuchlin's opinion of Qabbalah was not shared by everyone. For reasons that are still not totally clear but that are definitely related to the rise of interest in hermetic teachings[15] and the ever-present image of the Jew as sorcerer, Qabbalah from the 15th century onward (especially in Germany, and this is largely what stands behind Luther's invectives against Jewish superstition and sorcery) was increasingly identified with magic, especially black magic (word: cabal). In other words, like the Talmud, Qabbalah was seen as simultaneously destructive and salutary, though (and to this I will return in a moment) not always interchangeably so.

The fact that the same fate accrued to both the Talmud and the *Zohar* is not a coincidence. If one thinks about it, and I must admit that I've not found anyone who's said this, the deeply conflicted, contradictory attitude toward Jewish religious literature constitutes an exact reflection of the deeply conflicted, contradictory attitude of Western Christianity toward the Jews and Judaism. Following the model framed by Augustine, the Jew is to be excoriated and punished, yet he serves a positive function in society, so he must be preserved. He is both deicide and witness. Historically, rage and murderous hatred are visited upon him, yet there is a deep, abiding desire to convert him—to receive validation from his conversion. No less than Innocent III, who introduced the Jew-badge in Europe (though the patent, traditionally, belongs to Caliph Umar ibn al-Quttab), waxes lyrical as he speculates upon the wonderful addition that Israel will make to the Church when its branch is grafted thereupon. And, while Jeremy Cohen may well be correct that the Dominicans and Franciscans rejected the Augustinian position and wished to eradicate Judaism in Europe, their own logic (and papal policy) dictated that both sides of the contradiction must be maintained, as they were throughout the Middle Ages.

Once the early modern era dawned, however, and the Jews were placed into ghettoes (in those countries from which they had not been totally expelled), something did change. If one looks carefully at the material collected by Trachtenberg (and I am very much aware of the limitations of his analysis), one finds that the real jump in the extreme diabolization of the Jew took place in the 16th and, to an even greater extent, the 17th centuries. In other words, specifically (*davqa*) when the Jew was no longer a regular part of the Christian environment (and, as Jacob Katz has shown, the Jews put the finishing touches on a doctrine of tolerance vis-à-vis Christianity), the imagination of a not insubstantial number of Europe's Christians took flight and the image of the Jew took on dimensions of monstrosity that it had never before assigned (again, primarily in Germany, but not just there).[16]

The same thing happened to Jewish books. Now, the fact of the matter is that from the 15th century onward, one finds that attacks on the Talmud as pernicious and heretical far outweigh the number of disputations arranged with the intent of converting Jews based upon evidence from the Talmud. So there is a clear direction of development. Nevertheless, in the late 16th and early 17th centuries, the redeeming side of rabbinic literature nigh on disappears from the Jewish-Christian encounter, and the same appears to be true of Qabbalah. Johann Andreas Eisenmenger's *Entdecktes Judenthum* (Königsberg, 1711) is the ultimate expression of this development.

Furthermore, the Talmud and Qabbalah themselves undergo something of a transformation. From specific literary works, they are metamorphosed into something disembodied, secret, and sinister. The malevolent Jew, then, is left with his heretical, hermetical secret lore. And, as far as many were concerned, that is the Jew, and the Judaism, that emerged from the ghetto. Taken to its logical conclusion, this point of view could not but see the Jew and Judaism as lacking any redeeming features, unlike the situation that obtained in the Middle Ages.

Obviously, anti-Jewish and anti-Semitic discourse took on multiple forms and nuances, of which the *Protocols* is but one form. However, it appears clear that the image of the malevolent Jew and the secret Jewish sciences that the "learned elders" (again, a reference to Talmudism?) intend to use to achieve world domination grew out of the inner contradiction that lay at the root of medieval Christianity's attitude toward the Jews and Judaism and the diabolical way in which it resolved that contradiction during the age of the ghetto.

1. New York, 1982.

2. Cf. Peter Burke, *The European Renaissance. Centres and Peripheries* (Oxford: Blackwell, 1998).

3. Jakob Burkhardt, *The Civilization of the Renaissance in Italy* (1860; New York: Modern Library, 2002).

4. An interesting example of this sort of attitude is the deeply pained, though political correct, rumination by Stephen Eric Bonner, *A Rumor about the Jews: Reflections on Antisemitism and the Protocols of the Elders of Zion* (New York St. Martin's, 2000). See, for example, 1–11.

5. N. Cohn, *Warrant for Genocide: The Myth of the Jewish World Conspiracy and the Protocols of the Elders of Zion* (London: Serif, 1967).

6. C. Roth, "The Medieval Conception of the Jew: A New Interpretation," in *Essays and Studies in Memory of Linda R. Miller*, ed. I. Davidson (New York: Jewish Theological Seminary, 1938), 171–190.

7. J. Trachtenberg, *The Devil and the Jews: The Medieval Conception of the Jew and its Relation to Modern Antisemitism* (New Haven: Yale University Press, 1943).

8. J. Le Goff, *Medieval Civilization, 400–1500*, trans. J. Barrow (Oxford: Blackwell, 1988); E. Mâle, *The Gothic Image: Religious Art in France of the Thirteenth Century*, trans. D. Nussey (New York: Harper and Row 1972); A. Gurevich, *Categories of Medieval Culture* (London and Boston: Routledge and Kegan Paul, 1985).

9. Jean Baudrillard, *America* (Verso, 1989); Richard Landes, "Al Durah Investigation," *The Second Draft*, http://www.seconddraft.org/index.php?option=com_content&view=article&id=62&Itemid=80.

10. A related topic, to which I cannot relate here, is that of "Hebrew Truth," or *Hebraica Veritas*.

11. J. Cohen, *The Friars and the Jews: The Evolution of Medieval anti-Judaism* (Ithaca, NY: Cornell University Press, 1982), and Cohen, *Living Letters of the Law: Ideas of the Jews in Medieval Christianity* (Berkeley: University of California Press, 1999).

12. Interestingly, while the Tortosa Disputation was overwhelmingly devoted to the latter tact, toward the end of the proceedings Benedict XIII shifted gears and announced, without missing a beat, that, after using the Talmud to prove Christianity, authorities would then put it on trial for heresy. The truth is that, as demonstrated by Jeremy Cohen, the major work outlining the probative approach to rabbinic literature, Raimundus Martini's *Pugio Fidei Adversus Mauros et Judaeos*, also betrays this characteristic.

13. Cohen does note that, in his opinion, the mendicants who developed these strategies regarding rabbinic literature were merely manipulative.

14. See Johannes Reuchlin, *Recommendation Whether to Confiscate, Destroy and Burn All Jewish Books: A Classic Treatise against Anti-Semitism*, tr. Peter Wortsman (New York: Paulist Press, 2000).

15. On the hermetic movement in the Renaissance, see Francis Yates, *Giordanno Bruno and the Hermetic Tradition* (Chicago: University of Chicago Press, 1964); on Judaism and the Hermetic Tradition, see Moshe Idel, "Jewish Kabbalah and Patonism in the Middle Ages and the Renaissance," in *Neoplatonism and Jewish Thought*, ed. Lenn E. Goodman (Albany: SUNY Press, 1992), 319–351.

16. Of course, there was also significant scholarly interest in Judaism and in Jews, which serves as an important contretemps to this development.

5

Thomas of Monmouth and the
Protocols of the Sages of Narbonne

JOHANNES HEIL

Some years ago, Horst Fuhrmann published a book entitled *Überall ist Mittelalter* (*Middle Ages Everywhere*).[1] In this book, the former president of the Monumenta Germaniae Historica (MGH) tried to demonstrate how much of what we consider to be modern has its roots in the Middle Ages or is part of a medieval heritage. One point, however, he neglected: the impact of medieval anti-Jewish beliefs on modern ones, especially on the idea of "Jewish conspiracy."[2] *The Protocols of the Elders of Zion* is probably the most scandalous text of the 20th century, because of its content, its broad reception, and its unceasing attraction. It seems to us that the *Protocols* is something like an archetype or "ideal type" of modern, 20th-century anti-Semitism.

Of course, Thomas of Monmouth, who is mentioned in the title of this chapter, wrote, in the middle of the 12th century, a traditional "Life of a Saint," the "*Vita sancti Guilelmi*,"[3] and no *Protocols of the Sages of Narbonne* has ever been written, not by Thomas, nor by Rodulf Glaber, John of Winterthur, or any other medieval expert of conspiracy. The title of this chapter, however, indicates that the 20th-century fictions are by no means as modern as we usually believe them to be.[4]

Therefore, this chapter will add two arguments. First, it will point out that the narrative of the *Protocols* is neither unique nor exclusively modern but has a long prehistory that emanated from apocalyptic concepts of the High Middle Ages. Second, it will show that the long history of conspiracy beliefs reveals much of the mix of continuities and discontinuities that is so typical of the history of anti-Jewish beliefs or prejudices in general. Old and new conspiracy narratives share some of their characteristic elements, but they reveal also significant differences. Since early conspiracy ideas are framed by a cosmic-religious context, whereas modern concepts appear to be thoroughly secular, the focus of this chapter has to be on how this shift worked and by which factors it was driven.

The analysis starts with a fictional text from the end of the 19th century, which is not from the so-called *Protocols of the Elders of Zion*. Thereby it should become clear that the *Protocols* is by far not the only such text from the turn of the 20th century. Like others, the text of the *Protocols* is thoroughly scandalous, but with regard to form and literary quality it appears, when compared to others, weak and boring. Here is a section from a currently rather unknown but in its time widely read novel by (Ps.-) Sir John Retcliffe (Hermann Goedsche, 1815–1878), *Biarritz*, published in 1868–1876. In the chapter "Auf dem Prager Judenkirchhof" ("On the Jewish Churchyard in Prague"), we read:

> Once in hundred years, at a fixed time, representatives of the twelve Jewish tribes meet at Prague's Jewish cemetery. They will discuss the steps necessary to take to accomplish their aim: to gain the rule over the whole world. During their last meeting [in the 19th century] they counted all the resources which "Israel" had collected at London, Paris, Amsterdam and Frankfurt. Furthermore they discussed, what they could do to further impoverishment of artisans and farmers, what to blame the military institutions, what to improve the schism between the churches, and finally how to contribute to improving the annihilating liberal spirit. "Eighteen centuries our enemies dominated—the new century will be Israel's century" the assembly concluded.[5]

The author left no doubt that his text presumed to be fiction. However, does this mean that its content was also considered to be fictional? Why at all did he write this nasty story, and why was only this single chapter soon reprinted and widely distributed as a separate print? We can guess that the author and his audience believed the fiction to be factual.

Almost 650 years earlier, the English chronicler Matthew of Paris reported a story that has astonishing similarities to Goedsche's fact-fiction. The medieval author, too, told about Jewish aspirations, enmity, treason, and conspiracy when he reported on how enthusiastically the Jews of the continent reacted to the message of the arrival of the Mongols at the borders of Latin Europe in the 1230s.

> Many Jews from overseas [from the continent], especially from the Holy Empire, gathered secretly, since they believed, that they and the Mongols were of the same origin and these were their brethren, which once had been enclosed by order of Alexander the Great behind the Caspian mountains.

The one which was considered to be the most learned and richest among them, held a speech: "My brethren . . . our God Adonay has permitted for a long time, that we suffer from the power of the Christians. Yet, right now, the time has come, that we will be freed for that with God's permission we should oppress them. Since our brethren, the enclosed tribes of Israel, went out from their captivity to subvert the whole world. . . . So let us approach them with the most precious gifts and let us receive them in greatest honor."

What he said was gratefully accepted, therefore they brought all the weapons they could find, and in order to hide their crime better they put them in barrels. Then they told the Christian princes, whom they served, that the Mongols are Jews and that they would drink no other wine than kosher wine; . . . "But we want" [the Jews said] "to remove such inhuman and bad enemies from [our] midst and we want you [Christians] free from the impending danger of depopulation; therefore we have prepared thirty barrels with deadly poisoned wine, which we would like to send them." The Christians consented, yet when the Jewish convoy passed a bridge in the southern parts of Germany, a guard discovered the fraud. And now it became clear, "that those whom the Christians tolerate, with whom they do commerce, and to whom they are even allowed to lend money, aim at the destruction of the Christianity."[6]

Matthew Paris appears here to be a modern rather than a medieval author. In his report, God remains a rhetorical figure in the misguided beliefs of the Jews, and we hear nothing about the devil or the Antichrist, who were central to medieval ideas about conspiracy. The author provides a thoroughly secular account in which the Jews, with the help of the mysterious coreligionists from the Far East, aim at taking rule in the present world. If we had no other chronicle from the Middle Ages at hand than Matthew Paris's version of the Jewish-Mongol plot of 1240, we should conclude that there is no difference between medieval and modern concepts of conspiracy.

Yet, if we read a bit further in Matthew's works, we also meet different approaches. In his version of the blood libel legend of Lincoln (1255),[7] God and heaven are indispensable actors in the course of the events. The story of the murder of a Christian child during the Holy Week follows an already established narrative model, conceived of as an imitation and reactualization of the historical passion of Jesus; the "crime" of the Jews becomes obvious to the Christians through God's immediate intervention. Thereby, the narrative makes the Jews play an active role in the celebration of the Holy Week through their enactment of a kind of a negative Eucharist.

Such accounts I call "sacred legends" ("*Sakrallegenden*"), and I should explain in clearer terms what "sacred" here means. Therefore, I will refer to an even older story, taken from Ademar of Chabannes, who died in 1034. He also reported an event that took place on a Good Friday, but its narrative construction seems to be more archaic: On Friday during the Holy Week in 1018, after the end of the ceremony of the adoration of the cross, the Earth trembled in Rome and a heavy storm arose, since, as a (converted?) Jew from the "Greek Synagogue" (*de schola grecia*) told the pope, the Jews blamed at that moment in their synagogue the "Figure of the Crucified." The pope, then Benedict VIII, immediately took action and ordered the culpable members of the community beheaded. Thereby, the storm came immediately to an end.[8]

Ademar did not yet know of the ritual murder accusation; he lived more than a hundred years before Thomas of Monmouth, who was among the first to refer to this accusation and the first to put it into literary form (William of Norwich, 1144, *Vita S. Guilelmi*, c. 1150).[9] But Ademar already "knew" about the Jews' enmity toward the cross and about Good Friday as the appropriate date to dramatically express this enmity. In his eyes, already, the Jews were rebels against the divine order who would never accept their inferior status and would attack Christianity and Christ at any occasion.

Now we have a sample of paradigmatic accounts at hand, which permits us to compare the medieval and the modern versions of "Jewish conspiracy." It becomes clear that the alleged reunion of Jewish notables at Narbonne at which, according to Thomas of Monmouth, the murder of Christian children was planned annually and other stories have a lot of similarities with the "idea" of the modern Protocols. We shall therefore examine the differences between the older and the modern versions, and then their inter-relation.

Yet let us first consider what they have in common:

The first point is to emphasize the importance of meetings and planning in accounts of conspiracy. The Jews in Goedsche's novel gather every hundred years at a certain place, and their meeting follows the same agenda each time. Its sole purpose is to counsel on how to harm the Christians and how to get control over the world. The same happens in the medieval accounts. Not simply somewhere in the Jewish world, but at Narbonne, in this great community at the border between *Zarfat* (France) and *Sepharad* (Spain), the Jews held their assembly, as Thomas of Monmouth says. There they decided annually which community in the widespread Jewish world should provide the indispensable Christian victim for that year.

Narbonne was more than just an important community; it was a central community and a transfer place between North and South. In the past, the community with a veritable "Nasi" ("prince") at its head had enjoyed far-reaching autonomy and incomparable privileges.[10] The importance of communication is typical also for accounts of the later Middle Ages: according to them, the Jews would not only kill the victim or desecrate the sacrament but also would distribute the blood or the particles of the host among other communities. In order to commit "sacred crimes," the Jews would use their usual network of communication; they would gather for planning and committing the crime, or they would disseminate the portions of the desecrated host among their coreligionists in other towns and lands (as, e.g., illustrated in the desecration narrative of Passau from 1477).[11] The various destinations of host particles might delineate a certain area of local Jewish communication, which in the case of Passau included Bohemia and Austria and in the case of Sternberg (Mecklenburg/Germany) in 1492 not only [Berlin-] Spandau and Braunschweig but also places as far away as Frankfurt am Main, Nuremberg, and Venice.[12]

So far, the accounts by Thomas of Monmouth and others contain some basic realistic elements (i.e., the fact of intensive communication among the minority's members and its geographical extension), and this perhaps is the most important observation to make here: A successful account about hostile conspiracy should contain as many realistic elements as possible, and the plot should be the result of a few "logical" operations with a set of well-chosen elements and a mix of facts, knowledge, suspicion, and assumptions. There is almost no account of ritual murder, host desecration, or poisoning of wells that does not contain the element of precrime meeting, counseling, and planning.

Notably, there are many accounts that relate the alleged crime to Jewish holidays, and there are, in German sources from the end of the Middle Ages, finally those in which the crime has become the very purpose of the gathering for a holiday, a circumcision, or a wedding. The Jewish wedding at Sternberg in 1492 from which generated one of the best-documented host desecration allegations of the late Middle Ages (here, the fiancé delivers the stolen host to his bride as a spectacular overture to the wedding night) is only one among many examples.[13]

Indeed, in what historians consider to be the real world, Jews from different communities met from time to time, to discuss community affairs and rules (*Takkanot*) or to organize business matters. On the other hand, Christians also met for similar purposes. Since the Church, too, called its representatives regularly to councils, in the mind of medieval men the almost inevitable conclusion was that the leaders of the non-Christian "anti-Church" would do the same. Therefore, every account of a Jewish meeting of conspiracy is to a certain extent a mirror of social reality; the alleged purpose of the meeting was probably the only fictional element in such stories.

The second element that occurs in both medieval and modern accounts of conspiracy—the communication—is structurally related to the first one (and its social setting is also almost the same). The Jews in Goedsche's novel come from different places all over Europe, but they know the rules, and they arrive in time. Letters and messages are a central element also in medieval accounts. This could be a letter written in Hebrew that an ignorant Christian transmitted from France to England, it could be the distribution of particles of the desecrated host among the Jewish communities of the area, it could be poison that messengers brought from the south or from the east, or it could be instructions for how to use it.[14] Regardless of how this communication was believed to "work" in detail, all such accounts presented the Jews as a collective body spread over small communities but bound together through many forms of communication.

Already in 1010, the extensive network of Jewish communication played a key role in the belief that the Jews had sent a secret message to the "Caliph of Cairo" telling him to destroy the Holy Sepulcher in Jerusalem, a plot to destroy Christendom.[15] In Matthew of Paris's mid-13th-century account about the Jewish-Mongol plot, not a single person or the community but the Jews of "Alemannia" as a whole are the acting subject. This implies that an intensive communication preceded the execution of the conspiracy (which luckily failed). Here again, the idea of conspiracy reflected a given practice: The life of a minority group required intensive communication and a high degree of mobility.

There were many reasons to write letters, and, basically, the Christians had a realistic idea about it: a mid-15th-century Christian source informs us that Jews from Wroclaw communicated with Jewish sages in Legnica to get guidance on a complicated issue. So far, realistic. But the objective of this communication in 1453 was unrealistic: that the Jews had desecrated a host, and, after its astonishing reaction—the host started heavily to bleed and the Jews were unable to get rid of it—they forwarded it to their sages and asked how to deal with it.[16]

The third timeless element to mention here is the construction of a supralocal and supranational Jewish elite. In Goedsche's novel, the Jews gather from Amsterdam, Frankfurt, London, and Paris. Today he might add Tel Aviv, New York, the UN, and perhaps Moscow. They are the representatives of their communities, a meta-elite that constitutes Judaism as a supralocal collective body. Consider the difference: In Ademar's account on the Roman Good Friday, the Jewish community of Rome still acts as a whole and remains an anonymous body. But, by that time, an elite had emanated from this local collective, and soon its leaders became known by names: Thomas of Monmouth mentioned Eleazar, "the richest of the Jews of Norwich," as the head of the group of the murderers of young William.[17] John de Oxenedes, in his account of the blood libel allegation at Lincoln in 1255, made an explicit distinction between the ordinary Jews and the "main perpetrators" (*malefactorum . . . principalis*).[18] This Christian perspective is mirrored even in Jewish sources. The entry in the Nürnberg Memorbook on the host-desecration affair at Roettingen (Franconia, 1298) mentions the assaults against the "eminent men of the holy, eminent community."[19]

Again, this belief, too, has some real background. Reporting the case of Simon of Trent (1475), the late-15th-century "Austrian Chronicle" (by Matthias Kemnat or Jacob Unrest) puts the distance between the elite and the ordinary members of the community of Trent into a reasonable daily context: The leaders of the Jews planned a meeting during the Holy Week in their synagogue for a discussion of "what everyone lacks for the celebration of Easter," yet the assembly is said to have been postponed since "there were too many other people" (Gepovel) there. Even the Jew who was in the end charged with delivering the Christian victim, the boy Simon, argued later before the judges that he had no idea of the crime's purpose.[20]

The idea of an acting elite had, with regard to plausibility, a further advantage: Confronted with the alleged crimes of the Jews, the audience might have argued that they knew their own Jewish neighbors were not criminals but peaceful men. The distinction between elite and ordinary Jews served to abolish this contradiction. Consequently, when the Jews of Wroclaw were accused in 1453, the elders of the community were considered to be the initiators of the host desecration and were executed. The other members of the community, however, could evade death through conversion.[21]

The next point that old and modern versions of conspiracy beliefs have in common is the conviction that Jews pursue secret aims to the benefit of their coreligionists and to the misfortune of non-Jews. If the Jewish traitor had not reported to the pope the reason for the earthquake and storm at Rome in 1018, the "cause" would have remained undiscovered; similarly with the secret letters "the Jews" sent to al Hakim to destroy the Holy Sepulcher in 1009. The Jews, Christians argued, would plan and commit their crimes secretly. Reports about public blasphemies against the sacrament, the cross, or the statue of the Virgin are rather seldom.

However, the meeting at the Jewish cemetery at Prague was discovered by the modern novelist; the ritual murder and the host desecration through a miracle (through divine intervention); the poisoning of waters, at best, through watchful authorities or by the sheer number of victims of the disease. When the houses of the Jews were removed from Nuremberg after the pogrom of 1349, many subterranean rooms were discovered. This was hardly unusual for German city houses, and the author of the "Meisterlin chronicle" should have known this.[22] Nevertheless, in the case of the Jewish houses, he presented the discovery of ordinary basements as cause for alarm.

The issue of the "Jewish secret" leads to the point, where the specific account—the one about the Jewish conspiracy—reveals its embedding in a broader context. For Christian eyes, the Jewish world was full of secrets. We sense this in remarks about the un-understandable Hebrew letters, in ideas ("knowledge") about the content of the Talmud, and in reports about the purpose of synagogues and schools. The Jewish sphere, with its characteristic differentness, was in all regards a cause for confusion and concern. This is true not only for the propagators of alleged Jewish crimes, as we find this concern even in the Papal Bulls of protection for Jews. Here with the first words already, the inviolability of the Jews is subject to conditions: "*Sicut Judais non permittitur*"—"Such as that the Jews are not allowed to do anything in their synagogue contrary to the law"[23]—as if the Jews would otherwise permanently break the law. In 1298, Pope Nicolas IV wrote at the demand of German Jews to Emperor Rudolf and asked him to free Rabbi Meir of Rothenburg. The pope's good intention is obvious, yet he felt the need to argue twice that the noble captive "had nothing committed to subvert (*in subversione*) the Christian faith."[24] We may call this the "language of conspiracy" that precedes the idea of conspiracy.[25]

The last point to make here concerns the alleged aims of the Jews. Some modern and medieval authors tried to find out and to rationalize the aims of the Jews. In the case of modern authors, there was no doubt: The Jews try to overtake the society as a whole by dominating companies, money markets, the press/media, and government, and they use every means, even conversion, assimilation, charity, and sponsorship, to pursue their aims. The medieval case is more delicate, since the picture remains in many sources somewhat unclear. But it seems that with regard to Jewish aims, a considerable shift occurred during the centuries from 1000 to 1600. In Orléans in 1010, the Jews' aim was clear: they tried to undermine Christendom by getting a Muslim to destroy the Holy Sepulcher. In Rome, in 1018, the Jews tried to mock the cross and thereby to challenge heaven. Similarly, the blood libel legend was originally a narrative about the annual re-execution of the cru-cifixion. In 1235, however, a different story was told: The Annals of Marbach mention a "widespread rumor" (*"sicut fama communis habet"*) that the Jews need Christian blood for the celebration of Pesach (*"in parasceve necessa-rium habent"*). Here the audience learned that the Jews would prepare some kind of medicine from the blood (*"ad suum remedium"*).[26]

Accounts like this have led Gavin Langmuir to speak about ritual can-nibalism instead of ritual murder. There might be something correct in his observation, yet his terminological setting actually misses the most astonish-ing point. In the version that the Marbach Annals give for the ritual murder allegation at Fulda in 1235, the focus has moved from a sacred to a kind of empirical and scientific context. The reason for the misdeed of the Jews has left its former religious setting and is placed in the Jews' bodies and specific physical deficits. The former narrative, which had transformed the blood allegation from a re-actualization of the crucifixion into a sacred context, did not completely disappear (as the many images of the "martyrdom" of Simon of Trent and other examples indicate); however, the secularized rationale as given in the Marbach Annals spread in a parallel process over Europe during the next centuries. The late-15th-century *Cronica Gestorum in partibus Lom-bardie* (or *Diarium Parmense*) reported in 1480 a ritual murder committed by Jews from Treviso; here the reader learns that, through this crime, "many of them are saved from their disabilities (*sanantur*)."[27]

So what are the differences between old and modern conspiracy narra-tives? First, according to modern narratives, the Jewish conspirators no longer need Christian supporters. Once, in the imagination of Christians, they had been indispensable figures: the bad monk, who communicated the messages of the Jews of Orléans to the Caliph (1009), the deacon who fell in love with a Jewish girl and went to bed with her on the night following Good Friday, the Christian woman who saved the host under her tongue and delivered it to the Jews, the poor man who sold his *only* child to the Jews, the lepers whom the king of Grenada charged on advice from the Jews to distribute the poison in 1321 (as the continuator of Guillaume de Nangis relates), the wife of the sacristan who held the keys for the sanctuary, or the thief who broke into the sanctuary and stole the host[28]—they all have disap-peared from the stage of modern conspiracy beliefs. Admittedly, the Nazi propagandists still knew the figure of the *Judenknecht* ("servant of the Jews"), yet here it became a function of polemic and played no necessary role in the commission of the crime. In the Middle Ages, however, the Christian sup-porters were indispensable: They provided access to the sacrament, and—as the Jews are said to have argued (according to the continuator of Guillaume de Nangis, mentioned earlier, in 1321)—only the lepers could travel in the midst of the Christian world without provoking suspicion. This difference between the old and the modern versions is obvious, and the explanation for it is rather simple: In the old days, the story required Christian participation, whereas in modern times it does not.

The second difference is more subtle: The Jews themselves gradually lost their previous affiliations. We touch here on the broad complex of medieval and early modern apocalypticism, the Jews' position in both forms in the mind of Christians, and the changes undergone by this concept from the 10th to the 17th centuries. Sometime around the turn of the the 9th century, Christian exegetes, inspired by a selective reading of the Bible and apocryphal prophecies (Pseudo-Methodius, Tirbutian Sibylla), had started to consider the Jews to be the true followers of the Antichrist. In this version, the Jews would be the first to believe in the Antichrist; they would stay with him until his fall, and all of them or only some of them would perish together with him. According to the simple symmetries of sacred history in Christian eyes, the Messiah whom the Jews expected, since they did not believe in Christ, could be no other than the Antichrist.[29]

Haimo of Auxerre, the great exegete of the School of Auxerre, summarized these concepts in the mid-9th century: The Antichrist will be born out of the tribe of Dan, he will come to Jerusalem, there he will circumcise himself, and he will reveal himself to the Jews as their Messiah. In Jerusalem, he will order the temple rebuilt. In the end, all the nonbelievers, pagans, and Jews will perish with him, since God sent him into the world for no other reason than to bring about their fall.[30] Adso of Montier-en-Der in the 10th century designed a veritable *vita* of the coming life of the Antichrist in which the Jews played the same central role.[31]

Here we grasp the essence of premodern conspiracy beliefs. To the mind of medieval men, the reservations of the Jews toward the cross, Christ, and Christianity were no surprise and represented far more than an issue about belief only. Christians assumed that Jews would express their reluctance actively, as the almost necessary consequence of their fundamental opposition to the future course of history that God had provided. Today, we consider medieval stories about alleged Jewish crimes to be awful exceptions, but most probably to the medieval mind they were rather reasonable and "normal." To medieval men and women, it was highly likely that the Jews would mock the cross (Ademar), that they would conspire with the king of Babylon (Radulf Glaber), or that they would deliver Christianity to the hands of the Mongols (Matthew Paris). In this regard, the modern monstrosity *The Protocols of the Elders of Zion* is nothing but the continuation of a common medieval apocalyptic scenario.

Nevertheless, it would be too simple a conclusion if this essay were to end here. Aside from the fact that modern conspiracy beliefs originated in medieval apocalypticism, there is something else to mention, and it seems to me that this is no less important: The medieval version was contained in the order of the world. God himself would send out the Antichrist, as Haimo of Auxerre had emphasized. This means that all that the Antichrist in the future and his allies on Earth in the present would do would be directed against God and his people, but it would not happen without God's permission. In consequence, in the mind of medieval Christians, everything that had happened and that would happen corresponds to the course of the world as ordered and foreseen by God. Even in their loyalty to the Antichrist, the Jews would—as ultimate consequence—serve the Christians and contribute to the fulfillment of history.[32]

In the modern versions of conspiracy beliefs, however, the Jews are no longer under God's control. On their way through the ages, they not only lost their fellow supporters among the bad Christians; they lost also their metaphysical instigator. The belief in Jewish conspiracy survived the leveling of the apocalyptic rhetoric and finally the elimination of the Antichrist from mainstream discourse, which happened at some point during the 17th century.[33] Modern fancies about Jewish conspiracy and world domination expect a thorough triumph of the Jews and a lasting serfdom of the societies which they would overtake. Nothing and nobody would bind or control them, and there would be nothing in their deeds that in the end could work to the benefit and the perfection of the non-Jews. All that the Jews would undertake would contribute to their own profit only and to the thorough misfortune of the non-Jews. One might say, in the mind of (many) non-Jews, the Jews, like the Christians and post-Christians, had emancipated themselves from their medieval environment. And their aims had shifted from spiritual and salvific goods to secular, material ones: All that they will seek is financial and political domination.

I call this a process of desacralization, and I attribute this in a wider sense to the multifaceted process of secularization. How can this shift be explained, and what does it mean for the question of continuities and discontinuities between premodern and modern forms of anti-Jewish arguments? A simple answer would be that the process of secularization changed the concept of conspiracy and led to a complete overturn of the original setting, by which the Jews moved into the position once held by supranatural powers. Thus, the modern form of conspiracy beliefs would be nothing than a deplorable by-product of the process of emancipation and a dark heritage in the process of civilization. There is certainly some truth in this, yet this process is more complex, and further observations should be made, which are summarized here briefly.

Let us return to Matthew Paris and his perfect narrative realization of a world drama between good and evil. Matthew was a medieval writer, but the Jewish-Mongol plot, as he presented it, happened from its beginning to its end on the ground of this world. Heaven and hell remained quiet, no angels were sent out, no devils appeared on the stage, and no Antichrist is visible. Jews and Mongols act as true actors, not as functions of superior powers. One might argue that Matthew kept figures like the Antichrist silently backstage and that they were present in the audience's mind. This seems possible, but it is also true that he did not need these figures to tell his story. The same is true for many other medieval accounts, even for a considerable number of ritual murder and host desecration legends. It would be difficult to count them, but presumably the majority of these accounts give no indication about the aims for which the Jews should have committed the alleged crimes and also do not refer to God, Christ, or Antichrist.

Today, as we read these accounts, we know the rationale behind them— that in the Christian mind the Jews would repeat Christ's passion or would try to disenchant the holiness of the sacrament—and since we know that master narrative, we read silently all of these motives into a text where most of it is not written. In his *Vita* of Saint William, Thomas of Monmouth exten-sively discussed the reasons why the Jews killed the boy, as he believed them. Yet, in the chronicle written only a few decades later by Radulph of Cogge-shall, the details were rather short and imprecise: "a boy named William has been crucified by the Jews near Norwich." The author mentions no further circumstances or miracles. And it remains unclear why the Jews should have done this.

The same narrative negligence can be found in many other reports on the boy William of Norwich in England and, sometime later, in those on the con-tinent.[34] Robert of Torigni (d. 1186), abbot of Mont Saint Michel, reported for the time from 1144 to 1171 four cases of ritual murder—at Norwich in 1144, near Paris in 1163, at Gloucester in 1164, at Blois in 1171—but his comment on these is by no means clear: "One says that they [the Jews] commit this often during Easter, if they find an occasion to do it."[35] Why did Radulph and others not tell the full story as Thomas of Monmouth had given it? There are several possible answers to this question. One would be that Thomas's text was not much known. This indeed seems to be the case, since there are only few surviving manuscripts. But this does not mean that the narrative that his *vita* provides was not widely known. The story that Thomas had written about William had been retold many times in the successive decades and centuries, with other places and other names being substituted. And knowledge about the "circumstances" of William's death in 1144 also spread independently of Thomas's *Vita*, even on the continent.[36]

The second possibility is that chroniclers like Robert and Radulph, who had so many other things to report, felt no need to tell the whole story because they trusted that everybody knew the sacred background of the alleged crime. This means that authors included only textual signals that the readers were able to recognize on the basis of their own knowledge. We can assume that medieval chroniclers indeed intended the short story to be read as the full story, but if this was the case, then, in the long run, the outcome of this process has been the exact opposite of its intention. What was meant to continue a tradition in fact produced transformation.

The paradoxical conclusion is that the frequent story of the Jewish sacrilege was retold during the Middle Ages, and, the more people believed in it as a matter of fact, the more the story about the alleged crimes of the Jews became neglected, desacralized, and profane as a result; the more often the story was retold, the shorter and the more "worldly" it became. Sacred and semisacred explanations for the deeds of the Jews were replaced by accounts of a specific, even inborn, Jewish criminality, but these narratives focused on deeds and aims as typical criminality, and sometimes these were even mixed with comical narrative elements. In the end, people simply believed that Jews would kill Christians on any occasion, such as, in a story transmitted by Caesarius of Heisterbach and Gautier de Coinci, a pious scholar singing loudly "Salve Regina" in their street.[37]

The court records about the ritual murder accusation at Diessenhofen (Rhine, Switzerland) in 1401 report the argument that the Jews were accused of committing the crime in order to get rid of their "awful smell", but "on the question, why they try so forcefully to condemn the Christians," one of the accused is said to have answered that "we shall know that they all wish, that they have power over us, like we Christians have now the power over them."[38] Beyond any deterministic reading of the sources, one can conclude that this interrogation record—which was not a narrative account in a chronicle and which was written 250 years after the first narrative realization of the blood libel legend—had undertaken the argumentative step toward the modern, secular idea of Jewish conspiracy. Thomas of Monmouth, who had put the story about the holy boy William into a written hagiographic account around the middle of the 12th century, had hardly foreseen this move.

When at the end of the year 1348 the Jews of Kenzingen near Freiburg im Breisgau were forced to confess before the judges that "they had poisoned all the wells at Kenzingen," a veritable bundle of Jewish "crimes" was brought to light. Though in the whole account no single aim of the accused Jews is mentioned, it contains the confession of a Jew that two years previous the Jew had "slaughtered" (*geschächted*) two boys, one at Tübingen, the other at Munich. Abraham, another accused, confessed to have killed (*verderbet*) in 1347 a child at Strasbourg, whom he had bought for ten pounds. This was by no means the end of the Kenzingen protocol: The Jews were even charged with having poisoned the sauerkraut, and with having shit on (*beschissen*) the grapes in the wine press and done the same in the ditch, so that finally even fishes and frogs died. The ritual murder accusation was here only one element among many. If we read this protocol as a document of confessions made under the impression of torture and therefore as a mirror what authorities at the end of 1348 expected to hear from the mouth of a heavily threatened defendant, it is once more notable that the whole protocol mentions no sacred context in which all of these crimes were believed to have been committed.[39]

Admittedly, the Kenzingen protocol also permits an *extensive* reading: Taking seriously only half of the alleged crimes, one could conclude that the Jews committed sins against men and animals, meaning against creation as a whole. Then, the poison was more than simply an instrument; it was a veritable expression of the Jews' nature. One may argue that, between the lines, such court records consider the Jews to be enemies of God and rebels against the divine order (God's creation). However, once again, no God was mentioned in the Kenzingen protocol, and heaven remained silent. The Jews' enmity was directed completely against the world down here, and in this world the Jews, as our source reports, try to cause every possible damage and distress. Therefore, I read texts like the record of the investigation at Kenzingen in 1348 and many similar other reports that diligent authorities generated in the course of these years as documents that indicates a shift in the conception of the Jews: In Christian eyes, they had changed from enemies of God to enemies of men.

When observed throughout the long period from the High to the later Middle Ages, the idea of a "Jewish conspiracy," especially in its worldwide extension, appears to have been originally a by-product of internal Christian discourses that only consequently turned into negative concepts about the Jews and their alleged deeds. This leads to a paradoxical conclusion: that the narrative that was in its beginnings a dispute about faith, orthodoxy, and enmity and which was then externalized from intra-Christian discourses and consequently attributed to Jews returned some decades later into the middle of these Christian societies as the idea of a real threat by non-Christian "criminals" to Christians and their communities. Looking back from the 14th-century sources to the high medieval origins of conspiracy beliefs, it becomes clear there was no one-way development of the motive of Jewish conspiracy.

What we can see, then, are manifold roots and formation-contexts of the motive behind the Jewish conspiracy. We discover a tangled situation, where various narratives contain traces of elements that were to become typical components of anti-Jewish conspiracy beliefs. Therefore, we have to be careful when tracing back the prehistory of a text such as *The Protocols of the Elders of Zion*. The modern view tends to arrange the past according to its own knowledge and time-bound experiences in a linear way. Single cases in this brief overview prove repeatedly that specific elements of conspiracy concepts were given in anti-Jewish narratives, whereas others, especially in early examples, were lacking. Even this should be read not according to a simple scheme of gradual accumulation but as evidence for a wide range of rather different articulations, in which arose single elements of conspiracy beliefs and various anti-Jewish contextualizations, in the beginning independently and later on in a more interwoven fashion.

It seems to be significant that many observations about conspiracy ideas can be made in conjunction with respective anti-Jewish sacred legends leading to enchantment, ritual murder, and host desecration allegations, but each one of these legends as a whole was more than just a conspiracy narrative. At least in their formative period, roughly from 1150 to 1235 or so, these stories were meant to promote piety and faith, and they led to threats and death for Jews. But, during these early decades, the role of the Jews was a by-product of such narratives, and, though life threatening for those who had "to play" the role of the anti-Christian, these narratives presented the figure of the Jew as he appeared in many other Christian hagiographic texts. Later on, and in remarkable contrast to narratives about Jewish magic, violation of the human body, or desecration of the divine body in the sacraments, which were initially bound to sacred contexts, the libel of poisoned wells finally centered the Jews' activities and aspirations to the earthly sphere. Here the anti-Jewish allegation turned from a sacred legend into a thoroughly secular and simply criminal context, which overruled the attraction of sacred legends in part, be it temporarily or completely.

This observation has an impact on the evaluation of the relation between apocalypticism and conspiracy ideas that can hardly be overestimated. František Graus, in his groundbreaking study on the Black Death pogroms of 1347–1349, has argued that the idea of Jewish conspiracy became condensed as a result of anti-Jewish beliefs of the 14th century, which in turn culminated in the years of the plague.[40] However, conspiracy motifs in a distinct sacred and apocalyptic setting appear in narrative sources and in considerable number, as Arno Borst and Richard Landes have pointed out, as early as the 11th century.[41]

Apocalyptically alert chroniclers like Rodulf Glaber and Ademar of Chabannes or, to a much lesser extent, Otto of Freising in the 12th century[42] report many such examples from their own days and from the past. Within a few decades from the time of Adso of Montier-en-Der, shifts in theology and mentality, for which the construction of the Antichrist in a negative hagiographic framework is an indicator, had turned into a new construction of reality concerning past, present, and future, with the Jews as actors in its center: As the Jews would follow the Antichrist in the end of days, so they would behave in the present, and so significant deeds would also be discernible in the past.

Yet, given that the very characteristic of modern beliefs about Jewish conspiracy is their thoroughly secular conception, meaning that Jews would gain uncontested rule over politics and markets here in the world, the distance between medieval and modern concepts appears to be remarkable. In that respect, however, such "modern" concepts can be considered to be by-products of narrative strategies and rules rather than of reflected theological and ideological shifts. Many times retold and reshaped, the story of Jewish conspiracy was well known to audiences, and narrators could limit their account to sketches and catchword motifs. Such a condensed report concerned what the Jews would do, less why they would do so. In the 14th century, when lepers and/or Jews were repeatedly accused of poisoning the wells, waters, and world, the process of consecutive narrative reductionism and desacralization had been accomplished.

Now, in view of imagined and real crisis, the 14th century generated a new powerful and cruel narrative about enmity and conspiracy that was thoroughly secular. The number of logically consistent scenarios of conspiracy that deal with nothing else than worldly affairs come to considerable amounts in 14th-century sources and in the reports of informed courts, judges, city councils, and some chroniclers, as well. Since the 14th century, a consistent concept of Jewish conspiracy beyond any metaphysical alignment has been available: The Jews would direct their enmity immediately against the Christians and seek for ways to establish their uncontested rule.

The apocalyptic conspiracy, as reported so archetypically by Ademar in his account of Rome in 1018, still was included in the divinely ordered destination of this world and was therefore thought to fail in the end, since, with the Antichrist's defeat, the aspirations of his followers would necessarily fail. Yet, with the emergence of a noncosmic, secularized conspiracy narrative in the 13th and 14th centuries, things changed dramatically: The new narrative denied the possibility of any corrective intervention from above, and, if men would not put an end to it, the conspiracy would finally succeed. This is the medieval heritage that informed modern concepts of Jewish conspiracy, long before *The Protocols of the Elders of Zion* came into existence. The outlook of Jew hatred had become "modern" long before modernity, and there was basically nothing new in Goedsche's novel or in the *Protocols*.

NOTES

1. This chapter is based on a paper given in September 2003 for the Mosse Workshop at the University of Wisconsin, Madison, on invitation by Klaus Berghahn and David Sorkin. I am grateful for their comments and suggestions given during the discussion.

2. Interestingly Norman Cohen, in his seminal works on messianism, conspiracy ideas, and totalitarism, has failed to pinpoint the connection between medieval and modern narratives: see Norman Cohn, *The Pursuit of the Millennium. Revolutionary Millenarians and Mystical Anarchists of the Middle Ages*, revised and expanded version (London, 1970); the German version has a remarkably different title: *Das Ringen um das tausendjährige Reich. Revolutionärer Messianismus im Mittelalter und sein Fortleben in den modernen totalitären Bewegungen* (Bern, 1961); see also Cohn, *Warrant for Genocide. The Myth of the Jewish World Conspiracy and the Protocols of the Elders of Zion* (Harmondsworth, 1970).

3. See note 8.

4. For overviews, see also Henri Zuckier, "The Conspiratorial Imperative: Medieval Jewry in Western Europe," in *Changing Conceptions of Conspiracy*, ed. Carl F. Graumann and Serge Moscovici (New York, 1987), 87–103; Lucien Bély, "La place de l'étranger dans les conspirations," in *Complots et conjurations dans l'Europe moderne. Actes du colloque international organisé par l'École française de Rome, l'Institut de recherches sur les civilisations de l'occident moderne de l'Université de Paris-Sorbonne et le Dipartimento di storia moderna e contemporanea dell'Università degli studi di Pisa . . . 1993*, ed. Lucien Bély, Yves-Marie Bercé, and Elena Fasano Guarini (Collection de l'École Française de Rome, 220; Rome, 1996), 393–410; Robert Wistrich, "The Devil, the Jews, and Hatred of the Other," in *Demonizing the Other. Antisemitism, Racism, and Xenophobia*, ed. Robert Wistrich (Studies in Anti-Semitism, 4; Amsterdam, 1999), 1–15.

5. My translation; see Sir John Retcliffe [Hermann Goedsche], *Biarritz. Historisch-politischer Roman in acht Bänden*, Bd. 1 (Berlin, 1905), 130f.; see Volker Neuhaus, *Der zeitgeschichtliche Sensationsroman in Deutschland 1855–1878. "Sir John Retcliffe" und seine Schule* (Berlin, 1980).

6. Matthaeus Parisiensis, *Chronica majora*, ed. Henry R. Luard, 7 vols. (RBMAS; 57.1–7) (London 1872–1883; repr. 1964), 4:131–133; see Sophia Menache, "Jews, Saracens and the Jewish-Mongol 'Plot' of 1241," *History* 81 (1996): 321–342.

7. Matthaeus Parisiensis, *Chronica majora* (1880), 5:516–519; see Sophia Menache, "Matthew Paris's Attitudes toward Anglo-Jewry," *Journal of Medieval History* 23.2 (1997): 139–162.

8. Ademar de Chabannes, *Chronicon*, ed. Pascale Bourgain, *Ademari Cabannensis opera omnia* (CCCM, 129; Turnhout, 1999), 1:171; see Kenneth Stow, *The "1007 Anonymous" and Papal Sovereignty: Jewish Perceptions of the Papacy and Papal Policy in the High Middle Ages* (Hebrew Union College Annual Supplements, 4; Cincinnati, 1984), 28; Daniel F. Callahan, "Ademar of Chabannes. Millennial Fears, and the Development of Western Anti-Judaism," *Journal of Ecclesiastical History* 46 (1995): 23–34; Richard Landes, *Relics, Apocalypse, and the Deceits of History: Ademar of Chabannes, 9891034* (Harvard Historical Studies, 117; Cambridge, MA, 1995); Daniel F. Callahan, "The Cross, the Jews, and the Destruction of the Church of the Holy Sepulcher in the Writings of Ademar of Chabannes," in *Christian Attitudes toward the Jews in the Middle Ages - A Casebook*, ed. Michael Frassetto (New York, 2006), 15–23.

9. Thomas of Monmouth, *The Life and Miracles of St. William of Norwich*, ed. Augustus Jessopp (Cambridge, 1896); see Christopher Ocker, "Ritual Murder and the Subjectivity of Christ: A Choice in Medieval Christianity," *Harvard Theological Review* 91 (1998): 153–192; Jeffrey J. Cohen, "The Flow of the Blood in Norwich," *Speculum* 79 (2004): 26–65; Denise L. Despres, "Adolescence and Sanctity. 'The Life and Passion of Saint William of Norwich,'" *Journal of Religion* 90 (2010): 33–62. Israel J. Yuval ("Vengeance and Damnation, Blood and Defamation. From the Act of Martyrdom to the Blood Libel Accusation," *Zion* 58 (1993): 33–90; Hebrew with English summary pp. VI–VIII) has argued that the ritual murder narrative was known on the continent as early as 1147 (Würzburg).

10. Jeremy Cohen, "The Nasi of Narbonne. A Problem in Medieval Historiography," *American Jewish Studies Review*, 2 (1977): 45–76; Aryeh Graboïs, "Le 'roi juif' de Narbonne," *Annales du Midi* 218 (1997): 165–188; Shlomo H. Pick, "Jewish Aristocracy in Southern France," *Revue des Etudes Juives* 161,1–2 (2002): 97–121.

11. See Johannes Heil, ,*Gottesfeinde'—,Menschenfeinde'. Die Vorstellung von jüdischer Weltverschwörung, 13.-16. Jahrhundert* (Antisemitismus: Geschichte und Strukturen, 3) (Essen, 2006), 387–409; the pamphlet with pictorial scenes of the Passau desecration, printed at Nürnberg 1497–1498, in Heinz Schreckenberg, *Die Juden in der Kunst Europas. Ein historischer Bildaltlas* (Göttingen/Freiburg, 1996), 271.

12. See Heil, ,*Gottesfeinde'*, 402, passim.

13. *Die geschicht der Jüden tzum Sternberg ym landt tzu Mecklenburg* (Magdeburg?, 1492; Berlin: Staatsbibliothek Prs. Kulturbesitz, Inc., 1494), 10, fol. A2r ff.; also *Von der mishandelung des heiligen Sacraments von den iuden zu sternberg, o.O., o.J.* [Bamberg] ~ 1492]; see Wolfgang Treue, "Schlechte und gute Christen. Zur Rolle von Christen in antijüdischen Ritualmord- und Hostienschändungslegenden", *Aschkenas* 2 (1992): 95–116, 99; Volker Honemann, "Die Sternberger Hostienschändung und ihre Quellen," *Abhandlungen der Akademie der Wissenschaften in Göttingen, Philol.-Hist. Klasse*, 3rd series, 206, ed. Hartmut Boockmann, (Göttingen, 1994), 75–102; Caroline Walker Bynum, *Wonderful Blood: Theology and Practice in Late Medieval Northern Germany and Beyond* (Philadelphia, 2007), 69–74.

14. For the many examples see Heil, ‚*Gottesfeinde*', ch. 5, pp. 371–521.

15. Richard Landes, "The Massacres of 1010: On the Origins of Popular Anti-Jewish Violence in Western Europe," in *From Witness to Witchcraft. Jews and Judaism in Medieval Christian Thought*, ed. Jeremy Cohen (Wolfenbütteler Mittelalter-Studien; Herzog August-Bibliothek, 11; Wiesbaden 1996), 93.

16. ‚*De expulsione iudeorum*,' in *Monumenta Poloniae historica—Pomniki Dziejowe Polski* (Lwów, 1878), 3:787f.; see Heidemarie Petersen, "Die Predigttätigkeit des Johannes Capistrano in Breslau und Krakau 1453/54 und ihre Auswirkungen auf die Judengemeinden in Polen und Schlesien," in *In Breslau zuhause? Juden in einer mitteleuropäischen Metropole der Neuzeit*, ed.Manfred Hettling et al. (Studien zur jüdischen Geschichte, 9; Hamburg, 2003), 22–29.

17. Thomas of Monmouth, *The Life and Miracles of St. William of Norwich*, ed. Augustus Jessopp (Cambridge, 1896), I.6, 24f.; see also, II.13, 97f.

18. John de Oxenedes, *Chronica*, ed. Henry Ellis (RBSMA,13; London, 1859), 202.

19. *Das Martyrologium des Nürnberger Memorbuches*, ed. Siegmund Salfeld (Quellen zur Geschichte der Juden in Deutschland, 3; Berlin, 1898), 164; see Friedrich Lotter, "Hostien-frevelvorwurf und Blutwunderfälschung bei den Judenverfolgungen von 1298 (Rintfleisch') und 1336–1338 (‚Armleder')," in *Fälschungen im Mittelalter. Internationaler Kongreß der Monumenta Germaniae Historica, München, . . . 1986, vol. V: Fingierte Briefe, Frömmigkeit und Fälschung, Realienfälschungen* (MGH Schriften, 33.V; Hannover, 1988), 533–583.

20. Jakob Unrest, *Österreichische Chronik*, ed. Karl Grossmann (MGH Script. rer. germ., n.s., 11; Weimar, 1957), V.52, pp. 47, 49.

21. "De persecutione Iudaeorum Vratislaviensium anno 1453," ed. Wojciech Kętrzyński, in *Monumenta Poloniae Historica* (Lwów, 1884), 4:5; similar is the case for the pogrom in the duchy of Austria 1421, see *Die Wiener Geserah vom Jahre 1421*, ed. Samuel Krauss (Wien, 1920), 69f.; Thomas Ebendorfer, *Chronica Austriae*, ed. Alphons Lhotsky (Scriptores rerum Germanicarum, nova series 13, Berlin and Zurich 1967), 370f.; Eveline Brugger, "Von der Ansiedlung bis zur Vertreibung. Juden in Österreich im Mittelalter," in *Geschichte der Juden in Österreich*, ed. Eveline Brugger and Martha Keil (Österreichische Geschichte, 15, Wien 2006), 123–227 (Wiener Forum für Theologie und Religion, Vienna , forthcoming).

22. Sigmund Meisterlin, ‚Chronicle 1488,' III.22, in *Die Chroniken der deutschen Städte vom 14. bis ins 16. Jahrhundert*, ed. Hist Kom. Bay Ak Wiss (Historische Kommission bei der Bayerischen Akademie der Wissenschaften; München, 1864), 3:160; see Michael Toch, "'umb gemeyns nutz und nothdurfft willen.' Obrigkeitliches und jurisdiktionelles Denken bei der Austreibung der Nürnberger Juden 1498/99," *Zeitschrift für Historische Forschung* 11 (1984): 1–21. Johannes Heil, "Verschwörung, Wucher und Judenfeindschaft, oder: die Rechnung des Antichristen", *Aschkenas* 2012 (forthcoming).

23. Solomon Grayzel, "The Papal Bull 'Sicut Judeis,'" in *Studies and Essays in Honour of Abraham Newman*, ed. Meir ben Horin et al. (Philadelphia, 1992), 243–280; for Christian ideas about Jews see Yaacov Deutsch, "Polemical Ethnographies. Descriptions of Yom Kippur in the Writings of Christian Hebraists and Jewish Converts to Christianity in Early Modern Europe," in *Hebraica veritas? Christian Hebraists and the Study of Judaism in Early Modern Europe*, ed. Allison P. Coudert and Jeffrey S. Shoulson (Philadelphia, 2004), 202–233; Maria Diemling, "Anthonius Margaritha on the 'Whole Jewish Faith': A Sixteenth-Century Convert from Judaism and His Depiction of the Jewish Religion," in *Jews, Judaism, and the Reformation in Sixteenth-Century Germany*, ed. Dean P. Bell and

Stephen G. Burnett (Leiden, 2006), 303–333; Thomas Noll, "Albrecht Altdorfers Radierungen der Synagoge in Regensburg. Zur Wahrnehmung jüdischer Lebenswelt im frühen 16. Jahrhundert", in *Wechselseitige Wahrnehmung der Religionen im Spätmittelalter und in der frühen Neuzeit*, ed. Ludger Grenzmann (Berlin, 2009), 189–229.

24. Shlomo Simonsohn, *The Apostolic See and the Jews, Documents* (Studies and Texts; 94/110, 1; Toronto, 1991), No. 259, p. 267.

25. See Heil, ‚Gottesfeinde', 165–204.

26. *Annales Marbachenses*, ed. Roger Wilmans, in MGH Scriptores (1861), 17:178; Gavin Langmuir, "Ritual Cannibalism," in his *Toward a Definition of Antisemitism* (Berkeley, 1990), 263–281; see Christopher Ocker, "Ritual Murder and the Subjectivity of Christ: A Choice in Medieval Christianity," *Harvard Theological Review* 91 (1998): 153–192, 183f.

27. *Cronica Gestorum in partibus Lombardie et reliquis Italie (Diarium Parmense)*, ed. Giuliano Bonazzi (Rerum Italicarum Scriptores. Raccolta degli storici italiani . . . ordinata da L. A. Muratori, 2nd ed., vol. 22.3; Città di Castello, 1904), p. 72, lines 19–28; p. 106, lines 8–12; see also Thomas of Cantimpré, *Thomas von Cantimpré, Miraculorum, et exemplorum memorabilium sui temporis libri duo*, ed. Georg Colvener (Douai, 1605), 2.29.23, p. 305.

28. Guillaume de Nangis, *Chronique Latine de 1113 à 1300, avec la continuation de cette chronique de 1300 à 1368*, ed. Hércule Géraud (Paris, 1843; repr. New York, 1965), 2:31–35; further examples in Treue, *Schlechte und gute Christen*, 95–116; Heil, ‚Gottesfeinde', 454–495.

29. See Richard Kenneth Emmerson, *Antichrist in the Middle Ages. A Study of Medieval Apocalypticism* (Seattle, 1981); Bernard McGinn, "Portraying Antichrist in the Middle Ages," in *The Use and Abuse of Eschatology in the Middle Ages*, ed. Werner Verbeke, Daniel Verhelst, and Andries Welkenhuysen (Mediaevalia Lovanensia; I.XV; Löwen, 1988), 1–48; Johannes Fried, "Endzeiterwartung um die Jahrtausendwende," *Deutsches Archiv für Erforschung des Mittelalters* 45 (1989): 381–473; Gregory C. Jenks, *The Origins and Early Development of the Antichrist Myth* (Beih. zur Zeitschrift für die neutestamentliche Wissenschaft, 59; Berlin, 1991); Richard A. Landes, "'Millenarismus absconditus': L'historiographie augustinienne et le millénarisme du haut Moyen Âge jusqu'à l'an Mil," *Le Moyen Âge* 98 (1992): 355–377; David Burr, "The Antichrist and the Jews in Four Thirteenth-Century Apocalypse Commentaries," in *Friars and Jews in the Middle Ages and Renaissance*, ed. Steven J. McMichael and Susan E. Myers (Leiden, 2004), 22–38; Richard A. Landes and Andrew C. Gow (eds.), *The Apocalyptic Year 1000: Religious Expectation and Social Change, 950–1050* (Oxford, 2003); Felicitas Schmieder, "Christians, Jews, Muslims and Mongols. Fitting a Foreign People into the Western Christian Apocalyptic Scenario," *Medieval Encounters* 12, no. 2 (2006): 274–295; Johannes Heil, "Die ungeschriebene Bibel: Apokalypsen, Endzeit und das mittelalterliche 'Leben des Antichristen,'" in *Der Antichrist. Die Glasmalereien der Marienkirche in Frankfurt (Oder)*, ed.. Bernd Martin and Ulrich Knefelkamp (Leipzig, 2008), 19–37.

30. Haimo of Auxerre, *In II Thessalonicenses*, ed. Migne, *Patrologia Latina (PL)*, 117:779D–780A; see also his *In Apocalypsin, PL*, 117:1092D, 1186D; on Haimo, see Sumi Shimahara (ed.), *Études d'exégèse carolingienne. Autour d'Haymon d'Auxerre* (Collection de haut Moyen-Age, 4; Leiden, 2007).

31. Adso von Montier-en-Der, *De ortu et tempore Antichristi*, ed. Daniel Verhelst (CCCM, 45 ; Turnhout, 1976); see Daniel Verhelst, "Adso of Montier-en-Der and the Fear of the Year 1000," in *The Apocalyptic Year 1000: Religious Expectation and Social Change, 950–1050*, ed. Richard A. Landes and Andrew C. Gow (Oxford, 2003), 81–92.

32. See Cohn, *Warrant for Genocide*; Andrew Colin Gow, "The Red Jews. Antisemitism in an Apocalyptic Age 1200–1600" (*Studies in Medieval and Reformation Thought*, 55; Leiden, 1995).

33. See Hans J. Hillerbrand, "Von Polemik zur Verflachung. Zur Problematik des Antichrist-Mythos in Reformation und Gegenreformation," *Zeitschrift für Religions- und Geistesgeschichte*, 47 (1995): 114–125; Carlos Gilly, "The 'Midnight Lion,' the 'Eagle' and the 'Antichrist': Political, Religious and Chiliastic Propaganda in the Pamphlets, Illustrated Broadsheets and Ballads of the Thirty Years War," *Nederlands Archief voor Kerkgeschiedenis* 80 (2000): 46–77.

34. Radulphus of Coggeshall, *Chronicon anglicanum*, ed. Joseph Stevenson (RBSMA, 66; London, 1875; repr. 1965), 12; see also similar examples in Heil, ‚Gottesfeinde', 498f.

35. Robert of Torigny, "Chronik," in *Chronicles of the Reigns of Stephan, Henry II., and Richard I.*, ed. Richard Howlett (RBMAS 82.4; London, 1882), 4:251; for a translation see *The Gesta Normannorum Ducum of William of Jumièges, Orderic Vitalis and Robert of Torigni*, ed. and tr. Elisabeth M. C. Van Houts (Oxford, 1995); see also Robert Chazan, "The Blois Incident of 1171. A Study in Jewish Intercommunal Organization," *Proceedings—American Academy for Jewish Research* 36 (1968): 13–31; Jean-Paul Sauvage, "Le massacre des Juifs à Blois en 1171," *Mémoires de la Société des Sciences et Lettres du Loir-et-Cher* 49 (1994): 5–22; Joe Hillaby, "The Ritual-child-murder Accusation. Its Dissemination and Harold of Gloucester," *Jewish Historical Studies* 34 (1994–1996): 69–109.

36. John M. McCulloh, "Jewish Ritual Murder: William of Norwich, Thomas of Monmouth, and the Early Dissemination of the Myth," *Speculum* 72 (1997): 698–738.

37. Caesarius of Heisterbach, *Wundergeschichten*, vol. 1, app. 87, ed. Alfons Hilka (Bonn, 1933), 201f.; see also Gautier de Coinci, *Les miracles de Nostre Dame*, ed. Frederic Koenig (Textes littéraires français), vol. 4 (Geneva, 1970), II Mir. 13, p. 47f.; see Gilbert Dahan, "Les juifs dans les Miracles de Gautier de Coincy," *Archives Juives* 16 (1980): 59–68; Ivan G. Marcus, "Images of the Jews in the *Exempla* of Caesarius of Heisterbach," in *From Witness to Witchcraft*, ed. Jeremy Cohen, 247–256; Kirsten-Anne Fudeman, "Gautier de Coinci and the Literate Jew," in *Or le-Mayer. Studies in Bible, Semitic Languages, Rabbinic Literature, and Ancient Civilizations Presented to Mayer Gruber, et Shamir Yona* (Beer Sheva, 2010), 67–87.

38. See *Urkundenbuch der Stadt Freiburg im Breisgau*, ed. Heinrich Schreiber, vol. 2.1 (Freiburg im Breisgau, 1829), 169f.; Heil, ‚Gottesfeinde', 510f.

39. *Urkunden und Akten der Stadt Strassburg*, Part 1: *Urkundenbuch der Stadt Strassburg*, vol. 5 (Strassburg, 1896), No. 188, p. 177.

40. František Graus, *Pest—Geissler—Judenmorde. Das 14. Jahrhundert als Krisenzeit* (Veröffentlichungen des Max-Planck-Instituts für Geschichte, 86; Göttingen, 1987), 300f.; see also Reinhard Schneider, "Der Tag von Benfeld im Januar 1349. Sie kamen zusammen und kamen überein, die Juden zu vernichten," in *Spannungen und Widersprüche. Gedenkschrift für Frantisek Graus*, ed. Susanna Burghartz (Sigmaringen, 1992), 255–272.

41. Arno Borst, *Lebensformen im Mittelalter* (Frankfurt am Main, 1986), 611f.; Landes, "The Massacres of 1010," 79–112.

42. Otto of Freising, *Chronica sive historia de duabus civitatibus*, VIII.5–7; see Otto, Bishop of Freising, *The Two Cities: A Chronicle of Universal History to the Year 1146 AD*, tr. Charles C. Mierow, ed. Austin P. Evans and Charles Knapp (New York, 1966); Maria Dorninger, „Notizen zur Darstellung des Judentums bei Otto von Freising," *Chilufim—Zeitschrift für jüdische Kulturgeschichte* 5 (2008): 3–37.

PART III

The Early Years

The Apocalyptic Matrix of Genesis and Launch

6

"The Antichrist as an Imminent Political Possibility"

Sergei Nilus and the Apocalyptical Reading of
The Protocols of the Elders of Zion

——— MICHAEL HAGEMEISTER ———

Sergei Nilus, probably the most prominent editor and commentator of *The Protocols of the Elders of Zion*,[1] has become a kind of media star. His image is that of an enigmatic and at the same time surprisingly versatile figure. In Will Eisner's graphic novel *The Plot: The Secret Story of the Protocols of the Elders of Zion*, where the origins of the *Protocols* are presented as a conspiracy story—a conspiracy of cunning secret agents and sinister reactionaries—Nilus appears as a grey-haired mystic who is often invited to the Russian court, a competitor to Rasputin, a professor, and a wildly gesticulating fanatical anti-Semite.[2]

According to Umberto Eco, however, who wrote the introduction to Eisner's book, Nilus was not a professor but an "itinerant monk, . . . half prophet and half scoundrel."[3] Nilus "the monk" began his wanderings as early as 1988, namely in chapter 92 of Eco's novel *Foucault's Pendulum*, a book that can be seen as a fictionalized encyclopedia of occult teachings and conspiracy theories. Eco was probably influenced by the Serbian author Danilo Kiš. In his *Book of Kings and Fools*, Nilus appears as a "strange hermit," "for insiders simply father Sergius." Likewise, Nilus appears in books of which it is hard to tell whether they are based in fiction or fact, for example, in the occult conspiracy story *The Spear of Destiny* by Trevor Ravenscroft, in Hadassa Ben-Itto's semifictional story of the famous Berne Trial on the *Protocols*,[4] and in the international bestseller *The Holy Blood and the Holy Grail*. In the latter, Nilus is described as "a rather contemptible individual known to posterity under the pseudonym of Sergei Nilus."[5] In that book, which clearly inspired Dan Brown's blockbuster novel *The Da Vinci Code*, Nilus and the *Protocols* are part of the global conspiracy of a secret order, the "Prieuré de Sion," whose prominent members (including Isaac Newton, Victor Hugo, and Claude Debussy) are secretly attempting to bring the Merovingian dynasty—descendants of Jesus and Mary Magdalene—back to power.

When we turn to the scholarly literature on the *Protocols*, the picture becomes even more confused: The enigmatic Nilus appears in various guises: not only as a professor or a monk but also as a priest of the Russian Orthodox Church, an Orientalist, a court nobleman, a journalist, a half-crazy pseudomystic, a zoologist, a mediocre lawyer, a religious philosopher, an agent of the secret police, an Orthodox theologian, and even a former playboy. Some believe that Nilus was not his real name; some consider him the actual author of the *Protocols*. None of this is accurate.

Sergei Aleksandrovich Nilus, whose name is authentic and not a pseudonym, was born in Moscow on August 25 (Old Style), 1862, the son of a minor noble landowner.[6] Nilus's ancestors on his father's side were Lutheran and came from the Baltics, which explains his non-Russian last name—a derivation from Nicholas. Nilus's father was the first to be baptized in the Orthodox rite. His maternal ancestors were Russian landed nobility. Nilus studied law at the University of Moscow, worked briefly in the judicial system, but soon left the state service. He withdrew to his estate in the Orel district, which he managed ineffectively in the old-fashioned, patriarchal way. Although Nilus had always been indifferent to religion, toward the end of the century he succumbed to the apocalyptic mood that was spreading throughout the country. He thus joined those victims of rapid modernization and secularization who identified the downfall of their own world with the end of the world in general. On his pilgrimages, Nilus met the charismatic parish priest and wonder-worker John (Ioann) of Kronstadt (1829–1908, canonized 1990). From these experiences he fashioned his own mystical-apocalyptic faith based on miracles and signs.

Becoming active as a writer, Nilus won great fame among Orthodox believers for discovering and editing the teachings and apocalyptic prophecies of Serafim of Sarov (1754–1833, canonized 1903), one of Russia's most popular saints. Nilus's own description of the circumstances under which he supposedly found those records shortly before Serafim's canonization—in a basket with old papers at an attic—and his somehow "miraculously" deciphering them sound highly implausible and resemble the mystifications surrounding the *Protocols*. In both cases, the "originals"—if they ever existed—have been lost.[7]

Nilus published Serafim's teachings in 1903 in his devotional book *The Great in the Small: Notes of an Orthodox Believer*. In the second edition of this book, released at Tsarkoe Selo in December 1905 with a new subtitle, *The*

Antichrist as an Imminent Political Possibility, Nilus took up *The Protocols of the Elders of Zion* for the first time. Later editions of his book, also containing the *Protocols*, appeared under various titles in 1911 and 1912. The last edition was published in January 1917 by the famous Holy Trinity Monastery at Sergiev Posad and bore the menacing title *"It Is Near, Even at the Doors"*: *Concerning That Which People Do Not Wish to Believe and Which Is So Near.* As to the origins of the *Protocols*, Nilus gave differing accounts. At first, he described them as "secret documents" stolen from one of the most highly placed leaders of Freemasonry in France; later, he referred to the "Jewish plan to conquer the world" and claimed it had been presented at the First Zionist Congress in Basel (1897) by Theodor Herzl.[8]

In his commentary, Nilus interpreted the *Protocols* within the framework of his apocalyptic worldview as the unveiling of the hidden strategy of the satanic forces of darkness and their worldly allies—Jews and Freemasons—in their unremitting struggle against the Divine forces of light, embodied in the Russian Orthodox Church, a struggle which seemed to have entered its final stage at the turn of the century. Nilus felt deeply apocalyptic and was convinced of the Second Coming of Christ. He constantly noticed signs that the end was fast approaching; he regularly believed he saw the "Seal of the Antichrist" or the "Number of the Beast" around him. This belief that the end was nigh was shared with many of his contemporaries. The political, economic, and social transformations of the day—consequences of rapid industrialization, urbanization, and secularization—were interpreted to a large extent with the help of religious categories: as a foreboding of an imminent eschatological catastrophe and as evidence of the work of the Antichrist and his allies.[9]

Doomsday scenarios and the fear of revolution received special treatment in the subculture of Russian Judeophobia: The premodern or antimodern consciousness saw Jews and Freemasons—sponsors and beneficiaries of progress and enlightenment—as the henchmen of the Antichrist; indeed, they were often identified with him.[10] Thus, the common denominator of apocalyptic concepts blended anti-Jewish myths with fashionable occultism and the belief in—or even personal encounter with—demonic forces. The border between fiction and reality was hazy, and mystifications were not easily recognizable to many.

Nilus seems to have been favorably impressed by the famous *Short Tale of the Antichrist*, the last work of the renowned philosopher and alleged philo-Semite Vladimir Soloviev (1853–1900). In Nilus's understanding, Soloviev's depiction of the Antichrist as a "superman" and "benefactor" (*blagodetel'*) who gains world power with the help of the "mighty brotherhood of the Freemasons" and the *Comité permanent universel* (which in Judeophobic reading would stand for the *Alliance Israélite Universelle*) and builds his reign on the promise of universal peace and welfare was a visionary revelation of the satanic "Judeo-Masonic world conspiracy" and its goal, the foundation of a Jewish world kingdom as a diabolical perversion of the Kingdom of God. Nilus interpreted Soloviev's early and sudden death merely five months after the publication of his *Short Tale of the Antichrist* in a manner similar to Soloviev's own premonitions: the revenge of that same dark and sinister force whose secret plans he had exposed in his tale.[11] However, the actual "proof" of the accuracy of Soloviev's prophecy was, for Nilus, to be found in the *Protocols*.[12]

We see, therefore, that Nilus did not interpret the *Protocols* as politics—the interpretation that dominated in later years—but placed them in a religious, eschatological context: as *apokálypsis*, that is, the unveiling or uncovering of the struggle between the forces of Good and Evil, both in their invisible otherworldly incarnations and in their visible earthly allies.[13] This interpretation required no historical evidence; Nilus was not in the least interested in verifying the authenticity of the *Protocols*, either in the eyes of the law or through a critical appraisal of the sources.

> One could, correctly, criticize us for the apocryphal nature of this document [the *Protocols*]. But if it were possible to prove its authenticity by way of documentation or trustworthy witnesses; if one could reveal the faces of those sitting at the top of the world conspiracy, pulling the bloodied strings, then the very "mystery of lawlessness" would be broken which must remain intact until his incarnation as the "son of perdition."[14]

Nilus's reference here is to the famous revelation in the second letter of Paul to the Thessalonians, telling of the appearance of the Antichrist himself, who is expected soon, before the *parousia*, the Second Coming, of Christ:

> for that day will not come, unless the rebellion comes first, and the man of lawlessness is revealed, the son of perdition, who opposes and exalts himself against every so-called god or object of worship, so that he takes his seat in the temple of God, proclaiming himself to be God. [. . .] For the mystery of lawlessness is already at work. (2 Thess 2.3-4, 7)

The "mystery of lawlessness" was, for Nilus, indeed already at work. He saw the threatening signs everywhere; however, the time was not ripe, for the adversary had yet to appear and reveal his wickedness. His power was still being muzzled by a delaying, inhibitory, restraining power, by what Paul's letter calls the *katéchon*. Much has been speculated about the mysterious figure of the *katéchon*;[15] for Nilus it was clear: The only power that could hold back the Antichrist is Holy Russia—the autocratic power of the tsar and the Orthodox monasteries, bulwarks against the swelling flood of godlessness.[16]

Russians and Jews were, for Nilus, the peoples of the *éschaton*, the end of time: The role of the Jews in the history of salvation included, whether they knew it or not, struggling against Christianity and striving for world power, exactly as the *Protocols* revealed. This plan for world domination had, according to Nilus, been crafted by Solomon and other Jewish sages as early as 929 B.C. and was, over time, continuously amended and elaborated by the initiated. The apostle Paul, one of the most promising students of the Pharisees in his time, was surely also initiated into the plan, and it was *precisely this plan* that he meant when he referred to the "mystery of lawlessness" that was "already at work."[17] Nilus wanted to warn his Christian brothers of this "deadly danger that was fast approaching." But under no circumstances, he stressed, did he want to foment hatred of "the Jewish people, who, still blinded in their ardent and fiery—although false—belief, are not to blame for the satanic sins of their leaders: the scribes and Pharisees who have already once led Israel to ruin."[18]

Nilus was no racist anti-Semite, unlike, for example, Father Pavel Florenskii (1882–1937), the highly revered Orthodox priest and philosopher, who identified the Jews in racial terms as the enemies of the Aryans and as the polluters of the blood of other races and who proposed the castration of all Jews (which, however, as a Christian, he had to reject).[19] Nilus, by contrast, shared the traditional views of Christian anti-Judaism. Jews, according to this understanding, were part of the cosmic drama of Salvation in which they played a central predetermined role: they were pathbreakers and agents of the Antichrist who competed with God for rule over the world. Nevertheless, they always remained within the divine plan; indeed, they functioned as tools of God. Just as Judas's betrayal enabled the son of God to die a redeeming death (for which reason Christians also pray for Judas's salvation), so the Jews' actions help propel the historical process toward the final redemption. Nilus perceived a tragic dimension to this negative role that the Jews have had thrust upon them. He believed that their fateful part had to be played out according to the divine plan until the end of history. At the end of the world—after a brief reign of the Antichrist—the Jews will inevitably recognize and repent of their apostasy and turn to Christ, at which time, according to Paul's famous letter to the Romans, "all Israel will be saved" (Rom 11.26). The Jews must be spared. It is, after all, their conversion that will precipitate the Second Coming of Christ and the salvation of the world. Until that time, however, Jews in their impenitence are to blame for the suffering in the world and must themselves suffer the wrath of God. All of which means that they can be despised and oppressed but not physically destroyed, especially since, at the end of time, God's initial love will greet them once more. Christian anti-Judaism, despite its cruel tendencies, did not have the physical destruction of Jewry as its aim.[20] For Nilus, as for many other Russian religious thinkers, the "final resolution" of the "Jewish question" lies in *conversion*, that is, the elimination of Judaism, not of Jews.[21]

Nilus regarded the Russian Revolution, which to him seemed to bear out the plan of the "Elders of Zion," as an eschatological catastrophe and the beginning of the reign of the Antichrist, the false messiah of the Jews, who instead of the Heavenly Jerusalem promised a paradise on Earth. Nilus refused to leave Russia, instead joining the "Catacomb Church," the underground movement of Russian Orthodoxy that refused to compromise with the Bolsheviks. Together with his wife, he moved from place to place, living mostly in Ukraine. Arrested several times, tried, and imprisoned, he was always released, even though his identity was known to the authorities. Finally, utterly destitute, he found refuge with a parish priest in the village of Krutets, some eighty miles northeast of Moscow. There, on January 14, 1929, he died of a heart attack. His only son, Sergei (1883–1941) went to Poland after the Revolution of 1917. During the Bern trial (1933–1935) in which the *Protocols* was condemned as a fraud, he acted as an expert witness by sending a report that vouched for the authenticity of the book.[22]

Following the end of the Soviet rule, Nilus and his writings have been rediscovered in Russia. Nilus has become virtually a cult figure in ecclesiastical and nationalist circles. His restored grave in Krutets is looked after by the nuns of the nearby Ascension Convent and attracts pious pilgrims. His admirers are eagerly collecting records of miracles that occur at this grave and are documenting cases where a "blessed fragrance" emanates from his books—an unmistakable sign of holiness. Nilus, apocalyptic writer and fighter against satanic forces, seems to have a good chance to become at least a local saint of the Russian Orthodox Church.[23]

His books—especially those that contain the *Protocols*—are regularly republished[24] and can be found in bookshops in even the most distant provinces. His pious writings served as the basis for the play *Spiritual Eyes* (*Dukhovnye ochi*), which, starring several "People's Artists of the USSR," is being performed to great acclaim at the Moscow Orthodox Theatre, "The Voice" (*Glas*). In addition, congresses and annual "Nilus Lectures" (*Nilusovskie Chteniia*) are held on the anniversary of his death, where self-appointed experts on "Masonology" (*masonovedenie*), "Judeology" (*evreevedenie*), and "Conspirology" (*konspirologiia*) gather, and a "Sergei Nilus Prize" (*Premiia imeni Sergeia Aleksandrovicha Nilusa*) for "services to the spiritual life of the Russian people" has been inaugurated. This all points to the great reverence for Nilus both as a spiritual writer and as editor and commentator of the *Protocols*.

In this milieu, influenced by a strongly religious imagination, the *Protocols* is—just as Nilus would want—often interpreted as an "apocalypse," as the exposure of the hidden machinations of the Antichrist forces, and as the unveiling of their promise of peace and general welfare as satanic deception and a treacherous mask of evil. This incorporates the *Protocols* into a long tradition of apocryphal apocalyptic writings, including the widely distributed prophecies of Saint Serafim of Sarov about the end of the world and the coming of the Antichrist or the "Dream of Father John of Kronstadt," a bloodthirsty apocalypse contrived in the early 1920s as anti-Bolshevik, anti-Jewish propaganda and generally attributed to the miracle worker and clairvoyant of Kronstadt, a friend of Nilus's who shared similar views and died in 1908: Led by Serafim of Sarov, John wanders through the empire of Bolshevik terror and sees the triumph and downfall of the Jewish ruler of the world, the Antichrist.

In Russia today, there is a widespread belief in a conspiracy hatched by satanic forces and their earthly helpers.[25] Through countless tracts and brochures, these eschatological, demonological, and anti-Jewish predictions—evolved over centuries—are being revived and propagated: expectations of the Antichrist, a Jew from the tribe of Dan who was born in Israel in 1962 and will become the false messiah of the Jews;[26] rumors of the secret construction of the future base of the Antichrist, the third Temple under the Al Aqsa Mosque, in Jerusalem; manifestations of the "Seal of the Antichrist" and the "Number of the Beast," which are believed to be printed in bar codes and on tax IDs;[27] the appearance of demonic beings in the guise of aliens and unidentified flying objects;[28] and, significantly, Jewish ritual murder of Christians.[29]

A center of anti-Jewish apocalyptic thought is the famous Holy Trinity Monastery in Sergiev Posad, near Moscow, the home of the Moscow Theological Academy. In 1993, the monastery's publishing house published a book called *Russia before the Second Coming*, an anthology of apocalyptic and anti-Jewish conspiracy myths from the Church fathers until the present time. The book, which contains excerpts from Nilus's writings and from the *Protocols*, was published in a first edition of 100,000 copies. It became an instant bestseller and has been republished repeatedly since then (including numerous pirated editions). The text has now swollen to two fat folio volumes.[30] It seems that doctrines about the activities of the Evil Ones (the devil, the Antichrist, the demons) and their allies on Earth (the Jews) have forced the traditional Christian Good News off the stage.[31]

Among the public defenders of the *Protocols* are such well-known writers and publicists as Dmitrii Balashov (1927–2000), Petr Palamarchuk (1955–1998), and Stanislav Kuniaiev (b. 1932), as well as the renowned specialist in old Russian literature Iurii Begunov (b. 1932) and the late Metropolitan Ioann (Snychev, 1927–1995) of St. Petersburg and Ladoga, the second highest-ranking clergyman of the Russian Orthodox Church and a member of its Holy Synod. By far the most influential propagandist for the notion of a Jewish-Masonic conspiracy, however, is Oleg Platonov (b. 1950), an economist and historian, who apparently is quite well funded by Russian patriotic patrons and sponsors. Platonov, a notorious Holocaust denier who also advocates the canonization of Ivan the Terrible and Rasputin, publishes book after book obsessed with unveiling the conspiratorial Judeo-Masonic face of the "damnable non-Rus."[32]

Besides open propaganda, there are, of course, more subtle ways of fostering the *Protocols* and their apocalyptic message. Ilia Glazunov (b. 1930), probably Russia's best-known and most popular painter, who has been given his own pompous museum in the center of Moscow, is a good example of this.[33] In his gigantic canvas *The Grand Experiment* of 1990, Glazunov features eminent figures and events of 20th-century Russian history. In the painting's center— framed by a big, red, five-pointed star or pentagram, which, according to Glazunov, is "an ancient cabalistic sign, a symbol of evil"[34]—we see the portraits of Karl Marx and leading Marxists and Bolsheviks. At the center of the Red Star—in other words, in the center of evil—there is another star, a pentagram, covered with cabalistic, alchemic, and astrological signs—the "Seal of the Antichrist." Glazunov borrowed it from the title page of Nilus's book *Near Is the Coming Antichrist and the Kingdom of the Devil on Earth*, published in 1911 by the Holy Trinity Monastery at Sergiev Posad. This book contains the *Protocols*.

Tracing this key source makes the meaning of Glazunov's blunt and demagogical symbolism immediately clear: Marx and the—mostly Jewish—Bolsheviks are depicted as agents of the "Judeo-Masonic conspiracy" as described in the *Protocols*. And their victim is none other than Holy Russia. At this point, the serpent on Glazunov's painting can be decoded, too: it is the "Symbolic Serpent" that appears and is described in the *Protocols*. The serpent represents the progress of the Jewish conspiracy. Starting from Jerusalem at the time of Solomon, the serpent's head moves through the

European states until, with Zionist immigration, it returns to the point of its origin. The serpent signifies that the world is ruled from (and, literally, encircled by) Zion.[35] Glazunov's painting "exposes" those truly responsible for Russia's dismal fate and sufferings in the 20th century; in other words, it serves the same purpose as the *Protocols*.

The *Protocols* is an "open text" (Umberto Eco) that can be used and interpreted in various ways. The anti-Jewish interpretation is only one of these, albeit the most widespread. British and American conspirologists explain time and again that the *Protocols* is not connected to a Jewish conspiracy; they developed from the secret society of the Illuminati or are part of a thousand-year conspiracy of the Merovingians.[36] Aleksandr Dugin (b. 1962), the leading conspiracy theorist in Russia, has even expressed the opinion that the second part of the *Protocols*, which describes the foundation of a monarchy and a caste system, carries the "hallmark of a traditional Aryan mentality."[37]

The *Protocols* can also be read as a depiction of a future totalitarian welfare dictatorship with socialist traits (moreover, as a critical depiction, since they are meant to prevent such a dictatorship) and could, if they possessed any literary qualities, belong to the famous negative utopias of Russian literature of the 19th and 20th centuries: Dostoevskii's Grand Inquisitor (rather, a predecessor of the Antichrist), who—like the "Elders of Zion"—deems the majority of human beings weak and despicable and who deprives them of freedom in exchange for bread and games;[38] Valerii Briusov's benevolent dictatorship of the all-cognizant Board of Directors in the *Republic of the Southern Cross*; or Evgenii Zamiatin's Benefactor (*blagodetel'*), the all-powerful ruler of the totalitarian One State.[39]

Sergei Nilus saw in the *Protocols* a text that seemed to validate his Christian-apocalyptic worldview. The transition from Christian anti-Judaism to the Nazi's murderous anti-Semitism was to a large extent smooth—even Goebbels spoke of "Jewry as the Antichrist of world history." But still: Nilus expected the salvation of all of Israel, Goebbels, the extermination of all Jews.

NOTES

I am indebted to Felicitas Macgilchrist for help in translating this article.

1. *The Protocols of the Elders of Zion*, first published in Russia in 1903, is an anonymous work of undefined genre (dubbed "protocols" only by subsequent editors) that is still used today by anti-Semites across the globe to accuse the Jews of conspiring in a sinister quest for world domination and of seeking to establish a global, totalitarian welfare state. The text, which is largely a compilation of literary materials from the second half of the 19th century, was in all likelihood written at the beginning of the 20th century. Despite the most

intensive research, the details of its origins still defy clarification. In particular, the question of its authorship still remains open. There is a vast literature on the *Protocols*. Classic studies are Henri Rollin, *L'Apocalypse de notre temps: Les dessous de la propagande allemande d'après des documents inédits* (Paris, 1939; reed. Paris, 1991, 2005), and Norman Cohn, *Warrant for Genocide: The Myth of the Jewish World-Conspiracy and the Protocols of the Elders of Zion* (1967; London, 1996). The most important recent studies are Pierre-André Taguieff, *Les Protocoles des Sages de Sion. Faux et usages d'un faux* (Paris, 2004); Cesare G. De Michelis, *The Non-Existent Manuscript: A Study of the "Protocols of the Sages of Zion"* (Lincoln, UK, 2004); Vadim Skuratovskii, *Problema avtorstva "Protokolov sionskikh mudretsov"* (Kiev, 2001).

2. Will Eisner, *The Plot: The Secret Story of the Protocols of the Elders of Zion* (New York, 2005), 61–65, 134. For a critical discussion, see Michael Hagemeister, "The *Protocols of the Elders of Zion*: Between History and Fiction," *New German Critique* 35, no. 1 (2008): 83–95.

3. Umberto Eco, *Six Walks in the Fictional Woods* (Cambridge, MA, 1994), 137; Eco, *Serendipities: Language and Lunacy* (San Diego, 1999), 17.

4. Hadassa Ben-Itto, *The Lie That Wouldn't Die: The Protocols of the Elders of Zion* (London, 2005). The book is a peculiar mix of fact and fiction, in part a kind of historical novel with invented episodes, dialogues, and inner monologues.

5. Michael Baigent, Richard Leigh, and Henry Lincoln, *The Holy Blood and the Holy Grail* (London, 16th ed. 1990), 198–199.

6. For Nilus's biography as well as for literature by and about him, see my article in *Biographisch-Bibliographisches Kirchenlexikon* (Nordhausen, 2003), 21:1063–1067, available at http://www.bautz.de/bbkl/n/nilus_s_a.shtml. For a shorter version, see Michael Hagemeister, "Nilus, Sergei," in *Antisemitism: A Historical Encyclopedia of Prejudice and Persecution*, ed. Richard E. Levy (Santa Barbara, CA, 2005), 2:508–510.

7. See Michael Hagemeister, "Eine Apokalypse unserer Zeit.—Die Prophezeiungen des heiligen Serafim von Sarov über das Kommen des Antichrist und das Ende der Welt," in *Finis mundi—Endzeiten und Weltenden im östlichen Europa. Festschrift für Hans Lemberg zum 65. Geburtstag*, ed. Joachim Hösler and Wolfgang Kessler (Stuttgart, 1998), 41–60.

8. Sergei Nilus, *Velikoe v malom i antikhrist, kak blizkaia politicheskaia vozmozhnost'. Zapiski pravoslavnogo* (Tsarskoe Selo, 1905), 321–322, 405; Nilus, *"Bliz est', pri dverekh." O tom, chemu ne zhelaiut verit' i chto tak blizko* (Sergiev Posad, 1917), 88–89.

9. For a general survey on apocalypticism in Russia at the turn of the century, see James H. Billington, *The Icon and the Axe: An Interpretive History of Russian Culture* (New York, 1970), esp. 504–518; David M. Bethea, *The Shape of Apocalypse in Modern Russian Fiction* (Princeton, NJ, 1989); J. Eugene Clay, "Apocalypticism in Eastern Europe," in *The Encyclopedia of Apocalypticism*, ed. Stephen J. Stein (New York, 1998), 3:293–321; Leonid Katsis, *Russkaia eskhatologiia i russkaia literatura* (Moscow, 2000).

10. See Savelii Dudakov, *Istorija odnogo mifa: Ocherki russkoi literatury XIX–XX vv.* (Moscow, 1993); Konstantin Isupov (ed.), *Antikhrist. Antologiia* (Moscow, 1995). On Russian Judeophobia, see Heinz-Dietrich Löwe, *The Tsars and the Jews: Reform, Reaction and Anti-Semitism in Imperial Russia, 1772–1917* (Chur, 1993).

11. Nilus, *Velikoe v malom*, 317–318; Vasilii Velichko, *Vladimir Solov'ev: zhizn' i tvoreniia*, 2nd ed. (St. Petersburg, 1903), 171–172.

12. Nilus, *Velikoe v malom*, 316–319, 321–322. For the remarkable parallels between the content of Soloviev's *Short Tale of the Antichrist* and the *Protocols*, see Michael Hagemeister, „Vladimir Solov'ev and Sergej Nilus: Apocalypticism and Judeophobia," in *Vladimir*

Solov'ev: Reconciler and Polemicist, ed. Wil van den Bercken, Manon de Courten, and Evert van der Zweerde (Leuven, 2000), 287–296; Hagemeister, "Trilogie der Apokalypse—Vladimir Solov'ev, Serafim von Sarov und Sergej Nilus über das Kommen des Antichrist und das Ende der Weltgeschichte," in *Antichrist. Konstruktionen von Feindbildern*, ed. Wolfram Brandes and Felicitas Schmieder (Berlin, 2010), 255–275.

13. As far as I am aware, only the Orthodox theologian Anton Kartashev (1875–1960) refers to the *Protocols* as apocalypse. His 1923 foreword to a critical study, today almost forgotten, describes them as a "faked apocalypse" but does not elaborate on the idea. Anton Kartashev, "Predislovie," in Iurii Delevskii, *Protokoly Sionskikh Mudretsov. Istoriia odnogo podloga* (Berlin, 1923), 8.

14. Nilus, *Velikoe v malom*, 323.

15. For example, in the political theology of Carl Schmitt (1888–1985), the "crown jurist" for the Third Reich and "apocalypticist of the counterrevolution" (Jacob Taubes), who identified liberalism, Bolshevism, and Judaism with the Antichrist (or his agents) and who believed he recognized the *katéchon* in Hitler's dictatorship. Russian historiosophy, on the other hand, sees Moscow as the "Third Rome" (after the fall of Rome and Constantinople), the last power capable of restraining the Antichrist until the end of history. See Michael Hagemeister, "Das Dritte Rom gegen den Dritten Tempel—Der Antichrist im postsowjetischen Russland," in *Der Antichrist. Historische und systematische Zugänge*, ed. Mariano Delgado and Volker Leppin (Fribourg and Stuttgart, 2011), 461–485.

16. Sergei Nilus, *Dlia chego i komu nuzhny pravoslavnye monastyri* (Sergiev Posad, 1909).

17. Nilus, "*Bliz est', pri dverekh*," 161. Nilus's apocalyptic interpretation of the *Protocols* found no place in the German National Socialist's anti-Semitic concept. A German edition of his book with the title *The Jewish Antichrist and the Protocols of the Elders of Zion* was ready for publication in 1938 when Nazi censorship prevented its publication because of the "lengthy comments . . . on religious topics." Letter of Hans Jonak von Freyenwald to Sergei Sergeevich Nilus, March 3, 1940; Freyenwald Collection, Wiener Library, Tel Aviv (the library holds both the manuscript of the translation and the proof-sheets).

18. Nilus, *Velikoe v malom*, 323.

19. On Florenskii's anti-Semitism, see Michael Hagemeister and Torsten Metelka (eds.), *Appendix 2. Materialien zu Pavel Florenskij* (Berlin, 2001).

20. This is stressed by Steven Theodore Katz, *Continuity and Discontinuity between Christian and Nazi Antisemitism* (Tübingen, 2001), 24–27, 42–45. Referring to the Christian expectation of the "salvation of Israel" (even if only in the *eschaton*), the author argues against the "influential and widespread argument [. . .] that there was an essential continuity between Christian and Nazi anti-Semitism", since only the latter aimed at the annihilation of the Jewish people.

21. Thus, even on his deathbed, Vladimir Soloviev prayed for the conversion of the Jews. The Russian philosopher Nikolai Berdiaev (1874–1948) declared: "The final solution of the Jewish question is only possible from an eschatological perspective. This will also be the fateful resolution of world history, in the final struggle between Christ and Antichrist." Nikolai Berdiaev, *Smysl istorii. Opyt filosofii chelovecheskoi sud'by* (Berlin, 1923), 128. And Aleksei Losev (1893–1988), a Christian Neoplatonist and one of the most prominent figures in Russian philosophical and religious thought of the 20th century, called historical Judaism the "fortress of world Satanism." See „'Tak istiazuetsia i raspinaetsia istina . . .' A.F. Losev v retsenziiakh OGPU," in *Istochnik. Vestnik Arkhiva Prezidenta RF*, no. 4 (1996): 122.

22. See Michael Hagemeister, "Russian Émigrés in the Bern Trial of the 'Protocols of the Elders of Zion' (1933–1935)," in *Cahiers Parisiens /Parisian Notebooks*, ed. Jan Goldstein, no. 5 (2009): 375–391; Hagemeister, "The 'Protocols of the Elders of Zion' in Court. The Bern Trials, 1933–1937," in *The Global Impact of the Protocols of the Elders of Zion*, ed. Esther Webman (London, 2011), 241–253.

23. See Valentin Starikov, "Podvig Sergiia Nilusa," in *Russkij Vestnik*, no. 1–2 (2000): 12; Starikov, "Legendarnyi Nilus," in *Russkij dom*, no. 1 (2004): 14–15. A kind of a pilgrim's guide (with an exact description of the route to Nilus's grave) is provided by A. Pavlov, *K Nilusu v Krutets* (Moscow, 2002).

24. A complete edition of his works has been published: Sergei Nilus, *Polnoe sobranie sochinenii v shesti tomakh*, ed. Aleksandr Strizhev, 6 vols. (Moscow, 1999–2005).

25. See Vadim Rossman, *Russian Intellectual Antisemitism in the Post-Communist Era* (Lincoln, NE, 2002); Aleksandr Verkhovskii, *Politicheskoe pravoslavie. Russkie pravoslavnye natsionalisty i fundamentalisty, 1995-2001* (Moscow, 2003); *Eskhatologicheskii sbornik*, ed. Dmitrii Andreev et al. (St. Petersburg, 2006); Hagemeister, "Das Dritte Rom gegen den Dritten Tempel."

26. The date of birth of the Antichrist is easily explained: The square of 1962 is 18, in other words, 6+6+6. The notion that the Antichrist was born of the devil's union with a whore from the Jewish tribe of Dan is an old parody of the birth of the true Christ as the son of God and the Virgin Mary.

27. The Synod of the Bishops of the Moscow Patriarchate confirmed in March 2000 that the bar code included the number 666 and asked the authorities, in consideration of the believers in Russia, to change the bar code system to one deviating from the international standard.

28. See the widely distributed pamphlet *NLO: nepoznannye letaiushchie ob-ekty v svete pravoslavnoi very* by the priest-monk, wonder worker, and apocalypticist Seraphim (Eugene D. Rose, 1934–1982). The author, an American from California, was closely acquainted with Helen Kontsevitch, née Kartsova (1893–1989), Sergei Nilus's niece, who ended her days in Berkeley, California. Under her influence, Rose converted to Russian Orthodoxy and founded the Orthodox St. Herman of Alaska Brotherhood in Platina, California. Since 1969, the brotherhood has published Nilus's (carefully purged) works and posthumous materials.

29. When, in April 1993, three monks in the newly reopened monastery Optina Pustyn' were killed by a man who was apparently mentally disturbed, the extreme nationalist press, including the major Communist newspaper *Pravda*, appealed to the authority of Sergei Nilus as an "outstanding expert in Jewish symbolism, Zionism and Masonry" and thus interpreted the act as an attack by the Antichrist and as a Jewish ("Hasidic") ritual murder commissioned by conspiratorial satanic powers. Orthodox theologians do not consider "Jewish ritual murders" to be ordinary crimes but, rather, place them in the same vein as the desire for world domination and the alliance with the Antichrist, as the expression of deep—and deeply wrong, that is, deeply opposed to Christianity—religiousness. See Michael Hagemeister, "Ritualmordlegenden im post-sowjetischen Russland," in *Handbuch des Antisemitismus*, ed. Wolfgang Benz (Berlin, 2011), 4:338–340.

30. Sergei Fomin and Tamara Fomina (eds.), *Rossiia pered vtorym prishestviem. Materialy k ocherku Russkoi eskhatologii*, 2 vols. (Moscow, 1998).

31. This is obviously not a specifically Russian phenomenon, as a glance at the United States will show. A series of Antichrist thrillers published there by a Christian fundamentalist publishing house under the title *Left Behind* has become by far the greatest commercial success in modern apocalyptic literature, with more than 65 million copies (including related books) sold since 1995. See also Robert C. Fuller, *Naming the Antichrist: The History of an American Obsession* (New York, 1995); Michael Barkun, *A Culture of Conspiracy: Apocalyptic Visions in Contemporary America* (Berkeley, CA, 2003).

32. See, e.g., his *Sviataia Rus' i okaiannaia nerus'. Russkaia tsivilisatsiia protiv mirovogo zla* (Moscow, 2005) and his most recent edition of Sergei Nilus, *Tsarstvo antikhrista. "Bliz est', pri dverekh . . ."* (Moscow, 2005) in the series *Russian Resistance (Russkoe soprotivlenie)*. On Platonov, see James H. Billington, *Russia in Search of Itself* (Washington, DC, 2004), especially 85–86.

33. For details, see Michael Hagemeister, "Anti-Semitism, Occultism, and Theories of Conspiracy in Contemporary Russia—The Case of Ilya Glazunov," in *Anti-Semitism and Philo-Semitism in the Slavic World and Western Europe*, ed. Vladimir Paperni and Wolf Moskovich (Haifa, 2004), 235–241.

34. Ilia Glazunov in *Panorama*, August 31, 1994, 20. Quoted in Semyon Reznik, *The Nazification of Russia: Antisemitism in the Post-Soviet Era* (Washington, DC, 1996), 239.

35. On the "Symbolic Serpent" as an anti-Jewish symbol, see Cesare G. De Michelis, "Ot Ierusalima do Ierusalima. (Tsikl 'Simvolicheskogo Zmiia' v 'Protokolakh Sionskikh mudretsov')," in *Oh, Jerusalem!*, ed. Wolf Moskovich et al. (Pisa, 1999), 161–172.

36. See Daniel Pipes, *Conspiracy: How the Paranoid Style Flourishes and Where It Comes From* (New York, 1997), 130; Baigent, Leigh, and Lincoln, *The Holy Blood*, 198–203.

37. Aleksandr Dugin, "Krestovyi pokhod solntsa," in *Milyi angel* (Moscow, 1996), 2:71.

38. On the parallels between Dostoevskii's *Legend of the Grand Inquisitor* and the *Protocols*, see Léon Poliakov, *The History of Anti-Semitism*, vol. 4: *Suicidal Europe: 1870–1933* (New York, 1985), 59–60.

39. On the *Protocols* as an anti-Utopia, see Michael Hagemeister, "Die Protokolle der Weisen von Zion—eine Anti-Utopie oder der Große Plan in der Geschichte?," in *Verschwörungstheorien. Theorie—Geschichte—Wirkung*, ed. Helmut Reinalter (Innsbruck, 2002), 45–57; on Dostoevskii's hidden presence in the *Protocols*, see Skuratovskii, *Problema avtorstva*, 191–221.

7

Protocols of the Elders of Zion

Thoughts on the French Connection

JEFFREY MEHLMAN

A particularly cruel joke, astutely or apocryphally relayed to me by Steven Katz a quarter of a century ago, has it that if, in the year 1925, anyone had predicted that within twenty years close to six million Jews would be slaughtered in Europe, the only reasonable reaction would have been to say either that the claim was preposterous or "Ah, the French! Would they press their anti-Semitic madness to such an extreme?" The appropriateness of the quip to our present concern relates not only to the fact that the infamous forgery we are considering was, in all probability, concocted, admittedly by Russians, in Dreyfus-affair Paris but that it was in significant measure an act of plagiarism—by the sinister Mathieu Golovinsky, if recent reports are correct—of a French text. Yes, one is inclined to say, the country (France) that gave Edouard Drumont's *La France juive*, a thousand-page tract intent on demonstrating that anti-Semitism had a claim to being *the* political philosophy of modern times, a larger readership than any other work save one in the second half of the 19th century, might well have provided the script for what Norman Cohn has famously called a "warrant for genocide."[1]

Yet, no sooner has one leapt to that conclusion than one confronts a paradox. For the text of Maurice Joly on which the *Protocols* is based is in fact an admirably liberal document. The "Dialogue in Hell between Machiavelli and Montesquieu" pits a patron saint of political liberalism against an apologist for the cynical abuse of power and ends by all but stating that the Machiavellian system is already in place in the France of the Second Empire. Napoleon III's tyrannical designs on France, in the *Protocols*, are replaced by the Jewish conspiracy's designs on the entire world, which does not make any less enigmatic the transition from a politically liberal tract to a blueprint (or justification) for massacre. In Cohn's terms, there is a "cruel irony" in the fact that Joly's "admirable, incisive, ruthlessly logical, and beautifully constructed" work should issue in the "atrociously written piece of reactionary balderdash" that would sweep the world.[2]

There is, of course, a basis for associating Bonapartism with the Jews. Consider the role of the first Napoleon in the emancipation of the Jews, the fidelity, say, of Heine's "two grenadiers" to their so-called Kaiser during his one-hundred-day return from Elba, the ghetto-born rumors that Bonaparte in Jaffa, issuing his call to the Jews to come support him in his Middle Eastern campaign (with its designs on Jerusalem), might be the Messiah.[3]

But Joly's Napoleon III is less a messianic figure than a satanic one, and nothing could be more satanic than his ability to scramble the opposition between left and right. (Satan was, after all, as Walter Benjamin reminds us, the defeated rebel and the prince of this world.)[4] Democratic forms are to be exploited by the despot as a convenient cover for his tyranny.[5] That suggestion of an implicit link between democracy and tyranny would seem to point in the direction of Tocqueville (specifically on America). But the fact is that Napoleon III's ability to triangulate the binary opposition between left and right was a matter of both vexation and fascination in the 19th century. The critic Sainte-Beuve, for instance, a supporter of the emperor, claimed that if Napoleon III was a "césariste," a thorough-going autocrat, it was by reason of his commitment to socialism.[6] Renan thought one of the signal failures of the Empire was its growing commitment to . . . democracy.[7]

And most intriguing of all in this regard is Marx, in what is probably his best (and least Marxian) text, *The Eighteenth Brumaire of Louis Bonaparte*. In Marx's view, Napoleon III, who staged a coup d'état against his own presidency on December 2, 1851, declaring himself emperor of what he claimed was no longer a republic, marked a freezing or paralysis of the materialist dialectic of history.[8] In the wake of the crushing of the June insurrection of 1848, the expectation was that the proletariat would now be stronger in its ability to better assess what an error it had been to ever collaborate with the bourgeoisie. In Marx's terms: "The revolution is dead! Long live the revolution!"[9] And then the dialectic lapsed into paralysis (or "standstill," to use Walter Benjamin's term).[10] Instead of the proletariat overthrowing the bourgeoisie, both classes stayed put, as the dropouts of the class struggle, the lumpen-proletariat, organized as the Bohemian cohort of Napoleon III, ascended to the pinnacle of state power. History resembled nothing so much as a latrine backing up, with all those parasites of the class struggle who should have been flushed into nonexistence by the dialectic of history abruptly erupting on top.

I take it that the *Protocols'* insistence on the Jew as communist *and* capitalist is a residue of the inherent ambiguity—neither left nor right—of Napoleon III, whose designs on France, we have seen, would be transposed as the designs of the Jews on the world itself.

Now, the scrambling of left and right, which seems the hallmark of plebiscitary Bonapartism, is, when seen in a certain light, a prototype of what would later flourish as national socialism. In between, however, comes the Dreyfus Affair, with the populist violence of its anti-Semitic riots. It was Hannah Arendt who made the transition between the worlds of Napoleon III and Hitler most explicit by rewriting what Marx famously called the "farce" of Louis Bonaparte as what *she* called the "comedy" of the Dreyfus Affair—with the "mob," the "residue of all classes," replacing Marx's Bohemian lumpen-proletariat, dropouts of the class struggle, and Jules Guérin, the would-be artisan of his own putsch, his own coup d'état, during the Affair, "in whom high society found its first criminal hero," replacing Napoleon's infamous nephew.[11]

We can thus sketch a genealogy effecting the transition from Napoleon III, the implied target of the Dialogue in Hell on which the *Protocols* drew, to Jules Guérin, as depicted by Hannah Arendt, in the Dreyfus Affair, to Hitler in the 20th century. Things grow increasingly anti-Semitic, increasingly violent. The paradox is that the Second Empire matrix out of which anti-Jewish violence seemed to sprout and flourish is the same matrix out of which the mythology of Jewish violence emerged, as well.

It is almost as though the left/right ambiguity that so intrigued Marx and the others in Napoleon III was compounded by a second antinomy that might be termed Jewish/anti-Jewish. Which leads one to wonder: What if the persistence of the *Protocols* had something to do with the fascination exercised by the antinomy itself? What, that is, if the Machiavellian figure standing in for Napoleon III in Joly's dialogue in hell with Montesquieu had, in his contradictions, a kind of satanic appeal by which the West was mesmerized and to which it would soon, once that satanic appeal was transposed to the Jews, fall prey? (And here I might add that, toward the end of his life, Joly was being referred to as "the head of the secret Bonapartists, "*les bonapartistes masqués*," as though he himself had been seduced by the Machiavellian target of his own polemic.)[12] It should not be forgotten, moreover, that Joly was found guilty (for his dialogue in hell) by the same Sixth Chamber of the Correctional Tribunal of the Seine that found against Baudelaire in the trial over *Les Fleurs du mal*. (And here one may note that Joly, like Baudelaire, was known for the ferocity of his attacks against the self-importance of that arch-liberal Victor Hugo, of whom he wrote that, had he not profited from the charisma of exile resulting from his clash with Napoleon III, the "gigantic hodgepodge [*fatras*] of his poetry would have fallen away, his metaphors would have ended up looking like nothing so much as . . . a treasure-chest of fake jewels."[13]

When one considers that Walter Benjamin's famous and famously unfinished *Arcades Project* was built around the Baudelaire/Hugo opposition, that he claimed to be able to generate the nightmare of the 20th century from a matrix provided by the Paris of Baudelaire (i.e., of Napoleon III), and that nonetheless there is not a single mention of Maurice Joly, prime source of the *Protocols*, in the entire *Project*, one is inclined to say that passage to America was not the only boat that Benjamin may have missed.)[14]

At this point, one wants to recall just how satanic the image of the Jews was in the tradition culminating in the *Protocols*. In the book that Norman Cohn calls "the Bible of modern anti-Semitism," Gougenot des Mousseaux's *Le juif, le judaïsme et la judaïsation des peoples chrêtiens* (1869), the world appears to be "falling into the grip of a mysterious body of Satan-worshippers, whom he calls 'kabbalistic Jews.'"[15] Now, concerning that claim several comments are in order:

1. Norman Cohn's reaction is to quickly explain that, far from being a "secret demonic religion, a systematic cult of evil," Qabbalah "is nothing but a body of Jewish mystical and theosophical doctrine" with "nothing secret about it," a body of thought that had in fact "charmed" a number of Renaissance humanists.[16] In a word, a Qabbalist wouldn't hurt a fly. Here we encounter the danger of a certain philo-Semitic strand of thought: In wanting to demonstrate the inexistence of a "Jewish threat," one risks reducing the Jews to being innocuous.

2. The more this reader studied in Cohn the tradition that culminated in the *Protocols*, with its references to the Jews embracing a "systematic cult of evil," the more he felt himself to be in the world of Gershom Scholem's essay "Redemption through Sin."[17] Recall the proposition, a reaction to the conversion of Sabbatai Zevi, that, at this stage of the messianic process, the Jews, like their messiah, Sabbatai Zevi, must enter into evil in order to defeat it from within. Now consider a work by Gougenot's successor, the Abbé Chabauty, who made much, in his book *Les juifs nos maîtres* (1882), of a document that appeared in the *Revue des études juives,* a Jewish publication, of 1880. It was an alleged reply of the "Prince of the Jews of Constantinople," dated 1489, to a Letter of the Jews of Arles, and it contains the following lines: "You say that they are destroying your synagogues; then make your children canons and clerics, so that they may destroy their churches."[18] The anti-Semite Chabauty makes much of this, as may be imagined, but Norman Cohn dismisses it as a "joke." Perhaps. (One recalls the line quoted by Benjamin to the effect that an anti-Semite

is a man who takes seriously one-tenth of the jokes that Jews tell about themselves.) And yet how close it all seems to the afterlife of the Sabbatian heresy as elaborated by Gershom Scholem. Scholem, the best friend of Walter Benjamin, to whom *Major Trends of Jewish Mysticism* is dedicated and of whom Scholem wrote that the secret name he (Benjamin) assigned himself, "Agesilaus Santander," was an anagram of "Der Angelus Satanas."[19]

3. It was no doubt out of impatience with an attitude of the sort exemplified by Norman Cohn, one that seemed to reduce the Jews to harmlessness, that the hero of the Dreyfus Affair, the first Jew to stand up for Dreyfus, Bernard Lazare, once wrote an article in praise of Léon Bloy. Bloy was a great writer of baroque prose at the turn of the century and a heretical Catholic, a mystic of antinomian bent, paradoxically obsessed with two themes: (1) the abjection of the Jews and (2) the centrality of abjection in the Christian economy of salvation. By the end of his major statement on the subject, *Le Salut par les juifs*, a kind of infinitely risky traversal of anti-Semitism that pretends to emerge on the other side, the Jews emerge with a certain awful grandeur, and it was in response to that grandeur, or rather in reaction to the liberal philo-Semitic line that there was no need to worry about the Jews since Jews were at bottom insignificant, mere imitators, that Bernard Lazare could compare Bloy to the prophets Isaiah and Jeremiah.[20]

With Bloy we have returned to the world of religious mysticism, Catholic rather than Jewish (as with Scholem), which may serve as a transition to the world of the *Protocols* and its disastrous hold on the world's imagination, as exemplified by the Orthodox mystic and first purveyor of the forgery, Sergei Nilus. This is what he told a skeptical Frenchman, Count Alexandre du Chayla: "Let us admit that the *Protocols* are a forgery. Cannot God make use of a forgery in order to illuminate the iniquity of what is about to occur? Cannot God, in response to our faith, transform the bones of a dog into the relics of a miracle? He can thus place into the mouth of a liar the annunciation of truth."[21] That extraordinary statement, with its declaration of the *Protocols*' invulnerability to any and all refutation, brings the liberal academic up short. UNESCO, in its blindness, may have recently sponsored, at the new library of Alexandria, an exhibit on monotheism, in which the *Protocols* were placed alongside the Torah, with the two offered as the sacred texts of the Jews.[22] But it is clear from Nilus's statement that, if sacred text it be, it is rather that of the enemies of the Jews.

Curiously enough, the Nilus statement finds a secular prototype at a crucial juncture in the Dreyfus Affair. A key element in the dossier against

Dreyfus turns out to have been a forgery by one Lieutenant-Colonel Henry.[23] (Indeed, one of the reasons the General Staff of the Army was so intent on protecting the actual traitor, Esterhazy, was that if someone other than Dreyfus were guilty of the alleged crime of selling military secrets to the Germans, one would have to account for the forgeries used to clinch the case against Dreyfus.) Shortly after Henry was confronted with the discovery of his forgery, he committed suicide.

But it is precisely at that point that matters become interesting for us. For Charles Maurras, a relatively unknown journalist at the time, launched a campaign to honor Henry for what he called his "faux patriotique," his "patriotic," that is, heroic forgery. Henry *knew* the truth and decided to remedy the altogether contingent absence of an actual document establishing that truth—of Jewish perfidy—with a document of his own invention. Such is the secular anticipation in the Dreyfus Affair of Sergei Nilus's mystical statement about the truth of the forged *Protocols*. (It was as a result of his invention of the motif of a "patriotic forgery" that Maurras, the future leader of the royalist movement Action Française, was launched on one of the most influential political careers of the French 20th century.)

A collection was begun to build a monument to Henry, the forger, and it is a matter of some notoriety that Paul Valéry, one of the truly great poets of the 20th century, made a contribution, "not without careful consideration," to the campaign.[24] Out of anti-Semitism? Probably not. Rather out of disgust with the self-satisfaction of the virtue-trippers among the ranks of the Dreyfusards. (I should probably state that my own flirtation with Scholem earlier is probably dictated by a similar allergy to an all too comfortable—or melodramatic—vision of us virtuous victims and those dastardly villains.)[25]

Then there was Proust, the self-styled first of the Dreyfusards and France's greatest novelist (as well, I should add, as a longtime subscriber, on aesthetic grounds, he said, to the newspaper *Action Française*, founded by Maurras).[26] During the Affair, he was at work on the long and ultimately aborted manuscript of a book titled *Jean Santeuil*, an autobiographical novel so preoccupied with the vindication of persecuted innocence that it has been viewed by some as a Dreyfus Affair in miniature.[27] In the novel, the protagonist is depicted in feverish attendance at the trials of Emile Zola. What is most interesting in this context is Proust's treatment of Lieutenant Colonel Picquart, one of the heroes of the affair, the non-Jew and officer who risked his career arguing that Esterhazy, not Dreyfus, was the culprit. He is described at length by Proust as a "philosopher" and a man whose devotion to truth is such that the narrator rhapsodically evokes Socrates.

Then, at the conclusion of the section of the novel devoted to the Affair ("La vérité sur l'affaire Dreyfus"), in a series of quintessentially Proustian reversals, it is suggested that Esterhazy—as well as Dreyfus—was innocent, that the "philosopher" Picquart had in fact forged the notorious document establishing Esterhazy's guilt but that he had done so, in the envenomed and mendacious atmosphere of the Affair, in an effort to produce a counterlie that would alone validate his "philosophical" intuition of the truth.

This episode is plainly inspired by the incident of Henry's so-called patriotic forgery.[28] It speaks to the imaginative hold that that development had on France's greatest novelist, who chose to borrow a weapon from the anti-Dreyfusard arsenal, the heroic forgery, albeit for Dreyfusard ends, in his own fiction. (We have already seen the appeal that the plea to honor Henry's forgery had for France's greatest poet, Paul Valéry.) The next stop in the sequence would be the episode rewritten in a mystical idiom, as exemplified by Sergei Nilus's dumbfounding proposition that it was in God's power to turn even a forgery into a vehicle of truth. All of which is to say that if the *Protocols* retain their fascination for anti-Semites, the episode of the *Protocols*, in its structure, continues to retain its interest even for anti-anti-Semites.

As for *our* superior virtue, I suspect it would be enough to look back on the episode of the dubious document produced by Dan Rather in 2004 concerning the shabby military career of President George W. Bush, a document that may have come very close to establishing the truth but that suffered only from being (in all probability) forged, for us to admit that doubts (on the subject of our superior virtue) are permitted.

NOTES

1. Norman Cohn, *Warrant for Genocide: The Jewish World Conspiracy and the Protocols of the Elders of Zion* (New York: Serif, 1996).

2. Ibid., 74.

3. See Franz Kobler, *Napoleon and the Jews* (New York: Schocken, 1975).

4. Walter Benjamin, *Charles Baudelaire, Un poète lyrique à l'apogée du capitalisme* (Paris: Payot, 1974), 38.

5. Cohn, *Warrant for Genocide*, 75.

6. See my "Pour Sainte-Beuve: Maurice Blanchot, 10 March 1942," in *Genealogies of the Text*, ed. Mehlman (Cambridge: Cambridge University Press, 1995).

7. Ernst Renan, *La réforme intellectuelle* (Paris: Michel Lévy frères, 1872).

8. On this subject, see J. Mehlman, *Revolution and Repetition: Marx/Hugo/Balzac* (Berkeley: University of California Press, 1977).

9. Ibid., 10.

10. See Richard Wolin, *Walter Benjamin: An Aesthetic of Redemption* (New York: Columbia University Press, 1982), 124–126.

11. Hannah Arendt, *The Origins of Totalitarianism* (New York: Harcourt Brace Jovanovich 1973), 111.

12. Henri Rollin, *L'apocalypse de notre temps* (Paris: Allia, 1991), 308.

13. Ibid., 294.

14. W. Benjamin, *The Arcades Project*, trans. Howard Eiland and Kevin McLaughlin (Cambridge, MA: Harvard University Press, 1999).

15. Cohn, *Warrant for Genocide*, 41.

16. Ibid.

17. Gershom Scholem, "Redemption through Sin," in *The Messianic Idea in Judaism*, ed. Scholem (New York: Schocken, 1971).

18. Cohn, *Warrant for Genocide*, 46.

19. Gershom Scholem, "Walter Benjamin and His Angel," in *On Jews and Judaism in Crisis*, ed. Werner Dannhauser (New York: Schocken, 1976), 198–236.

20. See Antoine Compagnon, *Les antimodernes* (Paris: Gallimard, 2005), 204.

21. Eric Conan, "L'origine des *Protocoles des Sages de Sion*," *L'Express*, November 16, 1999.

22. See Eric Conan's review of Pierre-André Taguieff, *Prêcheurs de haine: traversée de la judéophobie planétaire* (Paris: Mille et une nuits, 2004), in *L'Express*, November 18, 2004.

23. On the Henry episode, see Jean-Denis Bredin, *The Affair: The Case of Alfred Dreyfus*, trans. J. Mehlman (New York: George Braziller, 1986), 324–335.

24. Arendt, *The Origins of Totalitarianism*, 107. On Valéry's flirtation with racist thinking and its repercussions in his work, see J. Mehlman, "Craniometry and Criticism: Notes on a Valéryan Criss-Cross," in my *Genealogies of the Text* (Cambridge: Cambridge University Press, 1995), 11–32.

25. See J. Mehlman, *Legacies of Anti-Semitism in France* (Minneapolis: University of Minnesota Press, 1983), 83–90.

26. See J. Mehlman, "Literature and Collaboration: Benoist-Méchin's Return to Proust," in *Genealogies of the Text*, ed. Mehlman (Cambridge: Cambridge University Press, 1995), 53–66.

27. See J. Mehlman, "The Dreyfus Affair," in *A New History of French Literature*, ed. Denis Hollier (Cambridge, MA: Harvard University Press, 1989), 825.

28. Ibid., 824–830.

8

"Jewish World Conspiracy" and the Question of Secular Religions

An Interpretative Perspective

PAUL ZAWADZKI

This text deals with history, but it is not a piece of historical work in the strictest sense of the term. It proposes a few general remarks—one hopes, *not too* general—on the subject of the myth of the Jewish world conspiracy, with respect to the problem identified by Raymond Aron as that of *secular religions*.[1]

Why introduce the notion of secular religions in this context? The answer, in the form of an hypothesis, is the following: The interpretative framework contained in the concept of secular religion is a very useful and important tool in terms of understanding the belief—the act of faith—incarnated in *The Protocols of the Elders of Zion*. Naturally, the topic of a Jewish world conspiracy may usefully be linked to the specificities of the history of anti-Semitism.[2] However, the *Protocols* can also be considered as a paradigm of the modern concept of conspiracy. If approached in this way, it can arguably be considered within the framework of the wider restructuring of belief taking place outside the traditional religious institutions, which effectively gave birth to the so-called *secular religions*.

I thus contend that much can be gained from considering the belief in a Jewish world conspiracy not merely in terms of the legacy of secularized superstitions from the past, but, more precisely, as a new phenomenon resulting, like the concept of secular religion, from a dialectical process directly linked to modernity. From this point of view, the true enigma of *The Protocols of the Elders of Zion* is revealed only when one ceases to view it merely as a relic of medieval demonizing of the Jews. On the contrary, one of the more perplexing aspects of the *Protocols* comes from the observation that it was precisely in the context of modernity that this patent forgery imposed itself as something not merely plausible but convincingly "true."

While working on his *History of Anti-Semitism*, Leon Poliakov was struck by the fascination exercised on the human mind by an elementary and exhaustive causality, equivalent from a psychological point of view to a "first cause." He saw at work in the heart of civilized Europe what Levy-Bruhl analysed in 1922 as the *primitive mentality*.[3] What needs to be understood is exactly why it was during the 20th century that conspiracy theories of society (Karl Popper), or what Manes Sperber referred to as the *"visions policières"* of history, became so important.[4]

Why do conspiracy theories seem to have flourished within a democratic modernity, to which, in many ways, they ran contrary? Why was such an astounding forgery as *The Protocols of the Elders of Zion* diffused in a wide range of languages during the century that witnessed the triumph of science, during the century that saw the rise of critical spirit and the deepening of historical consciousness, that, as Gadamer once remarked, is not only "the consciousness of the historicity of every present" but also the consciousness of "the relative character of our own opinions"?[5] It was this period of intense cultural agitation, which began in the 1880s and ended in the first decades of the 20th century—the "1900 moment"—that saw the birth of *The Protocols of the Elders of Zion*. This period was also characterized by the deepening of a movement of secularism in Europe in the context of a liberal process of separation between church and state. And, ironically, the same period that saw the fall in influence of the great religions also ushered in the delirious belief in a Jewish world conspiracy.

At the turn of the century, along with Nietzsche's nihilist diagnosis, it was Max Weber who undoubtedly gave the most acute analysis of this historical condition. The desperate situation sketched by Max Weber, most notably in his 1918 speech on the ethics of the scientist, described Western modernity as a void, an emptiness, a condition dominated by a loss of the ultimate meaning of things, a condition where this difficulty in believing in anything at all produced the *disenchantment of the world*.[6]

How, then, given this context, is it possible to conceive in the same historical period the fanaticism of ideological believers prepared to sacrifice themselves and others and the kind of nihilism that points to an attitude of conscious renunciation of all kinds of beliefs? Both positions should actually and logically exclude each other, just as absolutism excludes relativism, fullness excludes emptiness, and fire excludes ice.

To be sure, this feeling of perplexity is not ours alone only, I mean us *today*. By and large, it was a feeling shared by those who were confronted, sometimes in their very being, with the unforeseen power of political myths in the first half of the 20th century. More important, this feeling was acutely shared by those intellectuals who had been immersed in the culture of the Enlightenment and therefore had no clue about the looming advent of modern fanaticism. Far from kind of religious fanaticism that Voltaire had so indignantly condemned, this modern variant was deeply and violently anti-religious, as was the case in Hitler's Germany or Stalin's Russia.

If one had to take but one example to illustrate this point, the case of Ernst Cassirer serves well. After he left Germany, Cassirer wrote *The Myth of the State*. This work, which was published only posthumously at Yale in 1946, may be considered as Cassirer's intellectual will—a testament all the more moving in that it was written by one of the great figures of neo-Kantian rationalism. In this book, Cassirer dedicated his remaining intellectual strength to thinking about the power of myths. He first emphasized *"the rise of a new kind of power that of the mythical thought. [A power] which is probably the most remarkable trait of modernity,"*[7] before concluding his argument by a critical confession:

> we [intellectuals] have underestimated the power of myths. When we first heard about political myths, we found them to be so absurd, so ridiculous, and so crazy, that we had trouble taking them seriously.[8]

Beyond Cassirer's case, what is really striking about the mid-20th century is the large number of influential thinkers—people like Eric Voegelin, Hans Kohn, Arthur Koestler, Waldemar Gurian, Aleksander Hertz, Roger Caillois and members of the Collège de Sociologie, Raymond Aron, Czeslaw Milosz, and many more—who, coming from different political and philosophical backgrounds, have used the religious lexicon in order to approach the phenomenon taking place before their eyes. They talked about myths, mythical faith, sacredness, dogmas, cults, rites, and communion... And what they attempted to describe with language redolent of premodern culture was the emergence, in the mid-20th century, of a series of ideological beliefs, instituted by bloodthirsty political regimes, that took the form of millennial fanaticism. The experience of totalitarianism, together with the irruption on the political stage of powerful psychoaffective processes that one thought had been contained by the progress of rationalist optimism, deeply affected those intellectuals whose minds had been formed by the Enlightenment culture.

If, to repeat the words of Cassirer, a whole range of political beliefs, appeared to be "absurd," "ridiculous," and "crazy," it was because they could find a meaning only in a vision of history whereby the more the world becomes rational, the less "irrational" beliefs and fanaticism have a hold. If these thinkers underestimated the power of these myths, it was precisely because they approached them as simple relics of the past. Eric Voegelin criticized this lack of intellectual perspicacity in the preface to his book *Die politischen Religionen*, published in 1938. Voegelin affirmed: "It is unbearable constantly to hear that National Socialism is only a regression towards barbarianism, towards the dark Middle Ages, towards times anterior to the modern progresses of humanity."

We know today, however, that it is not sufficient to discard religion for prejudices and superstitions to disappear and for men to finally express their autonomy in accordance with the Kantian view of Enlightenment thought. Yet, a certain number of authors, and Max Weber in particular, had already perceived one of the important aspects of mythical restructuring going on in their time. Weber declared, in 1918: "The fate of our time is characterized by rationalization and intellectualization and, above all, by the 'disenchantment of the world.' Precisely, the ultimate and most sublime values have retreated from public life."[9] In saying so, Weber was very conscious of the fact that the void of meaning created by this disenchantment also created a longing for meaning. He was aware that it created a pressing need for more coherence and meaning among modern intellectuals. Effectively, because their role is to give meaning to the world, intellectuals are more exposed than others to the pathology of meaning embodied in modernity, and they are also the first to want to escape this pathology by recovering the global meaning of the world.

Again, this unsatisfied need for meaning, coupled with the difficulty of living in a meaningless world, was something that Weber found in the students he spoke with (students who would be thirty when Hitler came to power). He said: "the prophet for whom so many of our younger generation yearn simply does not exist."[10] And later he added: "If one tries intellectually to construe new religions without a new and genuine prophecy, then, in an inner sense, something similar will result, but with still worse effects. And academic prophecy, finally, will create only fanatical sects but never a genuine community. To the person who cannot bear the fate of the times like a man, one must say; may he rather return silently, without the usual publicity build-up of renegades, but simply and plainly. The arms of the old churches are opened widely and compassionately for him."[11]

This dimension we have outlined—the way political myths were produced in the 20th century and the role played by intellectuals in the process—could not have been approached with more simplicity and lucidity. If we have quoted these familiar pages, it is because, thanks to them, one is thrown into the heart of *the dialectic of skepticism and modern fanaticism*. With this, Weber unveils part of *the process of the restructuring of fanaticism beginning with doubt*—in other words, a process no longer beginning with faith but with the absence of certainty.

Effectively, when we study the intellectual atmosphere of Germany in the 1920, we find a striking combination of both fanaticism and nihilism. Max Weber provides perhaps the best-known case of an astute observer of the crisis, but he was only one of many. In 1930, for example, Karl Jaspers published a book entitled *Die geistige Situation der Zeit*. In this work, he was interested not in ideological fanaticism but in nihilism. The world described by Jaspers (prior to the seizure of power by Hitler) is less that of ideological faith than that of emptiness, skepticism, and the loss of substance.[12] Raymond Aron also described this kind of nihilism when, as a student, he experienced the moral atmosphere in Germany:

> Never was the Nietzschean methodology of critical analysis used with more virtuosity. Never did man perceive more lucidly the traps of interest and pride, the force of his desires and the frailty of his inner imperatives. Never did this realization come so close to anarchic skepticism.[13]

In the dissertation he completed, in 1938, on the limits of historical objectivity, Aron dedicated long pages to historicism—"a mix of skepticism and irrationality." To him, the kind of historicism that flourished in the early 20th century (even more strongly after the First World War) "did not only correspond to a time that was unsure of itself, but to a society without a future, rejecting the one it has predicted, and oscillating between Utopian revolt and so-called lucid fatalism."[14] Leo Strauss, it should be noted, also referred to German nihilism in a 1941 lecture. He emphasized the enthusiasm for Nietzsche among German youth, though he profoundly regretted "that these adolescents did not find teachers who could explain to them in clear terms the positive meaning, and not simply the destructive one, of their aspirations."[15]

It is within the context we have tried to illustrate with these three historical testimonies that *The Protocols of the Elders of Zion* produced devastating effects, that it became required reading in Germany, and that it was diffused by various political movements. And it is within this context that the concept of secular religion becomes useful. In effect, these peculiar ideologies attempt to reclaim the ultimate and absolute meaning in the immanent order of history, as well as in the political and ideological order.

Before continuing, we must briefly come back to some questions of terminology. Three terms are easily confused, namely *civil religion, political religion,* and *secular religion.*[16] I would like first to exclude the concept of civil religion such as it was conceptualized by Robert Bellah with relation to Rousseau's "The Social Contract" (Livre IV, ch. VIII).[17] If there is such a thing as religion in Rousseau, it is for the most part a refusal of any form of political absolutism. Civil religion provides a transcendental finality, a set of ultimate values, for political life, but it is still anchored in the liberal tradition. Civil religion is inscribed in the matrix of political liberalism and modern individualism; it has an affinity with pluralism. Secular religions constitute its negation.

The concept of political religion is favored by historians, especially by those who study Nazism and Fascism.[18] The expression, which one already finds in Condorcet,[19] was popularized by the book of Eric Voegelin on political religions, a work that was immediately confiscated by the Third Reich police. Voegelin analysed Nazism as a "worldly religion" (*religion intramondaine* in the French). However, Voegelin was not fully satisfied with that concept, and in his *Autobiographical Reflections* he wrote: "It is too vague and it is already distorting the real nature of experience by mixing it with dogma and doctrine."[20] Still, Voegelin was always attached to the analysis of modernity in terms of the rise of gnosticism. Among modern Gnostic movements (movements that, in the eyes of Voegelin, are founded on "the belief that it is possible to rid oneself of the evils of the world" through knowledge and historical understanding), Voegelin cited "Marxism, Communism, Fascism and National Socialism."[21]

The concept as used in historical literature has the advantages and the disadvantages of all loosely defined concepts: It has multiple meanings and yet is often indispensable (thinking here of concepts that are used in the social sciences, such as *alienation, anomie,* or even the aforementioned *disenchantment of the world*). With this degree of generality, the concept of political religion is often inspired by Durkheimian sociology of religion and refers imprecisely to all kinds of phenomena of sacralization in the political realm, without necessarily providing any explanation for their structure and origin.

This is why we prefer to use the concept of secular religion, regardless of its ironic dimension. Raymond Aron defined it quite simply when he was exiled in London in 1944. He had in mind National Socialism and Soviet socialism. Secular religions are "doctrines that replace faded faiths in the minds of our contemporaries and place the salvation of humanity in a future to come, in a new social order to be created. [. . .] The evangelists of these religions will mobilize all the means necessary, however terrible, so that nothing should compromise the sacred end in sight."[22]

There are three interesting points in this definition. First of all, Aron does not invoke the need for religion as an anthropological postulate. Second, his approach to secular religion prevents one from falling into a common misunderstanding, namely that these absolute beliefs are no longer of religions, while keeping a religious form. They are a new kind of ideology. They are hybrids born of modernity, a reconstituted mixture of heteronomy and autonomy, when politics are emancipated from religion. However, by recomposing a holistic political project, they express a form of hope and a search for salvation in and by history. By so doing, they revisit religious ambition in the political sphere, a kind of secular theocracy. As such, then, they need to be placed within the general framework of the recomposition of meanings in modernity.

Aron's definition points to three critical characteristics. First is an orientation toward the future: This element anchors secular religions in a world looking toward its future and structured by a project precisely defined as ideological. Second is an emphasis on the action of the men in history: in a future-oriented world, secular religions, contrary to the traditional millenarian movements,[23] deal not in theocentrism but in anthropocentrism; they are not passive apocalyptic expectation but active.[24] Third, the salvation of humanity occurs in the here and now. If salvation is found in history (written by men and no longer by gods), then this salvation is actually attainable.[25] It is a hope that can be realized on Earth, in the flesh, a secular millennialism.

The affinity between these new holistic beliefs and the myth of a modern conspiracy now becomes much clearer. Modern conspiracy theories still hope to explain everything, but they no longer do so with reference to fate. Instead, these theories affirm that history is man-made, and it is therefore within history that they search for a unique, elementary, and exhaustive causality. As Francois Furet indicated in his reflections on the French Revolution, "the idea of conspiracy as a category of political explanation" accompanies the development of the democratic imagination of power.[26] In terms of an ideological framework, the world is peopled with human wills. Jewish world conspiracies developed in the wake of the birth of mass political organizations, meaning a new type of collective actor aspiring to take power and to change society.

Conspiracy theories are fundamental elements of the secular religions of the 20th century, and they hold a crucial role in totalitarian practices. As secular religions, they have an important heuristic value. From meager evidence, interpreted ad infinitum, they offered an ersatz explanation of a simple, exhaustive, and global kind. In a secularized world, they claim to make sense of the enigma of evil and, more generally, of everything that has gone wrong (crisis, revolutions, wars and natural catastrophes). One could ironically say that they brought the Devil back, only this time it was a human Devil. And he is not a character from a Boulgakov novel but the real-life prosecutor Vichinksi, who, during the Moscow trials, questioned Zelenski, one of the accused who was the head of the distribution network of consumer goods, in these terms: "Were there instances when members of your organisation who were in charge of stocking butter put crushed glass in the butter? . . . Were there instance when your co-workers, your criminal accomplices, plotted against the Soviet state and the Soviet people by spreading nails in the butter?" A scene of such absurdity would be laughably comic if we did not know that eighteen of the accused were immediately executed.[27]

The idea of conspiracy was diffused in modern societies turning to democracy and carried an obvious nostalgia for unity. The modern idea of conspiracy supposes the disruption of democracy. One can say it "reintroduces religious principles within a secular vision of the world."[28] It re-enchants policy in secular societies. It made sense of crises and conflicts with reference to the workings of criminal conspirators, more often than not foreigners, or at least internal agents acting according to an external agenda: the "rootless cosmopolitans," the American imperialists, or the Zionists taking their orders from Tel-Aviv. Therefore, the conspiracy idea is in deep negation of the divisions and internal conflicts inherent in modern societies. It recomposes a holistic vision of a social group that is homogeneous, threatened by the outside world.

In that sense, it is not sufficient to say that conspiracy theories of society deal with "the secularization of religious superstitions."[29] Granted, they are efforts at the recomposition of beliefs resulting from a dialectical process belonging to modernity. But these conspiracy theories are to some extent a new phenomenon and not merely a secularised version of ancient beliefs.

Of course, there is hardly ever anything new in history. *The Protocols of the Elders of Zion* is just a recycling of old elements, just as modern anti-Semitism is a recycling of old representations. After all, the works of Norman Cohn, Gavin Langmuir, and others, including Johannes Heil and Jeffrey Woolf in this volume, do show that there existed already in the Middle Ages an anti-Jewish concept of conspiracy. Pierre- André Taguieff is correct to say that the myth of the world Jewish plot is a modern political myth "manufactured with materials of symbolic systems borrowed from medieval anti-Judaism and anti-Satanism."[30] It is therefore clear that modern fanaticism is a recycling of elements of medieval demonology. But, it is not only that. Secular religions and conspiracy theories are not simply the secularized version of traditional modes of thinking. In terms of representations, we find old structures, but they are recomposed in an ideological vision and no longer a religion, one of the world and not the hereafter.

Above all, they respond to new needs to which modernity itself gave birth. This allows us to put the emphasis on the new sociological meanings embodied in the *Protocols*. Modern fanaticism, in the 20th century, is not simply old-fashioned fanaticism; even if, when talking for example of the so-called Doctor's Plot in Soviet Russia or of Stalinst purges, one is reminded of medieval witch hunts. They cannot be explained only with reference to the persistence of fanatical faith or "the return to barbarianism." Claude Levi-Strauss once wrote that "the barbarian is foremost a man who believes in barbarianism."[31] Indeed, the barbarian believes that humanity is that of his own group. He perceives his beliefs and the norms to which he is subjected as natural. He sticks to the beliefs and values that make up his world. There is no place in it for self-doubt or skepticism.

Yet, what the history of the 20th century showed was a reverse trajectory taking place: Beliefs grew out of doubt and provided the fanatical a *scientific* answer to a lack of meaning in a world deemed to be a historical one.[32] Of this "leap of faith" G. Lukacs could provide the paradigm.[33] For Arthur Koestler, political myth (in his case the Soviet myth) offered "an admirable compensation for life's emptiness and the absurdity of death."[34] One of the great questions of the 20th century is this dialectic of skepticism and fanaticism, which Jean Grenier (Camus's teacher) analyzed in *L'Esprit d'orthodoxie*, published in 1937. As he wrote: "the sudden transition from absolute doubt to absolute faith, and in parallel the similar transition from unlimited despair to unlimited hope is a remarkable feature of the past decade."[35]

In the 19th century, Sergei Nilus was thought to be a disciple of Nietzsche and a free-thinker. Only later, when, after a sudden conversion, he actually turned back to mysticism and chose faith, did he incorporate *The Protocols of the Elders of Zion* into the second edition of his book *The Great in the Small* (1905).[36] Of course, one can observe a traditionalist use of the theme of Jewish conspiracy, as shown in the writings of Henri Gougenot de Mousseaux (1805–1876), a French traditionalist Catholic and counterrevolutionary, translated in German by Alfred Rosenberg, the "Reichsleiter für die Weltanschauung" of the Nazi party.[37] In Poland, the action of the famous abbot Trzeciak largely contributed to propagate the *Protocols* between two world wars. Churches in Warsaw still sold copies of the book until recently. But, in Poland, again, there were also nationalist and communist—or, to be more precise, national-communist—uses of the text. Roman Dmowski, leader of the nationalistic movement until 1939, was deeply convinced of the existence of a Jewish plot threatening the young Polish state. Child of positivism, formerly a biologist, Dmowski was certainly not a traditionalist spirit.[38]

Conspiracy theories allow an escape from a lack of meaning and permit new certitudes. They provide the means of the search of salvation by history. They therefore appear seductive to those who experience the pain of a "detraditionalization" they nonetheless embrace. Moreover, the theme of conspiracy lends itself easily to many ideological manipulations. It is a text open to all contexts.

The hyperplasticity and adaptability of *The Protocols of the Elders of Zion* may well explain why it provides a nice bridge between medieval anti-Semitism and demonological anti-Zionism. In Poland, the *Protocols* seemed to have "vanished" during the Stalinist years of the regime. It made a comeback during the anti-Zionist campaigns of 1967. I was able to collect testimonies according to which the book was then distributed to some journalists at the Polish press agency. Before the war, the equation was quite simple: Judaism equals Bolshevism, and Bolshevism equals Soviet imperialism. After the Six-Day War, however, this equation was recomposed. Then Judaism equaled Zionism, and Zionism equaled American imperialism. In each case, an external, hidden, malevolent enemy sought to destroy the Polish people.

For those "moderns" who live in a world where they presume that their fellow-citizens share a basic commitment to rationality and historical empiricism, the perennial success of the *Protocols* may seem incomprehensible. But, rather than dismiss it merely as a form of regression, they would do well to appreciate how it operates as a response to modernity, as a form of secular religion that fills the vacuum created by the destruction of traditional religious belief with secular certainties and reassurances. By embracing a narrative of global scope in which a historical conspiracy aims at destroying the collective identity of the believers, those who adopt these narratives re-enchant the world with an all-embracing narrative that explains everything and reassert the reassuring division between us (good and innocent victims) and them (evil, malevolent predators). It is little wonder, then, that conspiracy theories, among them the *Protocols* above all, provide one of the essential planks for modern "secular religions." And, given the propensity of these "secular religions" to offer the extravagant hopes of millennial salvation in *this* world, one must beware the conditions under which such theories become the basis of genocidal practices.

1. My thanks to Marion Guiral and Francine Simon Ekovich for the translation of this text.

2. Joshua Trachteneberg, *The Devil and the Jews. The Medieval Conception of the Jew and Its Relation to Modern Anti-Semitism* (1943; Philadelphia: The Jewish Publication Society, 1993); Norman Cohn, *Warrant for Genocide: The Myth of the Jewish World Conspiracy and the Protocols of the Elders of Zion* (1967; London: Serif, 1996), chapter 1; Gavin I. Langmuir, *History, Religion, and Antisemitism* (Berkeley: University of California Press, 1990), 341–342; Jeffrey Woolf and Johannes Heil in this volume.

3. *La causalité diabolique. Essai sur l'origine des persécutions* (Paris: Calmann-Lévy, 1980).

4. Manès Sperber, "La conception policière de l'histoire" (1953), in Sperber, *Le talon d'Achille* (Paris: Calmann-Lévy, 1957).

5. Hans-Georg Gadamer, *Le problème de la conscience historique* (1958; Paris: Seuil, 1996), 23.

6. Max Weber, "Science as a Vocation," in *From Max Weber: Essays in Sociology*, ed. H. H. Gerth and C. Wright Mills (New York: Oxford University Press, 1958), 129–156.

7. Ernst Cassirer, *Le mythe de l'Etat* (Paris: Gallimard, 1993), 17; English tr.: *The Myth of State* (New Haven: Yale University Press, 1946)], ch. 1. Author's translation.

8. Ibid., p. 400 [last page, ch. 18]. Author's translation.

9. Max Weber, "Science as a Vocation," 155.

10. Ibid., 153.

11. Ibid., 155.

12. K. Jaspers, *La situation spirituelle de notre époque* (1930), tr. W. Biemel et J. Ladrière, 2e éd. (Paris: Desclée de Brouwer, 1952).

13. R. Aron, "Tyrannie et mépris des hommes" [1942], in *Chroniques de guerre, la France libre, 1940–1945*, ed. Charles Bachelier (Paris: Gallimard, 1990), 471.

14. R. Aron, *Introduction à la philosophie de l'histoire. Essai sur les limites de l'objectivité historique* [1938], ed. S. Mesure (Paris: Gallimard, 1986), 376 and 368.

15. "Le nihilisme allemand" [1941], in *Nihilisme et politique*, tr. V. O. Seyden (Paris: Payot, Rivages, 2001), 44. Author's translation. See also Hermann Rauschning, *The Revolution of Nihilism: Warning to the West* (New York: Longman, Green, 1939), and *The Voice Of Destruction: Conversations with Hitler* (New York: Putnam, 1940).

16. An excellent introduction to the confused history of these concepts is given by Philippe Burrin, "Religion civile, religion politique, religion séculière," in *Riten, Mythen und Symbole—Die Arbeiterbewegung zwischen "Zivilreligion" und Volkskultur*, ed. Berthold Unfried and Christine Schindler (Vienna: Akademische Verlagsanstalt, 1999), 17–28.

17. Robert Bellah, "Civil Religion in America" [1967], in *Beyond Belief. Essays on Religion in a Post-Traditional World* (Berkeley: University of California Press, 1991).

18. See, for instance, Emilio Gentile, *Le religioni della politica. Fra democrazie e totalitarismi* (Roma: Laterza and Figli, 2001).

19. Nicolas de Condorcet, *Cinq mémoires sur l'instruction publique* (1791; Paris: GF-Flammarion, 1994), 93.

20. Eric Voegelin, *Autobiographical Reflections*, ed. Ellis Sandoz (Baton Rouge: Louisiana State University Press, 1989), ch. 14. Author's translation.

21. Eric Voegelin, "La religion des modernes. Les mouvements gnostiques de notre temps," in *Wort und Warheit—Monatsschrift für Religion und Kultur* [1960], tr. F. Manent, *Commentaire* 41 (1998): 318–327. His term "gnosticism" shares a great deal in common

with Norman Cohn's definition of millennialism: a belief in an imminent cataclysm that will, in the end, destroy evil and injustice and inaugurate a perfect society (*The Pursuit of the Millennium*, 3e éd. [London: Secker and Warburg, 1970]). Of course, since, by Cohn's definition, millennialism is about perfecting *this* world and gnosticism traditionally seeks to escape the lower spheres, the term may not be particularly appropriate. Voegelin uses "gnosticism" to refer to apocalyptic (i.e., revelatory) knowledge about the end-times.

22. Raymond Aron, "L'avenir des religions séculières," *Chroniques de guerre, la France libre, 1940–1945*, ed. Charles Bachelier (Paris: Gallimard, 1990), 45 (15 juillet 1944): 210–217; 46 (15 août 1944): 269–277; reprint in Aron, *L'âge des empires et l'avenir de la France* (Paris: Défense de la France, 1945), 287–318; *Commentaire*, 28–29 (1985): 369–383; *Chroniques de guerre, la France libre 1940–1945*, 925–948.

23. See the introduction to Cohn, *Pursuit of the Millennium*.

24. See Richard Landes's definitions in "Roosters Crow, Owls Hoot: On the Dynamics of Apocalyptic Millennialism," in *War in Heaven, Heaven on Earth: Theories of the Apocalyptic*, ed. Glen S. McGhee and Stephen O'Leary (London: Equinox Press, 2005), 19–46.

25. See the remarks of Marcel Gauchet, *Le désenchantement du monde: une histoire politique de la religion* (Paris: Gallimard, 1985), 257ff; English trans., Oscar Burge, *The Disenchantment of the World: A Political History of Religion* (Princeton: Princeton University Press, 1997).

26. François Furet, *Penser la Révolution française* (Paris: Gallimard, 1978), 77–81.

27. H. Carrère d'Encausse, *Staline, l'ordre par la terreur* (Paris: Flammarion, 1979), 58.

28. Marcel Gauchet, " Le démon du soupçon," *l'Histoire* 84 (1985): 54.

29. Karl Popper, " Prediction and Prophecy" [1948], in Karl Popper, *Conjectures and Refutations*, 4th ed. (London: Routledge and Kegan, 1972).

30. Pierre André Taguieff, *L'imaginaire du complot mondial. Aspects d'un mythe moderne* (Paris: Fayard/Mille et une nuits, 2006), 8.

31. Claude Lévi-Strauss, *Race et histoire* [1952], reprinted in *Le racisme devant la science* (Paris: Unesco/Gallimard, 1973), 15.

32. See discussion by Hannah Arendt, "Religion and Politics," *Confluence* 2, no. 3 (1953): 105–126.

33. Daniel Bell, "The Return of Sacred," reprinted in Bell, *The Winding Passage. Essays and Sociological Journeys, 1960–1980* (Cambridge, MA: Abt Associates, 1980), 342; see also the essay "After the Age of Sinfulness: Georg Lukàcs and the Mystical Roots of Revolution," tr. "Après l'âge du péché absolu. Georg Lukacs et les racines mystiques de la révolution," in Daniel Bell, *La fin de l'idéologie* (Paris: PUF, 1997), 333–360.

34. Arthur Koestler, "L'anatomie d'un mythe," in *Le Yogi et le commissaire*, ed. Koestler, tr. Dominique Aury et Jeanne Terracini (Paris: Livre de Poche, 1969), 185.

35. J. Grenier, *Essai sur l'esprit d'orthodoxie* (1937; Paris: Gallimard, 1961), 27.

36. Michael Hagemeister, "Wer war Sergei Nilus? Versuch einer bio-bibliographischen Skizze," *Ostkirchliche Studien* 40 (1991): 49–63; and this volume; André Taguieff, *Traversée de la judéophobie planétaire* (Paris: Fayard/Mille et une nuits, 2004), 647.

37. Jacob Katz, *Jews and Freemasons in Europe, 1723–1939* (Cambridge, MA: Harvard University Press, 1970), ch. 10; Cohn, *Warrant for Genocide*, ch. 11.

38. Paul Zawadzki, "Usages des Protocoles et logiques de l'antisémitisme en Pologne," in *Faux et usages d'un faux. Les Protocoles des Sages de Sion*, ed. Pierre-André Taguieff (Paris: Berg International, 1992), 2:279–324.

9

The Turning Point

The Protocols of the Elders of Zion *and the Eschatological War between Aryans and Jews*

DAVID REDLES

In 1918, Germany was reeling from an inexplicably lost war and threatened by what appeared to be an imminent Bolshevik-style revolution. Hunger had reached epidemic proportions, and the economy was beginning its steady decline, while society in general was politically and socially fragmented—all enacted against a modernist cultural backdrop that simultaneously celebrated and mocked the collapse of a once proud nation. At this time, rumors began to spread that a vast Jewish conspiracy was behind the war, its eventual loss, and the subsequent revolutionary upheavals in Russia, Hungary, and Germany. The sudden and intense nature of Germany's collapse and its seeming inexplicable causality led some individuals to search for a simple explanation for the chaos. They would find that explanation in an imaginary Evil Other, the so-called Jewish-Bolshevik.[1]

On November 9, 1918, a socialist revolution led by the Jewish journalist Kurt Eisner broke out in Munich. Members of the Thule Society, like other right-wing groups, were shocked by the sudden turn of events, especially when seven of its members were murdered by the revolutionaries.[2] Rudolf von Sebottendorff, the master of this semisecret lodge, gave an apocalyptic sermon to its members that was a thoroughly millennial diatribe on rebirth and resurrection through self-sacrifice in an eschatological struggle against the Jews:

> Yesterday we experienced the collapse of everything which was familiar, dear and valuable to us. In the place of our princes of Germanic blood rules our deadly enemy: Judah. What will come of this chaos, we do not know yet. But we can guess. A time will come of struggle, the most bitter need, a time of danger. . . . As long as I hold the iron hammer [a reference to his Master's hammer], I am determined to pledge the Thule to this struggle. . . . From today on our symbol is the red eagle, which warns us that we must die in order to live.[3]

On the surface, the Thule Society was an ariosophical education society. Ariosophy (meaning wisdom of the Aryans) was a form of occultism based on the thought of two Viennese pseudo-scholars, Guido von List and Lanz von Liebenfels.[4] Both men rejected modernity and found solace in a mythic past where Aryan supermen, perfect in body and soul, ruled over inferior humans of mixed blood. Combining theosophy, Social Darwinism, and eugenics, both men came to believe that the world had reached a turning point of either racial apocalypse or racial salvation.[5] If Aryan humanity continued in the direction of miscegenation, then apocalypse was sure to come. However, if the Aryans purified themselves through strict eugenic measures, they would become like god-men of old, save the world, and usher in a new millennium.

With the threat of a Bolshevik-style takeover of Bavaria looming, Sebottendorff and his lodge members dedicated the Thule Society to countering the alleged Jewish-Bolshevik threat. The belief that the turning point of apocalypse or salvation had arrived in 1918–1919 seems to have radicalized the ariosophists. No longer was a small group of racial elites sitting around studying rune symbols and listening to Wagnerian grail music enough to usher in the Aryan New Age. A turning point had arrived, and the Jewish-Bolsheviks appeared to be winning. The Thule Society now hoped to fight fire with fire. If the Jewish-Bolsheviks were attempting to raise class consciousness to win the workers and further their aim of world domination, then the Thulists needed to do the same, raising race consciousness among those same workers.

The ariosophists came to believe that a small group of Jews, three hundred elders or wise men, were using Bolshevism to attract workers to divide the Aryans by class and thus divide the race. The Thule Society dedicated itself to winning back German workers, their Aryan brothers, and to actively fighting the Jewish-Bolsheviks. To achieve this goal, Sebottendorff purchased a small working-class sports paper, the *Munich Observer*, which would later become the *Volkish Observer*, the official Nazi newspaper. The Thulists also started their own paramilitary group, the *Bund Oberland*, which fought under a swastika banner, to battle the Jewish-Bolsheviks (in reality German Communists, and mostly not Jewish) in the streets of Munich.

To figure out how best to attract workers away from the Communists, the Thule Society created a worker's circle, essentially a discussion group, led by Karl Harrer, Michael Lotter, and Anton Drexler. It was Drexler who then urged the creation of a political party, and the *Deutsche Arbeiterpartei* (DAP), the German Worker's Party, was formally founded in January

1919.[6] It was this party that one year later became the National Socialist German Worker's Party (NSDAP). Hitler would quickly push all other leaders aside, although his inner circle was replete with Thulists or Thule associates, including Gottfried Feder, Hans Frank, Alfred Rosenberg, Rudolf Hess, and Dietrich Eckart.[7]

But, it must be asked, what made the battle against the so-called Jewish-Bolsheviks suddenly so central? The earlier reference to three hundred Jewish elders is pertinent, for the belief that the chaos was being deliberately caused by Jews was seemingly revealed in a strange document that appeared a mere two months after revolution broke out in Munich and that seemed to explain the origins of the apocalyptic chaos.

The Protocols of the Elders of Zion *as an Apocalyptic Text*

Less than two months after Sebottendorrf made his apocalyptic sermon, a book by Ludwig Müller von Hausen, the editor of the journal *Auf Vorposten* (*On Outpost Duty*), appeared under the pseudonym Gottfried zur Beek. It told a fantastic tale; a group of three hundred Jewish elders had gathered in Basel in 1897 as part of a congress meeting of the Jewish Zionist Movement.[8] While the public meetings were about the establishment of a Jewish homeland in Palestine, secrets meetings had taken place that discussed the true hidden agenda—detailed plans for Jewish domination of the world. Entitled *Die Geheimnisse der Weisen von Zion* (*The Secrets of the Wise Men of Zion*), the book included a copy of the minutes of the alleged secret minutes. It quickly became a bestseller.[9] The German version of the *Protocols* would reach thirty-nine editions by 1939, and it continues to be a source of anti-Semitic propaganda to this day.[10] For the Nazis especially (they acquired the rights to the work in 1929), it proved to be a crucial source that shaped and intensified their millennial view of world history.

The *Protocols* is, of course, a hoax. But it was, and for some anti-Semites still is, a believed hoax. The forgery was probably concocted in 1903 within the Russian Empire, most likely in Ukraine.[11] It combined an obscure 19th-century anti-Napoleon III satire, Maurice Joly's *Dialogue aux Enfers entre Machiavel et Montesquieu* (1864), with *The Rabbi's Speech*, a portion of a novel by Hermann Goedsche titled *Biarritz* (1868).[12] While the hoaxers borrowed the basic structure and language of Joly's work and thus its critique of modernity, especially Napoleon III's cynical manipulation of democracy and the press, what it took from *The Rabbi's Speech* was its shifting of the blame for the horrors of modernity onto Jews, as well as its apocalyptic inversion of Jewish messianism. For *The Rabbi's Speech* is millennial, with references to the imminent coming of a Jewish messianic age that would see the House of David assume leadership of the world in fulfillment of the covenant with Jehovah. The covenant is realized by the Jews through manipulation of the evils of modernity, including capitalism, which is portrayed as centralizing wealth and power in the hands of Jews, and both democracy and socialism, which enable the Jews to manipulate the masses against the aristocratic elites. As described in the text: "By this means we will be able to make the masses rise when we wish. We will drive them to upheavals, to revolutions; and each of these catastrophes marks a big step forward for our particular interests and brings us rapidly nearer to our sole aim—world domination, as was promised to our father Abraham."[13] Jewish messianism and millennialism are thereby perverted into a satanic mirror of the desired Christian millennium, a paralleling of millennial desires and fears found later in Nazism.[14]

It was the antimodernism and the apocalyptic anti-Semitism that explained it that the Russian religious writer Sergei Nilus seized upon. Nilus was inspired by prophecies of the coming of the Antichrist in Russia made in the 18th century by Serafim von Sarov. Nilus elaborated on these prophecies by combining them with the apocalyptic writings of Fedor Dostoevsky and Vladimir Solov'ev, both of whom associated the coming end-times to varying degrees with the Jews.[15] Nilus was convinced he was chosen by heaven to save Russia, the believed Third Rome, site of the coming Christian millennium.[16] The second edition of his book *The Great in the Small: Anti-Christ Considered as an Imminent Political Possibility* contained the *Protocols* as an appendix. Nilus was convinced that the Antichrist would be a Jew, and the *Protocols* appeared to support his belief that world Jewry was preparing the ground for his appearance.

For Nilus, therefore, the satanic power behind the dark conspiracy of modernity was the Jew. In 1917, with the Russian Revolution unfolding before his eyes, Nilus published another edition of the *Great and the Small* with the chiliastic title, borrowed from Matthew 24:33, *He Is Near, at the Door . . . Here Comes Anti-Christ and the Reign of the Devil on Earth*. According to Nilus, the apocalyptic turning point had arrived. Either Russia and the true spirituality of the Orthodox Church would be saved, or Antichrist would rule and the world would end. Nilus combined fear and rejection of modernity with apocalyptic fear of the coming of the Antichrist, both of which he associated with Jews.[17] It was this apocalyptic rendering of the *Protocols* that traveled to the West with a number of emigrants fleeing Bolshevik terror, finding its way to Munich, Germany.[18]

In Munich the anti-Semitic writer and Thule associate Dietrich Eckart became convinced that the Jews were involved in a conspiracy to take over the world and that, consequently, a great world turning point had arrived. Using funds obtained from the Thule Society, Eckart began publishing his weekly newsletter, *Auf gut deutsch* (*In Plain German*), in 1918. He first mentioned the *Protocols* in the October 10 edition, writing that a British Protestant periodical originating out of Jerusalem had noted that a "Jewish lodge brotherhood 'The Wise Men of Zion'" had produced a "leaflet" in Russia in 1911 claiming plans for "Jewish world dominion" through the imminent destruction of the Russian and German imperial empires. Eckart then claimed that a map had appeared before World War I that showed the exact boundaries that would appear only after the Treaty of Versailles was promulgated after the war. Eckart exclaimed, "Oh, how wise are you Wise Men from Zion!"[19]

A little over two months later, Eckart returned to the subject of the *Protocols* in an article titled "The Midgard Serpent," a reference to the chaos monsters the Nordic god Thor has to defeat in the Icelandic epic the *Edda*. Eckart began by referring to a later section of the story that "describes the desperate struggle of the son's of light with the three monsters of darkness." This battle is Ragnarok, the Nordic apocalypse the results in the destruction of the world and its subsequent rebirth as a new Heaven on Earth. Linking this eschatological struggle with the supposed conflict between Aryans and Jews, Eckart concluded, "We do not need to read it, we experience it today." Eckart then connected this Nordic apocalypse with Revelation 20, which discusses the release of Satan, "the dragon, that ancient serpent," from one thousand years of imprisonment and the subsequent battle for the world. Eckart then associates the "loosing" of Satan with the Jews being released from a thousand years of imprisonment in the "ghettos" of Europe and their subsequent rise in power. According to Eckart, "the Jewish spirit is loosed, or as Christ expressed it, the 'Prince of the World,'" a reference to the Prince of Darkness. Eckart then cites Revelation 12, "for the devil has come down to you in great wrath, because he knows that his time is short!"[20]

This apocalyptic narrative leads Eckart directly into a discussion of Hausen's edition of the *Protocols*, of which Eckart says, "one reads again and again and yet one does not get to the end, because with almost every paragraph one lets the book fall as if paralyzed with unspeakable horror." Eckart once again refers to the "Jewish lodge brotherhood 'Wise Men of Zion'" and the supposed fact that "Russian Jews knew already in 1911 of the collapse of the Czarist empire, but also the German emperorship." He offers as explanation the "Bolshevistic chaos with the Jewish world dominion as background." He argues that "whoever wants to become thoroughly acquainted with Jewry should acquire this book."[21]

As the references to Ragnarok and Revelation attest, Eckart believed that the end-times had arrived, and the *Protocols* revealed the Jews' "satanic program" to take over the world.[22] It for this reason that he concluded in another article, "The hour of decision has come: between existence and non-existence, between Germany and Jewry, between all or nothing, between truth and lies, between inner and outer, between justice and caprice, between sense and madness, between goodness and murder. And humanity once again has the choice!"[23] The appearance of the *Protocols* during the unrelenting chaos of the nascent Weimar Republic seemed only to prove this eschatological narrative to be true, thus legitimating both the conspiracy theory of Jewish world dominance and the apocalyptic anti-Semitism that supported it.

Alfred Rosenberg, one of those who fled the spread of Bolshevism in the East, became Eckart's Russian expert, writing articles for *Auf gut deutsch* on the 1917 "Jewish revolution" and its supposed connection to the Jews. In 1923, when Germany fell into another cycle of political and economic chaos, Rosenberg wrote a gloss on the *Protocols* entitled *Die Protokolle der Weisen von Zion und die jüdische Weltpolitik* (*The Protocols of the Elders of Zion and Jewish World Policy*), which approximated an exegesis on Revelation, showing how contemporary world events were but confirmation of the insidious *Protocols*. Rosenberg presented a view that invoked the atmosphere of what Norman Cohn aptly called "apocalyptic prophecy." After citing Richard Wagner's infamous comment that the Jew was the "plastic demon of the decay of humanity," Rosenberg concurred, writing that "the Jew stands in our history as our metaphysical opposite." While he believed that most Germans had never truly perceived this, the apocalyptic chaos of postwar Russia and Germany, and the publication of the *Protocols* that explained it had finally exposed the demon. Rosenberg concluded his book with a passage replete with apocalyptic and millennial symbolism:

> That was *never* clearly grasped by us. . . . *Today* at last it seems as if the eternally foreign and hostile, now that it has climbed to such monstrous power, is felt and hated as such. For the first time in history instinct and knowledge attain clear consciousness. The Jew stands at the very top of the peak of power which he has so eagerly climbed, and awaits his fall into the abyss. The last fall. After that, there will be no place for the Jew in Europe or America. Today, in the midst of the collapse of a whole world, a new

era begins, a fundamental rejection in all fields of many ideas inherited from the past. One of the advance signs of the coming struggle for the new organization of the world is this understanding of the very nature of the demon which has caused our present downfall. Then the way will be open of a New Age.[24]

That Rosenberg believed the imminent attainment of world power would ironically signal "the last fall" of the Jews reflects a belief that Eckart and Hitler would share—that the Jews' will to world domination would ultimately result in their own extermination. I will return to this notion shortly.

For many anti-Semites, the *Protocols* was all the proof they needed that the Jews really were the force of evil in the world. Their long-held fear of a racial apocalypse had now found its Eschaton. With the loss of the war and Jewish-Bolshevik revolution spreading, the end-time was now. Looking back at the war, Eckart wrote, in 1919, "This war was a religious war, one can now see this clearly; a war between light and darkness, truth and lies, Christ and anti-Christ."[25] The signs of the time could not be more explicit. Hitler, at least, seems to have accepted the *Protocols* in this light.[26] On August 1, 1923, with Germany mired in economic chaos and with a new epidemic of hunger striking millions, Hitler gave a speech titled "Rising Prices, Republic, and Fascist State." His explanation of the chaos did not speak of modern economics or of the government's floating of worthless monies. The explanation was to be found in the alleged evil machinations of the Jews and their minions, the Bolsheviks and the Freemasons, as revealed in the *Protocols*. Was not the two-pronged attack of "international bank capital" and Soviet-style revolution revealed in this work? Hitler warned his audience: "We stand before a new revolution." Behind it lies the "Soviet star," which "is the star of David, the true sign of the synagogue. The symbol of that race over the world . . . the dominion of Jewry. The gold star signifies the Jews glistening gold. The hammer, which symbolizes the Soviet crest, represents the Freemasonic element. The sickle the inhuman terror! The hopeless Helots of the German Volk should create the Greater Jewish Paradise!" Jewish banking, combined with Bolshevik revolution and a little help from the Freemasons within Germany, was seen as an attempt to take over the world and therefore fulfill the covenant. Hitler continued, "according to the Zionist Protocols, the masses are to be made docile through hunger" and therefore ready "for the second revolution under the Star of David."[27]

The *Protocols* therefore became a key element in Hitler's conspiratorial thinking, for it was used to explain the apocalyptic chaos. Using the *Protocols* as a guide, Hitler argued that international Jewish bankers deliberately created the hyperinflation that forced Germans into epidemic hunger, making them pliant for a Jewish-Bolshevik type revolution, thereby taking another step in the plan to create the Jewish millennial paradise of world dominion. Hitler's conspiratorial mentality and its peculiar logic are also seen in his reaction to the disclosure that the *Protocols* were a fake. Since he believed that the press was controlled by Jews (part of the plan revealed in the *Protocols*), the accusations of forgery by the press only proved that it was true. Writing in *Mein Kampf*, Hitler stated that

> to what extent the whole existence of this people is based on a continuous lie is shown incomparably by the *Protocols of the Elders of Zion*, so infinitely hated by the Jews. They are based on a forgery, the *Frankfurter Zeitung* moans and screams once every week: the best proof they are authentic. What many Jews may do unconsciously is here consciously exposed. And that is what matters. It is completely indifferent from what Jewish brain these disclosures originate; the important thing is that with positively terrifying certainty they reveal the nature and activity of the Jewish people and expose their inner contexts as well as their ultimate final aims.[28]

We see here Hitler's belief that Jews instinctively strive toward world domination, even if unconscious of this striving. The covenant was now seen as a spiritual and a biological imperative. The *Protocols* revealed the eschatological "ultimate final aims," world domination and thus world annihilation—apocalypse. Hitler, as Rosenberg had, used the *Protocols* like a prophetic text, rereading history as prophecy fulfilled or, in this case, as the working out of the Jewish covenant with Jehovah, increasingly associated not with God but with Satan.

Years later, Hitler was still giving much the same explanation of modern economics as revealed by the *Protocols*. In Hermann Rauschning's controversial account of Hitler's monologues, the Führer credits the Jews with inventing the economics of "fluctuation and expansion that we call capitalism . . . an invention of genius, of the Devil's own ingenuity." Hitler continued, stating that "I have read *The Protocols of the Elders of Zion*—it simply appalled me. The stealthiness of the enemy, and his ubiquity!" Returning to the notion that two chosen peoples, mirror opposites of good and evil, faced each other, Hitler remarked: "Think of it—these people constantly on the move, and we with our new faith in unceasing activity, two groups so closely allied and yet so utterly dissimilar. It is in truth the critical battle for the fate of the world!" The Eschaton was imminent, and the *Protocols* a sign of the time. When Rauschning pointed out that he believed the work to be a fake, Hitler returned to the argument made in *Mein Kampf* that it was the inner truth of the supposedly destructive Jewish nature that was key, not the actual validity of the source. Further, he concluded, much as the members of the Thule Society had, that it was necessary to fight fire with fire: "We must beat the Jew with his own weapon, I saw that the moment I read the book." When Rauschning asked if the *Protocols* inspired Hitler in his struggle, he replied, "Yes, certainly down to the veriest detail. I found these *Protocols* enormously instructive. I have always learned a great deal from my opponents."[29] Indeed, in a speech titled "Why Are We Anti-Semites?," given on April 20, 1923, Hitler answered that question by paralleling the *Protocols*, calling Jews "a destroyer of peoples" who attempt to use democracy and Marxism to generate both pacifism and terrorism, ultimately destroying morality. Hitler therefore concluded that the Nazis were justified in using the same tactics as the Jews as revealed in the *Protocols*, concluding: "We may be inhuman! But if we save Germany, we have achieved the greatest deed in the world. We may do an injustice! But if we save Germany, then we have removed the greatest injustice in the world. We may be immoral! But if our people is saved, then we have once again broken a path to morality!"[30]

Corroborating Rauschning's account, Otto Wagener, a man much closer to Hitler at this time, recalls Hitler saying much the same thing. According to Wagener, Hitler claimed that the *Protocols* need not be true, for he believed the parasitism it revealed to be instinctive in all Jews, regardless of a conscious or rational plan to destroy the world. Wagener recalls Hitler stating: "It is hard for me to believe the Jew so purposeful and intellectually superior that he actually submitted these considerations so systematically in the councils of the Elders of Zion; that from the first he thought in the way I just elaborated—that would be uncanny. But his sixth sense guides him instinctively and unconsciously along the correct path, where, admittedly, consciousness has long since come to him."[31] The Nazi belief in the instinctive Jewish will to take over and thereby destroy the world needs to be further explored.

Dietrich Eckart, the Protocols, *and the Jewish Will to Exterminate*

Further insight into the conspiratorial world of Nazi millennialism and its indebtedness to an apocalyptic reading of the *Protocols* can be glimpsed from a relatively obscure early propaganda piece entitled *Bolshevism from Moses to Lenin: Dialogue between Hitler and Me*.[32] This brief work is a stylized conversation between Hitler and Dietrich Eckart, published in 1924, a few months after Eckart's death while Hitler was in Landsberg prison composing *Mein Kampf*, which he dedicated to Eckart, his intellectual mentor.[33] A young Heinrich Himmler would put it on his essential reading list, describing it as "an earthy, witty conversation between Hitler and Eckart that so genuinely and correctly characterizes both of them. It gives a perspective through all time and opens one's eyes to many points that one had not yet seen. I wish that everyone would read this."[34] Ironically, he was correct, for it reveals all to clearly the apocalyptic anti-Semitism of the Nazi inner circle.

Briefly put, such works should not be taken as anything like verbatim transcripts of individual conversations with Hitler. However, if understood as differing reconstructions and interpretations of Hitler's almost daily monologues, where the messianic Führer gave voice to his peculiar vision of the past, present, and future, then such sources are indispensable for understanding how Hitler perceived world history. Of course, such sources must be consulted as a group for purposes of verification and corroboration. The fact that those who produced these works often had diametrically opposed agendas but often present Hitler as verbalizing essentially the same ideas only strengthens their potential importance as sources. For instance, Rauschning was a man who lost faith in Hitler and produced his work as a warning to the West. Wagener, on the other hand, never lost faith in Hitler, even after the war, and saw himself as a keeper of the Grail whose notes on Hitler's pronouncements were treasured as the words of a misunderstood prophet. That both accounts, by two men on opposite ends of the Hitler cult, often betray a strikingly similar messianic and millenarian Hitlerian world view demonstrates the usefulness of these sources if taken as a group. Finally, it seems highly unlikely to me that two men with such different motives could fabricate the same Hitler.

Eckart's *Bolshevism from Moses to Lenin* attempts to reveal the hidden history of the Jews and their alleged desire, not simply for world domination but for world annihilation. The German reader of the time was clearly meant to see the loss of the First World War and the subsequent postwar chaos as the product of this same "hidden force." *Bolshevism from Moses to Lenin* in a sense reads the *Protocols* backwards into history, tracing the history of the Jews as a continuing attempt to fulfill the covenant of world domination by exterminating non-Jews. For example, the Book of Esther is explained as a Purim festival "murder" of seventy-five thousand Persians. It is an event that Eckart claimed "no doubt had the same Bolshevik background." The Egyptian expulsion of the Jews described in Exodus is used to justify the Nazis' desire to expel Germany's Jewish population.[35] Ignoring the bounds of time (a deliberate technique to show the allegedly eternal nature of the Jewish drive to world domination and annihilation), Eckart likened the alleged Jewish manipulation of the Egyptian "rabble" and "Bolshevik horde" to the calls for "Liberty, Equality, and Fraternity" that ignited the French Revolution. In this way, Eckart implies that the Jews used these catchwords of democracy to rile up the mob once again to murder the racial elites. The same implication is later attached to the Russian and German Revolutions of 1917–1918. Bolshevism therefore is defined not as a contemporary Marxist political theory but rather as an ancient Jewish technique to manipulate the mixed-race subhumans against the racial elites.

Joshua 6 is cited as further proof of the Jewish tendency to "exterminate" Gentiles "root and branch," a phrasing, perhaps not ironically, the Nazis liked to use for their solution to Jewish Question. Hitler referred to the destruction of Jericho as an "uninterrupted mass murder of bestial cruelty and shameless rapacity and cold-blooded cunning," a "Hell incarnate."[36] The reader was intended to see a connection between the biblical description of the fall of Jericho and the horror stories that came out of Hungary and Russia after the Communist revolutions.

The continuing references to Jewish extermination of non-Jews is deliberate and, from an apocalyptic standpoint, crucial. For *Bolshevism from Moses to Lenin* is proposing that the final battle is approaching. The pamphlet concludes with Hitler discussing the "final goal" to which the Jew is instinctively "pushed":

> Above and beyond world domination—annihilation of the world. He believes he must bring the entire world down on its knees before him in order to prepare a paradise on earth. . . . While he makes a pretense to elevate humanity, he torments it into despair, madness and ruin. If he is not commanded to stop he will annihilate all humanity. His nature compels him to that goal, even though he dimly realizes that he must therefore destroy himself. . . . To be obliged to try to annihilate us with all his might, but at the same time to suspect that that must lead irrevocably to his own destruction. Therein lies, if you will: the tragedy of Lucifer.[37]

Even if we are to take these to be solely the words of Eckart, Hitler expressed exactly the same explanation of Bolshevism and its supposed "Jewish" origins. Indeed, in *Mein Kampf*, which was composed at roughly the same time and which is dedicated to Eckart, Hitler argues repeatedly that the

Jews were promised in the Old Testament not eternity in the heavenly New Jerusalem but dominion of the temporal Earth. It was to this end that the Jew conspired. Hitler explains that his "historical research" led him to question whether or not

> inscrutable Destiny, perhaps for reasons unknown to us poor mortals, did not with eternal and immutable resolve, desire the final victory of this little nation. Was it possible that the earth had been promised as a reward to this people which lives only for this earth?

Later in the book, Hitler, speaking of these alleged Jewish machinations, states: "[F]or the higher he climbs, the more alluring his old goal that was once promised him rises from the veil of the past, and with feverish avidity his keenest minds see the dream of world domination tangibly approaching." This situation would lead to the fulfillment of the "Jewish prophecy—the Jew would really devour the peoples of the Earth, would become their master."[38] The end result of the "Jewish doctrine of Marxism" would be a realization of the covenant and consequently the literal end of the world:

> As a foundation of the universe, this doctrine would bring about the end of any order intellectually conceivable to man. And as, in this greatest of all recognizable organisms, the result of an application of such a law could only be chaos, on earth it could only be destruction for the inhabitants of this planet. If, with the help of his Marxist creed, the Jew is victorious over the other peoples of the world, his crown will be the funeral wreath of humanity and this planet will, as it did thousands [millions in later editions] of years ago, move through the ether devoid of men.[39]

Hitler continued this theme in his then-unpublished second book. After discussing the supposed parasitic nature of the Jews and their compulsive striving for world domination, Hitler explained, again using the *Protocols* as a guide, that

> [h]is ultimate aim is the denationalization and the chaotic bastardization of other peoples, the lowering of the racial level of the highest, and the domination of this racial mush through the eradication [*ausrottung*] of these people's intelligentsia and their replacement with the members of his own people.

The Jews having taken over individual countries and eventually the world through race poisoning and the policy of extermination, Hitler again concludes, exactly as in *Bolshevism from Moses to Lenin*, that the result will be apocalypse:

> The Jewish international struggle will therefore always end in bloody Bolshevization–that is to say, in truth, the destruction of the intellectual upper classes associated with the various peoples, so that he himself will be able to rise to mastery over the now leaderless humanity. . . . Jewish domination always ends with the decline of all culture and ultimately of the insanity of the Jew himself. Because he is a parasite on the peoples, and his victory means his own end just as much as the death of his victim.[40]

Otto Wagener recalled Hitler saying much the same thing in the early 1930s. Using the metaphor of the gardener, Hitler stated:

> Nothing upsets Jewry more than a gardener who is intent on keeping his garden neat and healthy. Nothing is more inimical to Jewry than order! It needs the smell of decay, the stench of cadavers, weakness, lack of resistance, submission of the personal self, illness, degeneracy! And wherever it takes root, it continues the process of decomposition! It *must*! For only under those conditions can it lead its parasitic existence.

Echoing *Bolshevism from Moses to Lenin*, Hitler claimed this parasitic chaotic nature led to the expulsion of Jews from Babylonia, Egypt, Rome, England, and the Rhineland, for "in each of these a gardener was at work who was incorruptible and loved his people." Hitler saw in Weimar an increased parasitism of apocalyptic proportions: "But since Weimar, you can once again see an enormous acceleration in the proliferation, the taking root, the stripping of corpses. Truly, if something does not happen soon, it may be too late!" Since Hitler viewed this will to exterminate as being endemic to Jewish nature, it was to a degree an inevitable part of human experience: "For it *will* repeat itself, it will always return, as long as people live on this Earth. And the last ones, God help us, who will proliferate even when the end of man has come—that will be, in spite of everything, the Jews, until they breathe the last of their miserable parasites' lives on the piled cadavers of their victims." To forestall this Jewish apocalypse was his mission and, by extension, the mission of the Nazi movement: "To postpone this point in time as far into the future as possible is our duty, our God-given mission—yes, it is the substance of Divine Creation altogether." This mission was to counter the promise made by Jehovah that the Jews would "one day rule over all mankind." The Nazis, then, had been chosen by God to act the role of end-time gardener: "But the Jews are *here*, in the world, whether or not we deplore their vile, sadistic parasitism and their will to destroy and exterminate us. . . . The gardener *must* intervene, and he must do soon—as soon as possible!"[41] There could be no salvation without extermination.

The Aryan-Jewish conflict was, quite literally, interpreted as an eschatological war, and the *Protocols* revealed that the final battle was imminent. In *Mein Kampf*, Hitler defined Marxism as a "poison" deliberately produced by the Jewish "prophet" Karl Marx "in the service of his race" to bring about the "swifter annihilation of the independent existence of free nations on this earth."[42] The final battle would come in a fight to the death with Jewish-Bolsheviks. In his first important speech after leaving Landsberg prison in 1925, Hitler explained that the Nazi aim was

> clear and simple: Fight against the satanic power which has collapsed Germany into this misery; Fight Marxism, as well as the spiritual carrier of this world pest and epidemic, the Jews. . . . As we join ranks then in this new movement, we are clear to ourselves, that in this arena there are two possibilities; either the enemy walks over our corpse or we over theirs.[43]

A year later, Hitler reiterated in another speech that "there is going to be a final confrontation, and that will not come in the *Reichstag* but in an overall showdown which will result in the destruction of either Marxism or ourselves." It was the Nazis' mission to prepare Germany for this impending final conflict. He continued, using imagery taken from Revelation 12, the same reference used by Dietrich Eckart some nine years earlier and similarly transforming Satan into the mythical Jewish-Bolshevik:

> It is our mission to forge a strong weapon—will and energy—so that when the hour strikes, and the Red dragon raises itself to strike, at least some of our people will not surrender to despair. I myself represent the same principles that I stood for a year ago.
>
> We are convinced that there will be a final showdown in this struggle against Marxism. We are fighting one another and there can be only one outcome. One will be destroyed and the other will be victorious.
>
> It is the great mission of the National Socialist movement to give our times a new faith and to see to it that millions will stand by this faith, then, when the hour comes for the showdown, the German people will not be completely unarmed when they meet the international murderers.[44]

This notion of the satanic power of the Jews was no mere rhetorical device for Hitler. When Hitler stated, in *Mein Kampf*, that "the personification of the devil as the symbol of all evil assumes the living appearance of the Jew," he meant it literally that the Jew was the force of evil and destruction in the world.[45] Hitler's mentor, Eckart, had written as early as 1919 that "when light clashes with darkness, there is no coming to terms! Indeed there is only struggle for life and death, till the annihilation of one or the other. Consequently the World War has only apparently come to an end."[46] The Nazis believed themselves involved in a cosmic battle between the forces of good and evil, light and darkness. World War I was but one stage in an evolving eschatological war that the publication of the *Protocols* laid bare.

Hitler, in an early speech of 1922, *Die 'Hecker' der Wahrheit!* ("*The 'Agitator' of Truth*"), prophesied on this impending apocalypse and on Germany's choice between slavery and annihilation at the hands of the Jewish-Bolsheviks and victory and salvation for Aryan humanity if it followed National Socialism:

> There are only two possibilities in Germany! Do not believe that the *Volk* will wander everlasting in the midst of compromise! It will devote itself first to the side that has prophesied on the consequences of the coming ruin and has steered clear of it.
>
> Either it will be the side of the left: then God help us, that leads us to the final corruption, Bolshevism; or it is the side of the right, which is resolute . . . it allows no compromise. Believe me, the German *Volk* lost this World War because it had not understood that there is allowed on this Earth only victor and slave.
>
> And here it is precise; this powerful, great contest can be reduced to but two possibilities: Either victory of the Aryans or its annihilation and victory of the Jews.[47]

This "politics of either-or," as the historian Robert Wistrich so aptly labeled it, was rooted in the internal logic of Nazi apocalyptic belief.[48] Hitler and his inner circle believed that world history was essentially the struggle of racial groups and that there were two chosen races, one Aryan, chosen of God, and one Jewish, chosen of Satan. These two races were locked in mortal combat, with a final reckoning imminent. In this scenario, "the Jew" became an abstract and symbolic Evil Other whose extermination was essential for world salvation. This was not simply rhetoric designed solely for audience effect but a believed vision of a coming eschatological battle that could have only one end possible: extermination of either the Aryans or the Jews. The

Protocols was taken to be a revelation of the Jews' attempt to take over the world in fulfillment of the covenant. The Nazis then extended this myth to include the notion that, once the covenant was fulfilled, the Jews would attempt to exterminate the Gentiles. Only a counterextermination of Jews could prevent this apocalypse. While exactly how this apocalyptic scenario would play out certainly was unknown to Hitler and his inner circle, the belief that it would occur in their lifetimes was absolutely an article of faith. Germany, and the world for that matter, had arrived at an eschatological turning point. It was a time of apocalypse or salvation in a millennial Third Reich. In this way, an imaginary enemy, involved in an imaginary world conspiracy as revealed in the imaginary *Protocols*, led to a very real genocide.

NOTES

1. For more on the Weimar culture of apocalypse and its importance for the rise of Nazism, see David Redles, *Hitler's Millennial Reich: Apocalyptic Belief and the Search for Salvation* (New York: New York University Press, 2005).

2. The Thule Society was affiliated with the occultist *Germanenorden*. The most complete work on the Thule Society is Hermann Gilbhard, *Die Thule Gesellschaft: Vom okkulten Mummenschanz zum Hakenkreuz* (Munich: Kiessling 1994). The word "Thule" refers to the mythical northern homeland of the ancient Aryans that, like Atlantis, sank under the sea. The Aryans then purportedly migrated around the Eurasia continent, creating wondrous civilizations from India to Greece to Rome to Germanic Europe. For many in the *volkish* movement, Thule came to represent both an ideal past where Aryans, perfect in body and soul, ruled a Golden Age and an ideal future, a New Age that would see a resurrection of the Aryan god-men of old. See the essay by Jost Hermand, "Ultima Thule. Völkische und faschistische Zukunftsvisionen," in his collection *Orte, irgendwo: Formen utopischen Denkens* (Königstein: Athenäum, 1981), 61–86.

3. Quoted in Nicholas Goodrick-Clarke, *The Occult Roots of Nazism: Secret Aryan Cults and Their Influence on Nazi Ideology* (New York: New York University Press, 1992), 145.

4. By far the best work on the ariosophists is Goodrick-Clarke, *Occult Roots of Nazism*. On the Nazi indebtedness to the ariosophists, see also Jackson Spielvogel and David Redles, "Hitler's Racial Ideology: Content and Occult Sources," *Simon Wiesenthal Center Annual* 3 (1986): 227–246.

5. On the fusion of Social Darwinism and occultism, see Helmut Zander, "Sozialdarwinistische Rassentheorie aus dem okkulten Untergrund des Kaiserreich," in *Handbuch zur "Völkischen Bewegung" 1871–1918*, eds. Uwe Puschner et al. (Munich: K. G. Saur, 1996): 224–251.

6. Michael Lotter discusses the origins of the German Worker's Party and its early association with the Thule Society in "Der Beginn meines politischen Denkens!" This typescript manuscript can be found in the *NSDAP Hauptarchiv*, Hoover Institute microfilm collection, roll 3, folder 78. Lotter was drawn into the worker's circle after hearing Drexler speak on the "will to exterminate everything Germanic through Jewry and Freemasonry Lodges" (p. 3 of this document).

7. Discussed in Goodrick-Clarke, *The Occult Roots of Nazism*, 149–150; Gilbhard, *Die Thule Gesellschaft*, 148–154.

8. On the origins of this myth, see Michael Hagemeister, "Die 'Protokolle der Weisen von Zion' und der Basler Zionistenkongress von 1897," in *Der Traum von Israel: Die Ursprünge des modernen Zionismus*, ed. Heiko Haumann (Weinheim: Beltz Athenäum Verlag, 1998), 250–273.

9. Gottfried zur Beek, ed., *Die Geheimnesse der Weisen von Zion* (Charlottenberg: Verlag Auf Vorposten, 1919). Müller von Hausen had received a copy of the *Protocols* from Piotr Shabelskii-Bork, a former Russian officer who had fled to Germany from Bolshevik Russia. Shabelskii-Bork was closely associated with Fyodor Vinberg, a fellow Russian refugee who published a version of the *Protocols* in *Luch Sveta* (*Ray of Light*), a yearbook that presented the combat against the Jewish Elders as a religious mission. According to Vinberg, if the Germans and the Russians joined together to defeat the Jews, there would be peace on Earth. For more on this and other aspects of the *Protocols*, see Norman Cohn, *Warrant for Genocide: The Myth of the Jewish World Conspiracy and Protocols of the Elders of Zion* (London: Serif, 1996). A useful historiography concerning the *Protocols*, including a few corrections to Cohn's work, is Ronald S. Green, "Scholars Contending with Delusional Ideology: Historians, Antisemitic Lore, and *The Protocols*," *SHOFAR* 18 (2000): 82–100.

10. An English translation by Victor Marsden continues to be sold today as a true document. I was able to purchase a copy through Amazon.com that used a vendor that specializes in conspiratorial nonsense. Reader comments at that time showed purchasers found themselves "enlightened" by the "facts" found therein. Editions continue to appear around the world, and Egyptian television recently ran a multipart dramatic series that used the *Protocols* as if they were true. On some of the modern uses this of pernicious forgery, see Dina Porat, "*The Protocols of the Elders of Zion*: New Uses of an Old Myth," in *Demonizing the Other: Antisemitism, Racism, and Xenophobia*, ed. Robert S. Wistrich (Amsterdam: Harwood Academic, 1999), 322–334. This is a very useful collection for understanding the construction of Jews as an Evil Other in its multifarious expressions.

11. The possible origin of the document, based on a close analysis of available copies, is discussed in Cesare G. De Michelis, *The Non-Existent Manuscript: A Study of the Protocols of the Sages of Zion* (Lincoln: University of Nebraska Press, 2004), esp., 73–86.

12. Maurice Joly, *Dialogue aux enfers entre Machiavel et Montesquieu ou La politique de Machiavel au XIXe siècle, par un contemporain* (Brussels: A. Mertens, 1864). Goedsche's book, written under the name Sir John Retcliffe the Younger, was entitled *Biarritz* (Berlin: C. S. Liebrecht, 1868). The "Rabbi's Speech" section was later republished as a supposedly factual document as *Die Geheimnisse des Judenfriedhofes in Prag* (Praha: Orbis, 1942).

13. Quotations from *The Rabbi's Speech* as found in Appendix I of Cohn's *Warrant for Genocide*, 279–284.

14. I talk about this process at length in *Hitler's Millennial Reich*. See also James M. Rhodes, *The Hitler Movement: A Modern Millenarian Revolution* (Stanford: Hoover Institute Press, 1980).

15. Michael Hagemeister, "Eine Apokalypse unserer Zeit: Die Prophezeiungen des heiligen Serafim von Sarov über das Kommen des Antichrist und das Ende der Welt," in *Finis Mundi: Endzeiten und Weltenden im östlichen Europa*, ed. Joachim Hösler and Wolfgang Kessler (Stuttgart: Franz Steiner Verlag, 1998): 41–60; Michael Hagemeister, "Sergej Nilus und die 'Protokolle der Weisen von Zion,'" *Jahrbuch für Antisemitismusforschung* 5 (1996): 127–147.

16. This line of thought would later be picked up by the Nazis, who reconceptualized the Third Rome as the Third Reich, combining Russian millennialism with German apocalyptic musings on the medieval thought of Joachim of Fiore. See David Redles, "The Nazi Endtimes: The Third Reich as Millennial Reich," in *End of Days: Essays on the Apocalypse from Antiquity to Modernity*, ed. Karolyn Kinane and Michael A. Ryan (Jefferson, NC: McFarland, 2009), 173–196.

17. Discussed in Cohn, *Warrant for Genocide*, 99–100.

18. On the passage of the *Protocols* to Germany and later to the Nazis, see Michael Kellogg, *The Russian Roots of Nazism: White Émigres and the Making of National Socialism* (Cambridge: Cambridge University Press, 2005).

19. Dietrich Eckart, "Tagebuch," *Auf gut deutsch* (October 10, 1919), 512–513. The map in question is most likely the one that appears as an appendix to Hausen's translation of the *Protocols*, titled "The Kaiser's Dream." Eckart noted in this article that this supposed pre-war map labeled the Russian territory "Russian Desert," exactly as the "Kaiser's Dream" map does. This map actually first appeared in the English periodical *Truth* in 1890 and was meant as a satire of the then German Kaiser's imperial ambitions. Hausen and Eckart claimed that it was a true document that betrayed Jewish desires to redraw the map of Europe by organizing a world war between the European empires. The origins of the "Kaiser's Dream" is discussed in Cohn, *Warrant for Genocide*, 154.

20. Dietrich Eckart, "Die Midgardschlange," *Auf gut deutsch* (December 30, 1919), 680–681. This article is directly preceded by two images. One, labeled "Before the World War," shows a woman wearing a crown and holding a sword, representing the European monarchies, standing upon a snake with a stereotypical Jewish head. The second image is labeled "After the World War" and shows the woman now being strangled by the "Jewish" snake, the crown and sword on the ground.

21. Ibid., 681, 683.

22. Ibid., 692.

23. Dietrich Eckart, "Die Schlacht auf den Katalaunischen Feldern" *Auf gut deutsch* (February 20, 1920), 86.

24. Alfred Rosenberg, *Die Protokolle der Weissen von Zion und die jüdische Weltpolitik* (Munich: Deutscher Volksverlag, 1923), 147. Cohn's comment can be found in *Warrant for Genocide*, 216–217. Interestingly, in 1923, Lanz von Liebenfels, one of the founding fathers of ariosophy, published a brief work titled *Weltende und Weltwende. Der Zusammenbruch der europäische Kulturwelt* [*World Turning Point and World Transformation. The Collapse of the European Cultural World*] (Lorch: Karl Rohm Verlag, 1923). Liebenfels likewise used the *Protocols* as proof that a millennial turning point had arrived and that the dawn of a New Age was at hand—but only if the Jews could be defeated.

25. Dietrich Eckart, "Immer lächeln, und doch ein Schurke!" *Auf gut deutsch*, (February 7, 1919), 83.

26. For analysis of Hitler's early speeches and their indebtedness to the *Protocols*, see Günter Schubert, *Anfänge nationalsozialistischer Außenpolitik* (Köln: Verlag Wissenschaft und Politik, 1963), 33–35. Also instructive is Alexander Stein, *Adolf Hitler: Schüler der "Weisen von Zion"* (Karlsbad: Verlagsanstalt Graphia, 1936).

27. Adolf Hitler, *Adolf Hitlers Reden*, ed. Ernst Boepple (Munich: Deutscher Volksverlag, 1925), 71. Interestingly, Sergei Nilus earlier had interpreted the Jewish star as the sign of the Antichrist.

28. Adolf Hitler, *Mein Kampf*, trans. Ralph Manheim (Boston: Houghton-Mifflin, 1971), 307–308.

29. Hermann Rauschning, *The Voice of Destruction* (New York: Putnam, 1940), 238–239. On the careful use of this source, one of a number I have termed the Hitler gospels, including the works by Wagener and Eckart cited later, as well as Hitler's wartime Table Talk, see "The Hitler Gospels and Old Guard Testimonials: Reconstructing a Mythical World," appendix of Redles, *Hitler's Millennial Reich*, 191–201.

30. Hitler, *Adolf Hitler Reden*, 56.

31. Otto Wagener, *Hitler: Memoirs of a Confidant*, trans. Ruth Hein, ed. Henry Ashby Turner Jr. (New Haven: Yale University Press, 1985), 70–71.

32. Dietrich Eckart, *Der Bolschewismus von Moses bis Lenin. Zwiegespräch zwischen Adolf Hitler and mir* (Munich: Hoheneichen-Verlag, 1924). Hereafter cited as Eckart, *BML*. For the sake of clarity, I will ascribe quotations from *BML* to Eckart and Hitler, respectively, although they should be understood, as with other examples of the Hitler gospels, as Eckart's rendering of Hitler's sentiments as expressed in many conversations, discussions, and monologues.

33. Hitler later said of Eckart, "He shone in our eyes like the polar star. . . . At the time, I was intellectually a child still on the bottle." Adolf Hitler, *Hitler's Table Talk 1941-1944: His Private Conversations*, trans. Norman Cameron and R. H. Stevens (New York: Enigma Books, 2008), 166–167.

34. This portion of Himmler's recommended reading list can be found in Manfred Messerschmidt, *Die Wehrmacht im NS-Staat: Zeit der Indoktrination* (Hamburg: R.v. Decker, 1969), 241.

35. Eckart, *BML*, 7–8.

36. Ibid., 9. The reference is to Joshua 6:21, "Then they utterly destroyed all in the city, both men and women, young and old, oxen, sheep and asses, with the edge of the sword." Interestingly, a modern partial translation of *BML*, which appeared in the American neo-Nazi periodical *National Socialist World*, (Fall 1966): 13–33, translates the original text's *Massenmorden* (mass murder) with the modern post-Holocaust word "genocide," a not so subtle attempt to shift the blame for the Nazi genocide of Jews back to the Jews themselves by perpetuating the Nazi myth of Jewish genocidal tendencies, which forced the Nazis to act first.

37. Eckart, *BML*, 49–50.

38. Hitler, *Mein Kampf*, 64, 313, 452.

39. Ibid., 65.

40. Adolf Hitler, *Hitler's Second Book: The Unpublished Sequel to Mein Kampf*, trans. Krista Smith (New York: Enigma Books, 2003), 231. For a detailed discussion of the origins of this book and why it was not published, see the introduction by the book's editor, Gerhard L. Weinberg.

41. Wagener, *Hitler: Memoirs of a Confidant*, 64–65. On the Nazi idea of Jews as parasites, see Alexander Bein, "'Der jüdische Parasit,' Bemerkungen zur Semantik der Judenfrage," *Vierteljahrshefte für Zeitgeschichte* 2 (1963): 121–149. On animalization in general, see Philippe Burrin, "Nazi Antisemitism: Animalization and Demonization," in *Demonizing the Other: Antisemitism, Racism, and Xenophobia*, ed. Robert S. Wistrich (Amsterdam: Harwood Academic, 1999), 223–235.

42. Ibid., 382.

43. Adolf Hitler, *Die Rede Adolf Hitlers in der ersten grossen Massenversammlung bei Wiederaufrichtung der Nationalsozialistischen Deutschen Arbeiterpartei* (Munich: Ehrer, 1925), 8.

44. Louis L. Snyder, *Hitler's Third Reich: A Documentary History* (Chicago: Nelson-Hall, 1981), 51–52.

45. Hitler, *Mein Kampf*, 324. This is in line with the thinking expressed in Eckart's *Bolshevism from Moses to Lenin*, which again validates the usefulness of this source.

46. Dietrich Eckart, "Immer lächeln, und doch ein Schurke," *Auf gut deutsch*, (February 7, 1919): 84.

47. Hitler, *Adolf Hitlers Reden*, 17.

48. Discussed at length in Robert Wistrich, *Hitler's Apocalypse: Jews and the Nazi Legacy* (New York: St. Martin's Press, 1985), 27–47. This book is essential for understanding the apocalyptic nature of Nazi anti-Semitism, as well as its continuing appeal.

PART IV

Post-Holocaust *Protocols*

Non-Western Variations

10

The *Protocols* in Japan

DAVID G. GOODMAN

In the mid-1980s, books with titles like *The Jewish Plot to Control the World*, *The Expert Way of Reading the Jewish Protocols*, and *The Secret of Jewish Power That Moves the World* flooded the Japanese market.[1] They were written not by quacks but by people of stature in Japanese society: a Shintō priest, a university professor, and a senior parliamentarian.[2] Major bookstores set up "Jewish corners" to display these bestsellers, which were being advertised widely and ostentatiously in all of Japan's mass-circulation daily newspapers.[3] On television, an animated program titled *An Introduction to the Japanese Economy* aired nationally in prime time, depicting the machinations of an "international Jewish capitalist," showing President Ronald Reagan in the Oval Office discussing U.S. government policy toward "Jewish capital," and portraying Judaism as a belief in sunspots and the prophecies of Nostradamus.[4] Magazines like *Weekly Post* (circulation 688,000) warned, in its July 10, 1992 edition, that "the Jews" had engineered the recent drop in the Japanese stock market and were "poised to destroy the Japanese economy whenever they desire."[5]

To anyone familiar with *The Protocols of the Elders of Zion*, the provenance of these images of Jews as a cabal of nefarious schemers intent on destroying Japan and taking over the world will be immediately apparent. But this raises a number of disturbing questions. What is the *Protocols* doing in Japan? How did it get there? What does the popularity of the *Protocols* in Japan mean? Is it a passing fad, or does it have perdurable "cultural roots" in Japan? Who is responsible for promoting and popularizing the century-old forgery, and why are they doing it? And, finally, does the *Protocols* pose a danger to anyone, or does its popularity in Japan represent, as some have suggested, a new kind of benign, "innocent" anti-Semitism?

1. What Are the Protocols *Doing in Japan?*

The *Protocols* has been in Japan as long as it has been in Europe and the United States. Higuchi Tsuyanosuke (a.k.a. Kitagami Baiseki, 1870–1931) introduced its main tenets in 1921 in a series of lectures titled "The Jewish Peril" (*Yudayaka*, Higuchi's coinage). The entire text was published in 1924 under the title *Behind the World Revolution* (*Sekai kakumei no rimen*) in a translation by Yasue Norihiro (a.k.a Hō Kōshi, 1888–1950).

In 1918, Japan dispatched a force, eventually totaling seventy-two thousand troops, to Siberia as part of a joint attempt by American, French, British, Canadian, and Czech armies to reverse the Russian Revolution. While they were there, Japanese personnel, including Higuchi and Yasue, who were there as language instructors and interpreters, received copies of the *Protocols* from their White Russian allies. Higuchi had trained as a Russian Orthodox priest at the Nikolai Seminary in Tokyo and had received a divinity degree from the Theological Seminary in St. Petersburg; Yasue had studied Russian at the Tokyo School of Foreign Languages. Japanese forces remained in Siberia until 1922 and were the last of the allies to leave.

Needless to say, the Siberian Intervention ended in failure, but the *Protocols* gave veterans of the campaign a way to explain their lack of success: A shadowy and indomitable Jewish conspiracy was behind the Russian Revolution. This self-serving version of events and the veracity of the *Protocols* did not go unchallenged, and liberals like the Tokyo University law professor Yoshino Sakuzō (1878–1933) energetically opposed it, but, during the 1920s, the *Protocols* nevertheless gradually became part of the Japanese intellectual landscape.[6]

In the 1930s, as Japan drew closer to Nazi Germany, the notion that a global Jewish conspiracy was threatening Japan became widespread. "Books describing 'the Jewish global conspiracy' and 'the Masonic threat' were available," the historian Saitō Takashi later recalled, "and our knowledge was so poor that we readily believed the theories they presented."[7] In his autobiography, the highly respected liberal historian Irokawa Daikichi also recalled blaming the Jews for the war. "Stalin, Chiang K'ai-shek, Roosevelt, and Churchill are all puppets of International Jewry," he recalled having written in his high school diary. "The roots of their strategy lie in secret organizations of Jewish military industrialists, international businessmen, finance capitalists, members of secret societies, speculators, and the like; Hitler and the Nazis are the saviors of mankind for combating them!"[8] The dean of Japan's nationalist writers, Tokutomi Iichirō (Sohō), inveighed against the Jews in his *Citizen's Reader for Certain Victory*: "The Jews are the curse of mankind!" "Under the guise of democracy they wield their plutocratic hegemony in the United States. American democracy has become a Jewish den!"[9] All of this amounted, the historian John Dower has noted, to "an outburst of anti-Jewish race hate" that was especially pronounced early in the war.[10]

Between 1921 and 1945, that is, *The Protocols of the Elders of Zion* entered Japan and was integrated into Japan's intellectual discourse. Its history in Japan does not differ appreciably from its history in other countries.

2. How Does the Protocols *Relate to Japanese Culture?*

At the end of his classic essay "The Paranoid Style in American Politics," Richard Hofstadter emphasized that a politics based on the belief in a vast conspiracy—what he so memorably called the "paranoid style"—is not unique to any particular nation but is a "persistent psychological complex" that appears across cultures. "The recurrence of the paranoid style over a long span of time and in different places," he wrote in 1964, "suggests that a mentality disposed to see the world in the paranoid's way may always be present in some considerable minority of the population."[11]

Japan confirms this hypothesis. A paranoid political mentality was evident in Japan long before *The Protocols of the Elders of Zion* arrived on its shores and facilitated its acceptance there.

Of particular interest for our purposes are the anti-Christian and anti-foreign polemics that flourished in Japan in the 19th century, when Japan was struggling to defend itself against the encroaching Western powers.[12] An example comes from *Comments on Heresy* (*Hekija shōgen*), written in 1857 by the Confucian scholar and political activist Ōhashi Totsuan (1816–1862).[13] Ōhashi was fulminating against the "Western barbarians," but, to illustrate how late Tokugawa-period xenophobia prefigured later Japanese anti-Semitic rhetoric, I will substitute the word "Jews" for "Western barbarians" in Ōhashi's text. The result is an anti-Semitic rant.

The fundamental aim of the [Jews] is to annex all countries of the world, to treat them as undifferentiated members of the same world order, and to make their national polities, their institutions, and their religions uniform throughout. In order for them to achieve this goal, the [Jews] must first involve themselves in every aspect of life and subvert people's minds. Thus, they first employ sonorous phrases, intoning, "The people of all nations walk the same earth and under the same sky, and as they are brothers, it is God's will that they be compassionate toward one another." So saying, they impress the ignorant, and with even more skillful subterfuges stimulate the mind. Simultaneously, they provide their sympathizers with money and other incentives. That they appeal to the stupid masses in this way goes without saying, but they also lure those with some small powers of discernment into their realm of darkness. Making people respect them is part of their insidious plot. . . . Thus, as time passes, they abscond with the hearts of men and convert the multitudes who flock to them. With even more vulgar trinkets, they offer the necessities of life, and sucking out the marrow of the nation, they sap its inimitable strength. Then waiting for the time when the nation is most vulnerable to conquest, they devour it in a single gulp.[14]

The "Western barbarians," all adherents of an "occult religion" (yōkyō—in Ōhashi's case, Christianity), were conspiring to dominate the world and would stop at nothing to subvert every area of culture to achieve this end. Trade and finance were the major tools of their plot, which aimed to destroy Japan's national identity and create a single world order that they alone would control. Long before *The Protocols of the Elders of Zion* entered Japan, in other words, the Japanese had an indigenous theory of a global religious conspiracy bent on their destruction. The cultural roots of the *Protocols* and Japanese anti-Semitism are to be found in important part in this preexisting conspiratorial mentality.[15]

A second tradition that facilitated acceptance of the *Protocols* in Japan was its history of millenarian beliefs. By "millenarian beliefs" I mean beliefs that, under certain prescribed conditions, time will be fulfilled, history as we know it will come to an end, and a new ontological order free of suffering and death will be introduced.[16] The *Protocols* is a millenarian text in the sense that it purports to document the deliberations of an odious conspiracy whose aim is to obstruct the achievement of this ultimate and universal salvation. The *Protocols* is part of a long tradition that equates Jews with the Antichrist, who frustrates and obstructs the Second Coming of Christ and the millennium. While Japan is not a Christian country, it has its own history of millenarian thought that has made the *Protocols* and the notion of a conspiracy to obstruct the achievement of ultimate salvation credible.

Buddhism, Christianity, and Shintō have all contributed to Japan's millenarian tradition. The first Buddha to be introduced to Japan—in the form of a statue brought from Korea in 584—was Maitreya (Japanese: Miroku), who is often called the "Buddhist messiah." "In Buddhist conceptions," Wolfgang Bauer has written,

Maitreya was a future Buddha, one "who had not yet appeared." According to some schools, his birth lay in the remote future while others . . . thought his advent might occur at any time. . . . [Maitreya] would not merely proclaim the teaching like the historical Buddha, but simultaneously and at a single stoke free the world of misery and injustice and create conditions of undiluted joy and happiness in it.[17]

Another strand of Japanese Buddhist millenarianism derives from Nichiren (1222–1282), a 13th-century Buddhist activist who taught that the *Lotus Sutra* was the only true scripture of the Buddhist canon and that Japan had been specially chosen to save the world through it. According to Nichiren, Japan had entered the final stage of *mappō*, the "end of the Law," and an apocalyptic climax to history was imminent. The attempted Mongol invasion of Japan in 1274, which Nichiren predicted, was only one indicator that the end-time was near. In the new age that would follow the apocalypse, Japan would assume its rightful place as the center of the world, and Nichiren would be its founding sage. I am "the pillar of Japan, the eye of the nation, and the vessel of the country," Nichiren proclaimed.[18]

Christian chiliasm was introduced to Japan following the arrival of Francis Xavier in Japan in 1549. Ninety years after Xavier's arrival, in 1637, impoverished Christian peasants in Shimabara, an area in Kyushu not far from Nagasaki, rose up in revolt against the Tokugawa regime under the leadership of Amakusa Shirō, a sixteen-year-old youth whom the faithful believed to be God incarnate. As many as forty thousand Japanese Christians joined the Shimabara rebellion, and, by the time it was suppressed in the spring of 1638, they had been wiped out and as many as seventy thousand government troops had lost their lives.[19]

The millenarian character of the Shimabara Rebellion is evident in a cryptic poem composed in Chinese at the time, proclaiming that, with the appearance of the savior Amakusa Shirō,

> Heaven will make the flowers bloom before their time.
> The counties and the provinces will rumble then and roar,
> And the dwellers of this realm will see their trees and plants consumed
>   by fire.
> All people shall wear the nine-jeweled Cross about their necks,
> And suddenly white banners will be fluttering in the fields and hills.
> All other faiths will be engulfed by the True Creed,
> And Our Heavenly Lord will save the people of this world.[20]

The antinomian, apocalyptic, and millenarian quality of this prophecy is unmistakable. With Amakusa Shirō's miraculous appearance, the prevailing laws of nature and of humankind will be revoked; history will end in a fiery apocalypse; all other faiths will be destroyed; and universal redemption will be achieved.

There are hints of millenarianism in early Shintō beliefs about a paradise called Tokoyo, "the eternal land." These indigenous beliefs quickly became entwined with Chinese Taoist ideas about immortality and with the Pure Land Buddhist notion of the Western Paradise, where the Buddha Amida (Amitabha) welcomes the faithful after death. Tokoyo came to be understood as a place where aging and death do not exist and where life is eternal.[21]

Organized Shintō as we know it today, however, dates from the 18th and 19th centuries and the innovations of nativist thinkers of the "National Learning" (*Kokugaku*) school, such as the great scholar Motoori Norinaga (1730–1801) and his self-proclaimed disciple, Hirata Atsutane (1776–1843). Motoori deciphered the long-incomprehensible *Record of Ancient Matters* (*Kojiki*, 712), Japan's first mythohistory, and Hirata married Motoori's ideas to aspects of Christian theology culled from Chinese sources. This new Shintō, which became Japan's official state religion after the Meiji Restoration of 1868, proclaimed that Japan, "Land of the Gods," ruled over by an incarnate god, was the predestined redeemer among nations.

In the modern period, these three millenarian traditions—Buddhist, Christian, and Shintō—were joined by Social Darwinism, nationalism, Marxism, and fascism, producing many variations, some of which inspired acts of political violence and legitimized Japan's "holy war" with Asia and the West. Kita Ikki (1883–1937), for example, a follower of Nichiren, was the main ideologue behind the attempted coup d'état of February 26, 1936, which sought to restore power to the emperor that had allegedly been usurped by corrupt politicians and to establish a utopia of "imperial communism" in Japan.[22] Similarly, Ishiwara Kanji (1889–1949) combined Nichiren beliefs with German military science to postulate a theory of an apocalyptic "final war" between the West, led by the United States, and Asia, led by Japan. Ishiwara believed that Japan would emerge victorious from this titanic struggle and establish an age of universal peace. In order to bring about this apocalyptic "final war," Ishiwara, a lieutenant general in the Japanese army, engineered the 1931 Manchurian Incident and conceived the puppet kingdom of Manchukuo, which led directly to the Asia-Pacific War.[23]

In sum, while Japan does not share Christianity's long tradition of animosity toward Jews, it does have intellectual traditions that made the *Protocols* credible and facilitated its integration into Japanese political and religious discourses.

3. Who Has Been Responsible for Promoting the Protocols, and Why?

Strange as it may seem, the *Protocols* has been read in Japan as both a philo-Semitic and an anti-Semitic text. During the war years (1931–1945), there were two groups of influential "Jewish experts" devoted to the *Protocols*: those who read the *Protocols* and concluded that the Jews were so powerful that they should be befriended and convinced to aid the Japanese empire and those who read the *Protocols* and concluded that the Jews were enemies who posed a mortal threat to Japan.

Prominent in the former group was Inuzuka Koreshige (1890–1965), who, in addition to his copious anti-Jewish writings, in 1939 coauthored the so-called fugu plan, a proposal to create an East Asian homeland for Jews, who in gratitude would put their knowledge and resources at the service of Japan.[24] The proposal was never taken seriously and never became government policy. As the navy captain responsible for the more than twenty thousand Jewish refugees in Shanghai between 1939 and 1942, however, Inuzuka was moved to protect the Jews under his control in hopes of using them to dissuade the United States from declaring war on Japan. After war with the United States broke out, Inuzuka was relieved of his post in February 1942, and Japanese policy toward the Jews became harsher. A ghetto was established in Shanghai, but Japanese policy remained relatively humane. After the defeat, Inuzuka continued his efforts to win Jews over to Japan, and to that end he established the Japan-Israel Association (*Nihon-Isuraeru kyōkai*) and other organizations to promote Japanese-Jewish amity.

Foremost among the latter group of "Jewish experts" was Shiōden Nobutaka (a.k.a. Fujiwara Nobutaka, 1879–1962), a cosmopolitan military officer who had been stationed in Harbin and Paris and who spoke Russian and French. Shiōden retired from active service in the Japanese army at the rank of lieutenant general in 1929 but continued to serve as an adviser to the military. He had been interested in the Jewish question since his days in France during World War I, and he became openly sympathetic to the Nazis in the 1930s. In a July 1939 letter to Julius Streicher's *Die Stürmer*, he wrote, "I am pleased to inform you that the copious information and material collected during my journey in Germany has now been translated into Japanese by experts. This will contribute to the enlightenment of the Japanese about the Jewish plan for world domination."[25] Shiōden wrote his own five-hundred-page tome, *The Jews: Their Thought and Movement*, in 1941, that included as an appendix his own translation of the *Protocols* from the French.[26] In the 1942 Diet election, he ran on an explicitly anti-Semitic platform and polled more votes than any other candidate. Contra Inuzuka and his group, Shiōden argued strenuously that the Jews were too dangerous and cunning to be manipulated and that attempts to harness their power could lead only to disaster.[27] His views gained ascendancy after Pearl Harbor and contributed to the harsher treatment of Jewish refugees in Shanghai that began in 1942.

After the war, as Japan worked to reinvent itself as a peace-loving, democratic nation, all expressions of xenophobic ethnic nationalism were discouraged, including the *Protocols*. Despite the efforts of Japanese writers, scholars, and theologians to discredit it, however, the *Protocols* continued to be republished.[28] Matsumoto Fumi reprinted it in her 1958 book, *Building the Altar at Mount Fuji*; Nagafuchi Ichirō republished it in *The Jews and World Revolution* in 1971; and, in 1977, the intellectual journal *L'Esprit d'aujourd'hui* (*Gendai no esupuri*) published learned articles on the international Jewish conspiracy in a supposedly serious special issue on the Jews.[29]

It was in the 1980s, however, in the context of friction with the United States over trade issues, that the *Protocols* reemerged as a popular text. Numerous writers exploited the theory of a global Jewish conspiracy bent on destroying Japan, and the *Protocols* became a staple of Japanese popular culture. Two writers from opposite ends of the political spectrum serve to illustrate the diverse motives of those responsible for this recrudescence.

Uno Masami: Christian Xenophobe

The author who did the most to repopularize the *Protocols* in the mid-1980s was Uno Masami (1941–), a Christian fundamentalist minister in the Osaka Bible Christian Church (*Osaka seisho kirisuto kyōkai*) and a self-proclaimed authority on world affairs. Uno began his publishing career with explicit works of Christian prophecy like *Great Prophecies of the Old Testament: The Jews and Armageddon*, which appeared in 1982. His breakthrough came in 1986, however, when he published two bestsellers—*If You Understand the Jews, You Will Understand the World* and *If You Understand the Jews, You Will Understand Japan*—that sold a combined total of more than a million copies in less than a year.[30] His theories were accorded a high degree of credibility in mainstream journalistic, business, and political circles, alarming foreign and some Japanese observers.[31]

Uno's basic argument was that the United States was controlled by a secret Jewish "shadow government"; that Japanese-U.S. relations were in fact Japanese-*Jewish* relations; and that the Jews manipulated American policies in order to destroy Japan.[32] Uno decried Japan's postwar democratic institutions, including the American-drafted constitution, as part of the Jewish plot to destroy Japan.[33] In his view, democracy and globalization were simply part of a far-reaching attempt to "Judaize Japan," and he recommended the policies of Adolf Hitler to protect the interests of the Japanese *volk* (*minzoku no rieki*).[34]

There was a distinct millenarian dimension to Uno's views. He preached that the ultimate aim of the Jews was to precipitate World War III in order to bring about the Messianic Age.[35] As supposedly foretold by the prophet Ezekiel,[36] a Soviet invasion of Israel would precipitate the war, which the Jews would win.[37] Echoing the *Protocols*, he predicted that a Jewish dictator would be anointed and benevolently rule the world from the rebuilt Temple in Jerusalem but would be overthrown in three and a half years, when the resurrected Jesus, the real Messiah, would appear on the Mount of Olives to usher in the true Millennium.[38]

Uno's arguments owed much to American Christian fundamentalists and right-wing groups. Much of his biblical exegesis is identical to the apocalyptic theology of the American premillennialist preacher Hal Lindsey and his immensely popular *The Late Great Planet Earth*.[39] In 1987, Uno established a Japanese branch of the Liberty Lobby, an extreme right-wing American group, and began publishing a Japanese edition of its newsletter, *New American View*.[40] In 1989, he invited Dale P. Crowley Jr., a self-proclaimed "fanatically insane, raving right-wing"[41] Baptist minister, to share the stage with him during a well-attended lecture in Osaka. "A staunch America firster," the Liberty Lobby's weekly tabloid *The Spotlight* wrote of the event, "Crowley spent two weeks in Japan as the guest of Pastor Masami Uno, an economist and clergyman who is concerned about the growing Zionist influence in his country. Crowley, who is fluent in Japanese, addressed groups of business executives, many of whom were CEOs of their companies."[42] The lecture was videotaped and was distributed to Japanese video stores.[43]

Uno also had links to the American political extremist Lyndon LaRouche and wrote *Confessions of the Jews* with Paul Goldstein and Jeffrey Steinberg, two well-known LaRouche supporters. Both were indicted in 1987 for obstruction of justice in connection with LaRouche's trial for fraud in his 1984 presidential campaign.[44]

Uno's work was well received in Japan. His books were advertised prominently in all of Japan's major newspapers; he was quoted in news articles about the Japanese economy;[45] and in May 1987 he was invited by a conservative faction of Japan's ruling Liberal Democratic Party to speak at a Constitution Day rally.[46] Emboldened by his extraordinary success, many other writers followed his example, making *The Protocols of the Elders of Zion* and its theory of a Jewish conspiracy to rule the world and destroy Japan common knowledge.

Ohta Ryū: Left-Wing Ideologue

Right-wing figures like Uno Masami were not the only ones who exploited the *Protocols*. Leftists like Ohta (or, Ōta) Ryū have also promoted it, and the downward trajectory of Ohta's thinking has closely paralleled the general decline of leftist politics in postwar Japan. From an orthodox Communist in the immediate postwar period, Ohta degenerated into Japan's most prolific proponent of what the German socialist August Bebel called "the socialism of fools."

Ohta's career can be divided into several phases. Born Kurihara Ryūichi on the island of Sakhalin, in 1930, Ohta joined the Japanese Communist Party (JCP) in 1947. After Khrushchev's revelations of Stalin's crimes in 1956, he left the Party to form the Trotskyist League of Japan (*Nihon Torotsukisuto renmei*); in December 1957, he founded the League of Revolutionary Communists (*Kakkyōdō*, short for *Kakumei-teki kyōsanshugisha dōmei*), with Kuroda Kan'ichi and others. The two most important sects of the Japanese New Left, the Revolutionary Marxist Faction (*Kakumaru*, short for *Kakumei-teki Marukusu-shugi ha*) and the Nucleus Faction (*Chūkaku-ha*), were offshoots of the League of Revolutionary Communists. Calling himself a "pure Trotskyist" (*jun-Toro*), Ohta left Kakkyōdō in July 1958, but he remained a seminal thinker in the Japanese New Left movement and was involved in the establishment and dissolution of numerous left-wing sects and movements and even attempted at one point to infiltrate and hijack the Japan Socialist Party.

In the late 1960s and early 1970s, the Revolutionary Marxists engaged in urban warfare with their Nucleus Faction rivals, resulting in numerous deaths and injuries. In 1970, another left-wing sect, the Red Army Faction, hijacked a Japan Airlines jet to North Korea, and in 1972 the United Red Army (*Rengō Sekigun*), consisting of members of the Red Army Faction and members of another extreme left-wing sect, the Japanese Communist Party Revolutionary Left (*Nihon kyōsantō kakumei saha* or *Kakusa*), were found to have murdered a dozen of their own members in an ideological purge. This terrorism and sectarian violence alienated the Japanese public and contributed importantly to the general loss of sympathy for the left in Japan in the 1970s and beyond.

As the New Left degenerated and it became increasingly clear that it would never achieve its revolutionary goals, Ohta turned away from political revolution to the ethnic liberation and ecology movements. He became an advocate for Japan's dwindling Ainu minority and a proponent of an ecological revolution to protect the environment. He promoted what he called "Natural Life Learning" (*Tenju no gaku*), which casts humans as the enemies of the Earth, demands their repentance, and calls grandiloquently for the peaceful coexistence of all species throughout the universe.

A search of the Kinokuniya Book Web, an Amazon-like website, produces more than eighty hits with Ohta as either author or translator. Before 1991, his books focused primarily on Marxist theory, with titles like *The Road to World Revolution* (*Sekai kakumei e no michi*, 1978) and *The Revolution in Revolutionary Theory* (*Kakumei riron no kakumei*, 1979, with Saeki Yōsuke). In books like *Introduction to Japan's Indigenous People* (*Nihon genjūmin josetsu*, 1981) and *Japan's Indigenous People and the Emperor System* (*Nihon genjūmin to tennōsei*, 1982), Ohta concerned himself with the Ainu minority. In other books like *Manifesto of a Japanese Ecologist* (*Nihon ekorojisuto sengen*, 1986) and *Toward the Elimination of Animal Domestication* (*Kachiku seido zenpai-ron josetsu*, 1985), Ohta took up the cudgels for the environmental and animal rights movements.

Although he had written about religion as early as 1980, in *Religion and Revolution* (*Shūkyō to kakumei*), Ohta did not turn his full attention to matters of religion and the occult until 1991, when he published *The Principle of UFOs and Celestial Civilization* (*UFO genri to uchū bunmei*). His first book about Jews, *The Global Strategy of the Seven Great Jewish Cartels* (*Yudaya shichi-dai-zaibutsu no sekai senryaku*), appeared in 1991. Since 1991, Ohta has published at least a book a year with the word "*Yudaya*" (Jew) in the title, along with many more volumes of conspiracy theory that detail the "Jewish threat." In addition to his original writings, Ohta has produced numerous translations of works including Martin Luther's *The Jews and Their Lies* (2003) and works by the American conspiracy theorists Eustace Mullins and John Coleman. In August 2004, he published a revised and updated edition of Shiōden Nobutaka's translation of the *Protocols*. In his forty-page afterword, Ohta argued that the 1.3 billion Muslims who recognize the *Protocols* as an accurate account of the true character of Jews and Israel could not be wrong and that the Japanese, too, should awake to this reality. Until his death, in 2009, Ohta Ryū, the erstwhile Communist, New Left ideologue, defender of minority rights, ecological crusader, and dabbler in the occult, was Japan's most prolific recent exponent of *The Protocols of the Elders of Zion*.

Ohta also sought to translate his ideas into political action. He ran unsuccessfully for a seat in the lower house of the Japanese Diet in 1990. As founder of the Society for Global Restoration (*Chikyu ishin kai*), he was probably behind the Global Restoration Party (*Chikyū ishin tō*), which fielded several candidates in Tokyo, the Osaka-Kobe area, and Gunma prefecture in the 1992 upper-house Diet election. These candidates ran on a platform opposing "the ambitions of the Jews (Pharisees) to conquer the world and turn it into a global pasture for the human race."[47] Although the Global Restoration Party polled only 11,883 votes, or 0.03 percent of the electorate,[48] it was the first time since 1942 that candidates for public office in Japan had run on an overtly anti-Jewish platform.

Ohta Ryū is not the only Japanese leftist to be seduced by *The Protocols of the Elders of Zion*. In the October 28, 1993, issue of *Sapio*, a biweekly news magazine with a circulation (in 1989) of 230,000, for example, Hirose Takashi, a prominent left-wing journalist, asserted that a Jewish conspiracy headed by the Rothschilds controlled the world's banks, media, military, and governments and produced a detailed flowchart to prove it.[49] Ohta Ryū's career, however, offers the clearest example of the descent of a Japanese leftist from orthodox Communism to "the socialism of fools."

4. Does the Protocols Pose a Threat in Japan?

To borrow Charles Strozier's phrase, *The Protocols of the Elders of Zion* is an "atrocity-producing narrative." It posits an immense secret conspiracy out to destroy "us" and everything "we" hold dear. Its purpose is to provoke a response in its readers.

How widely the *Protocols* is believed in Japan is hard to ascertain. Certainly only a small minority of Japanese take the *Protocols* at face value. Moreover, Jews living in Japan have never been persecuted because of it; as noted earlier, a familiarity with the *Protocols* actually accrued to the benefit of Jewish refugees in Shanghai during the war. On the other hand, the sense that Jews are extraordinarily powerful and dangerous is widespread in Japan.[50] And, in today's world, it does not take a mass movement for the *Protocols* to constitute a danger. A handful of true believers on the lunatic fringe suffices.

Aum Shinrikyō (Supreme Truth), a religious cult founded in 1984, constituted such a handful. On March 20, 1995, members of the cult released poison sarin gas on the Tokyo subway, killing twelve people and sending another five thousand to the hospital. It was the most devastating act of urban terrorism in the industrialized world before 9/11.

Three months before the attack, Aum had devoted ninety-five-pages of a special issue of its organ publication, *Vajrayâna Sacca*, to a diatribe against the Jews. Quoting liberally from the *Protocols*, Aum's "Manual of Fear" began with a "declaration of war" on the Jewish enemy: "On behalf of the earth's 5.5 billion people," the editors wrote, "*Vajrayâna Sacca* hereby formally declares war on the 'world shadow government' that murders untold numbers of people and, while hiding behind sonorous phrases and high-sounding principles, plans to brainwash and control the rest. Japanese, awake! The enemy's plot has long since torn our lives to shreds."[51]

A conspiracy theory identical to that promoted in the books of "authorities" like Uno Masami and Ohta Ryū was central to Aum's worldview.[52] As the scholar Ian Reader has written, Aum's founder and guru Asahara Shōkō, who was a longtime admirer of Hitler, was obsessed with "the notion that Aum was surrounded by hostile forces and that a vast conspiracy bent on world domination was seeking to destroy Aum as part of its fiendish plans. . . . Aum was the only force left standing between the conspirators (who included the US and Japanese governments, the Freemasons, the Jews and numerous others) and their evil intentions."[53]

In an environment saturated with books and articles, videos and public speeches about the global Jewish conspiracy bent on destroying Japan, where candidates had run for parliamentary office on an anti-Semitic platform, it is hard to conclude that Asahara and Aum were not influenced by the *Protocols* and were not motivated, at least in part, by its provocation. The *Protocols* did not produce their paranoia or their violence, but it focused and shaped them. In Aum's paranoid imagination, everyone was against them, everyone was a conspirator, everyone was a Jew.[54]

5. Conclusion

The Protocols of the Elders of Zion has been in Japan as long as it has been in the West. Its reception was mediated and facilitated by indigenous strains of political paranoia and millenarian thinking. Both the left and the right have promoted it, forming alliances with like-minded groups abroad; in 1995, a religious cult on the lunatic fringe of society acted out its "atrocity-producing narrative." All of this is significant as we move into the 21st century and as more and more non-Western peoples are exposed to the *Protocols*. The Japanese example demonstrates that the *Protocols* will adapt to the new age. A knowledge of Jews is not necessary. In the process of globalization, not only good ideas spread around the world; evil ones proliferate, too.

1. Portions of this essay have previously appeared in a different form in David G. Goodman, "The Protocols of the Elders of Zion, Aum, and Antisemitism in Japan," *Posen Papers in Contemporary Antisemitism 2* (Jerusalem: Vidal Sassoon International Center for the Study of Antisemitism, Hebrew University, 2005); and in Esther Webman, ed., *The Global Impact of the Protocols of the Elders of Zion: A Century-Old Myth* (Routledge, 2011).

2. Yamakage Motohisa, *Yudaya no sekai shihai senryaku: miezaru sekai seifu no kyōi* [The Jewish Plot to Control the World: The Threat of the Invisible World Government] (Management-sha, 1985); Yajima Kinji, *Yudaya purotokōru no chō-urayomi-jutsu* [The Expert Way of Reading the Jewish Protocols] (Seishun shuppansha, 1986); and Saitō Eisaburō, *Sekai o ugokasu yudaya pawaa no himitsu* [The Secret of Jewish Power that Moves the World] (Nihon keizai tsūshinsha, 1984). Unless otherwise noted, all books were published in Tokyo.

3. All of Japan's major newspapers, including the *Asahi*, *Yomiuri*, and *Nihon keizai* (*Nikkei*), routinely carried lurid advertisements for blatantly anti-Semitic books and, when challenged, retorted angrily that they saw nothing objectionable in doing so. See "Anti-Semitic Book Ad Assailed," *Japan Times*, July 31, 1993.

4. Aired on TV Tokyo (*Terebi Tōkyō*) on December 27, 1987. The program was an animated version of Ishinomori Shōtarō's graphic novel *An Introduction to the Japanese Economy*, vol. 2, ch. 4 (Nihon keizai shimbunsha, 1987), 215–276. The first volume of this work (which does not contain the offensive material) has been translated into English and published by the University of California Press. See Shotaro Ishinomori, *Japan, Inc.: Introduction to Japanese Economics (The Comic Book)* (Berkeley: University of California Press, 1988).

5. "Kinkyū keikoku: 'kabuka ichiman-en' de 'Yudaya shihon' ni nerawareru Nihon kigyō" [Urgent Alert: Japanese Industry Threatened by "Jewish Capital" When the [Nikkei] Stock Average Hits 10,000], *Shūkan Post*, July 10, 1992, 31–35.

6. For a recent contribution to our understanding of the way the *Protocols* were domesticated in Japan in the 1920s and 1930s, see Christopher W. A. Szpilman, "Fascist and Quasi-Fascist Ideas in Interwar Japan, 1918–1941," in *Japan in the Fascist Era*, ed. E. Bruce Reynolds (New York: Palgrave, 2004), 81–85.

7. Saitō Takashi, "Rekishi to no deai," *UP* (Tokyo University Press), September 1975.

8. Irokawa Daikichi, *Aru Shōwa-shi: jibunshi no kokoromi* [One Man's History of the Shōwa Era: an Attempt at a Self-History] (Chūō kōronsha, 1975), 91–92, 115. See also Kimura Hiroshi, "Yudayajin-netsu ni toritsukarete" [Taken Captive by the Jewish Fever], *Shokun*, January 1971; and Mizuta Hiroshi in "Issatsu no hon, 137," *Asahi shimbun*, October 13, 1963.

The Japanese were not unique. As Frank Dikötter notes, "Contempt for the Jews [among Chinese intellectuals], and even a feeling of hatred towards them, remained vivid for decades. Wu Zelin, an outstanding anthropologist active in the 1930s, recently recalled that he and his colleagues used to find the Jews 'laughable, despicable, pitiable, admirable, enviable, and hateful." Frank Dikötter, *The Discourse of Race in Modern China* (Stanford: Stanford University Press, 1992), 114.

9. Tokutomi Iichirō, *Hisshō kokumin tokuhon* [A Citizen's Reader for Certain Victory] (Mainichi shimbunsha, 1944), 69–71, 139–140. Quoted in Ben-Ami Shillony, *Politics and*

Culture in Wartime Japan (New York: Oxford University Press, 1981), 161. Tokutomi is referred to as "the dean of Japan's nationalist writers" in Ryusaku Tsunoda et al., eds., *Sources of Japanese Tradition* (New York: Columbia University Press, 1964), 2:291.

10. John W. Dower, *War without Mercy: Race and Power in the Pacific War* (New York: Pantheon, 1986), 258.

11. Richard Hofstadter, *The Paranoid Style in American Politics and Other Essays* (New York: Knopf, 1965), 38–39.

12. For a more extended discussion of this topic, see David G. Goodman and Masanori Miyazawa, *Jews in the Japanese Mind: The History and Uses of a Cultural Stereotype*, expanded ed. (Lanham, MD: Lexington Books, 2000), 18–28; and Miyazawa, "Hai-Yaso to Han-Yudaya—kindai Nihon no haigai shisō" [Anti-Christianity and Anti-Semitism: Xenophobic Thought in Modern Japan], in *Shakai kagaku kenkyū*, Waseda daigaku shakai kagaku kenkyūjo (February 1984), 84:311–334.

13. For a general introduction to Ōhashi's thought, see Carmen Blacker, "Ōhashi Totsuan: A Study in Anti-Western Thought," *Transactions of the Asiatic Society of Japan* 3, no. 7 (November 1959): 147–168.

14. Ōhashi, "Hekija shōgen," in *Meiji bunka zenshū* (Tokyo: Nihon hyōrunsha, 1927), 15:130.

15. It should be acknowledged that in the case of Christianity, Japanese polemicists like Ōhashi Totsuan had a point. The Japanese were aware of the complicity of Christian missionaries in Western imperialism in China, the Philippines, and Southeast Asia and had reason to be concerned that they not repeat the same mistakes and be subjugated like their Asian neighbors.

16. For a succinct discussion, see Norman Cohn, "Medieval Millenarism: Its Bearing on the Comparative Study of Millenarian Movements," in *Millennial Dreams in Action*, ed. Sylvia L. Thrupp (The Hague: Mouton, 1962), 31–43.

17. Wolfgang Bauer, *China and the Search for Happiness: Recurring Themes in Four Thousand Years of Chinese Cultural History*, tr. Michael Shaw (New York: Seabury Press, 1976), 163–164, 222–223.

18. Tsunoda et al., *Sources of Japanese Tradition*, 219.

19. Ivan Morris, *The Nobility of Failure: Tragic Heroes in the History of Japan* (New York: New American Library, 1975), 151–152.

20. Ibid., 144.

21. Yasunaga Toshinobu, *Nihon no yūtopia shisō: komyūn e no shikō*, Kyōyō sensho 13 (Tokyo: Hōsei Daigaku Shuppankyoku, 1971), 99.

22. Ben-Ami Shillony, *Revolt in Japan: The Young Officers and February 26, 1936 Incident* (Princeton: Princeton University Press, 1973), 66.

23. Mark R. Peattie, *Ishiwara Kanji and Japan's Confrontation with the West* (Princeton: Princeton University Press, 1975), 42, 57–58, 72.

24. Marvin Tokayer and Mary Swartz, *The Fugu Plan: The Untold Story of the Japanese and the Jews during World War II* (New York: Paddington Press, 1979).

25. See Norman Cohn, *Warrant for Genocide: The Myth of the Jewish World Conspiracy and the Protocols of the Elders of Zion*, Brown Judaic Studies 23 (Chico, CA: Scholars Press, 1981), 242–243.

26. Shiōden Nobutaka, *Yudaya shisō to undō* (Tokyo: Naigai shobō, 1941; repr. ed., Tokyo: Shinkōsha Publishers, 1987).

27. For more details on Shiōden, see Goodman and Miyazawa, *Jews in the Japanese Mind*, 126–128 and *passim*.

28. These efforts are detailed in Goodman and Miyazawa, *Jews in the Japanese Mind*, 135–182.

29. Matsumoto Fumi, *Fuji kaidan'in konryū* (n.p.: Fujisan Myōkōin, 1958); Nagafuchi Ichirō, *Yudayajin to sekai kakumei* (Tokyo: Shinjinbutsu ōraisha, 1971); Nara Hiroshi, ed., *Yudayajin*, a special issue of *Gendai no esupuri*, no. 121 (August 1977). A much superior special issue on the Jews was published this same year. See *Yudayateki chisei to gendai* [Jewish Intellect and the Present], a special issue of *Gendai no shisō* [*Revue de la pensée d'aujourd'hui*] 5, no. 12 (November 1977).

30. Sales figures from an advertisement by the publisher, Tokuma shoten, in the *Yomiuri shimbun*, April 6, 1987.

31. "Japanese Writers Are Critical of Jews," *New York Times*, March 12, 1987. For a more detailed discussion, see also Goodman and Masanori, *Jews in the Japanese Mind*, 1–2, 225–232.

32. Uno Masami, *Yudaya ga wakaru to sekai ga miete kuru* [If You Understand the Jews, You Will Understand the World] (Tokuma shoten, 1986), 147. Hereinafter, *Sekai*.

33. Uno, *Sekai*, 149–150; and Uno Masami, *Yudaya ga wakaru to Nihon ga miete kuru* [If You Understand the Jews, You Will Understand Japan] (Tokuma shoten, 1986), 161. Hereinafter, *Nihon*.

34. Uno, *Nihon*, 127, 135, 193–196.

35. Uno, *Sekai*, 241–242; Nihon, 237–252.

36. Uno, *Sekai*, 7, 234–236.

37. Uno, *Nihon*, 244.

38. Uno, *Nihon*, 225–226, 249–252.

39. Hal Lindsey, *The Late Great Planet Earth* (New York: Bantam Books, 1973), esp. 135–168.

40. In 1988, the Anti-Defamation League of B'nai B'rith described the Liberty Lobby as "the most active anti-Semitic organization in the [United States]."Anti-Defamation League of B'nai B'rith, *Extremism on the Right* (New York: Anti-Defamation League of B'nai B'rith, 1988), 35. See also Anti-Defamation League of B'nai B'rith, "Liberty Lobby: Network of Hate," ADL Research Report, 1990, 11–12.

41. "Religious Tug of War Delays Burial of Arlington Man," *Washington Post*, January 6, 1988.

42. *The Spotlight*, February 27, 1989, 13.

43. *Yudaya ga wakaru to Amerika ga miete kuru* [If You Understand the Jews, You Will Understand America] (Chūtō mondai kenkyū sentaa [Middle East Problems Research Center], 1989). The lecture took place at the Osaka Nakanoshima Kōkaidō on September 18, 1989. A twelve-minute excerpt with English subtitles can be viewed at http://netfiles. uiuc.edu/dgoodman/shared/unovideo.htm. In 1991, Uno published Crowley's views as *Yudaya no kokusai senryaku: Amerikajin kara no shōgen* [The International Jewish Conspiracy: An American Account] (Nihon bungeisha, 1991).

44. Uno Masami, Paul Goldstein, and Jeffrey Steinberg, *Yudaya no kokuhaku: Nihon keizai o rimen kara miru* [Confessions of the Jews: Behind the Scenes of the Japanese Economy] (Osaka: Enoch shuppan, 1990). Goldstein and Steinberg appeared on the masthead of LaRouche's magazine *EIR* (*Executive Intelligence Review*) as "Directors of Counterintelligence."

45. "En: haisui no kōbō" (The Yen: Last Ditch Defense), *Yomiuri shimbun*, January 17, 1987.

46. "Backers, Protesters Mark Constitution's 40th Year," *Japan Times*, May 4, 1987.

47. This slogan appeared on a campaign poster.

48. *Asahi shimbun*, July 27, 1992.

49. *Sapio*, October 28, 1993, 20–21.

50. See William Watts, "Anti-Semitism in Japan: A Survey Research Study—A Report to the Anti-Defamation League of B'nai B'rith," December 19, 1988, 3-4, 18, and *passim*. See also Goodman and Miyazawa, *Jews in the Japanese Mind*, 3–5. Numerous ostensibly philo-Semitic books on the Jews' supposedly extraordinary ability to make money are constantly appearing and represent the flip side of anti-Semitic stereotypes of Jews. See, for example, Honda Ken, *Lessons of a Wealthy Jew: 17 Secrets for Becoming Rich and Happy* [*Yudaya daifugō no oshie: shiawase na kanemochi ni naru 17 no hiketsu*] (Tokyo: Daiwa shobō, 2003), which the publisher claimed had sold 380,000 copies by April 2004. See ad in *Nihon keizai shimbun*, April 4, 2004.

51. *Vajrayâna Sacca*, ed. Aum editorial staff, no. 6 (January 25, 1995): 3.

52. Hirose Takashi is cited on page 34 of "The Manual of Fear," and his chart is reproduced on page 71. The editors obviously also cribbed extensively from Uno, Ohta, and others.

53. Ian Reader, *Religious Violence in Contemporary Japan: The Case of Aum Shinrikyō* (Honolulu: University of Hawaii Press, 2000), 11.

54. In Aum's "Manual of Fear," the crown prince and princess (the current emperor and empress), the prime minister, the leader of the Sōka Gakki neo-Buddhist sect, and other prominent Japanese are identified as Freemasons (i.e., Jews) who had "sold their souls to the devil." See *Vajrayâna Sacca*, ed. Aum editorial staff, 6 (January 25, 1995): 16–18.

11

The Protocols of the Elders of Zion

An Authentic Document in Palestinian Authority Ideology

ITAMAR MARCUS AND BARBARA CROOK

Are the Jewish Elders of Zion conspiring to subjugate the entire world under a Jewish world government? It sounds too ridiculous to consider, let alone necessitate a denial. But if you were a 10th-grade student in a school under the Palestinian Authority (PA), that is precisely what you would have been learning from your new history book. The schoolbook, published in 2004 by the Palestinian Ministry of Education, teaches that among the foundations of Zionism agreed upon at the First Zionist Congress in 1897, "there is a group of confidential resolutions adopted by the Congress and known by the name 'The Protocols of the Elders of Zion' the goal of which was world domination."[1] It has been one hundred years since the publication of the infamous *Protocols of the Elders of Zion* and nearly a century since Henry Ford published his apology for arguing that the *Protocols* were authentic documentation of a Jewish conspiracy. It's been decades since the enlightened world has relegated the *Protocols* to the shelves of hate propaganda, along with the blood libels and poisoned-well accusations of the Middle Ages. Why, then, would the PA resurrect this vicious libel in the 21st century and pass it off as authentic to its children?

The striking truth is that this depiction of Jews as plotting against the world in a kind of conspiracy theory never went out of favor and has been actively espoused in PA society, whose political, religious, and educational leaders have incorporated the *Protocols*—and the hate ideology it represents—as basic components of their world view.

This is not merely one among the many PA libels against Jews. The *Protocols* libel is critical for Palestinian society, especially while teaching children that it represents the First Zionist Congress, because it backs up the global ideology of delegitimization of Jews, Israel, and, especially, Zionism, which is the foundation of Palestinian Authority propaganda.

Defining the Zionist movement as one aspect of a global Jewish plot toward world domination leads to three important conclusions:

152

1. Zionism is inherently an illegitimate and sinister movement.
2. Zionism is dangerous and threatening not merely to Arabs but to the entire world.
3. Fighting Zionism is, for Arabs and the world, an act of self-defense and a service to all humanity.

As such, references to the *Protocols* appear regularly in the PA media, presented as authentic by academics, educators, political leaders, and journalists.

A dominant preoccupation of PA academia is the repeated and varied denials of Israel's historical right to exist. These denials entail the erasure of Jewish history in the land, the creation of a Palestinian Islamic history in the land, and, finally, a motivation for the establishment of Zionism—other than its being an authentic national renaissance movement. Thus, a history is invented in which the Land of Israel has always been Arab Islamic "Palestine," with no Jewish roots, and Palestinian historians created reasons to explain Zionism's occurrence. The essential narrative created by Arab and Palestinian educators teaches that Zionism in Israel was a European idea with two goals:

1. To set up a bridgehead for European imperialism to control the Middle East;
2. To serve as a form of self-defense for Christian Europeans, who sought to be rid of the danger and burden of having Jews living among them.

The *Protocols* libel fits nicely into this, as can be seen in the following discussion by senior PA historians:

Dr. Issam Sissalem, history lecturer at Islamic University and Educational TV host:

"The Jews lived in isolated areas, in ghettos in Poland and in Russia. They were the remains of the Khazars . . . with no connection to our land. . . . *At that time, Britain wanted to plant a cancer* [in the Middle East to control it]. *It did not occur to them* [the Jews] *that Palestine would be theirs. They wanted . . . any Homeland. Our people wisely sensed this, as they planted on the land and lived in peace and security, continuing a twelve thousand year journey on this land.*"

"Britain wanted to plant here the Jews in order to protect the Suez Canal. . . . Britain decided to plant in this land a foreign secluded entity—a cancer—in order to drive a wedge in the [Arab] nation."

Riad Al-Astal, history lecturer at Al-Azhar University in Gaza:

"There are two major elements for which Britain and the other European states were striving: the first element was to get rid of the Jews, who were known as those who provoke civil wars, disturbances, and financial crises in Germany, in France and in other European states . . . second: the European plan, . . . to torpedo any hope for an Arab unity.

In these circumstances [of European nationalism] developed what is known as the Zionist Renaissance, and the seeds of what is called *The Protocols of the Elders of Zion* appeared at the end of the 18th century. They are the *Protocols* that were presented in the Basel Congress in Switzerland [the First Zionist Congress in 1897]."[2]

Once established as factual, the *Protocols* is cited by historians as textual proof of the necessity of fighting Israel. One example:

Dr. Attallah Abu Al-Farah:

"Can there be, in practice, co-existence on Palestinian land between ourselves and the Jews, in light of their mentality which stems from *The Protocols of the Elders of Zion*?"

Dr. Issam Sissalem, history professor and host:

"This question comes from 'My Beloved Friend.' I say: Dr. Attallah, who is a learned expert . . ."[3]

This conversation was important for numerous reasons. The date was May 14, 1999, the eve of Israel's Independence Day, and the purpose of the program was to reject Israel's right to exist. Citing the *Protocols* as authentic confirms the illegitimacy of Israel. Also note that this was said in 1999, before the PA terror war (also called "Intifada") was launched. Some suggest that the hatred expressed on PA TV was a result of the war, but, in fact, the opposite is true: The hate promotion is not a result of the war but preceded it by many years and was in all likelihood a major cause of the war.

Finally, note the political implications expressed by the professor:

"Can there be co-existence on Palestinian land between ourselves and the Jews, in light of their mentality which stems from *The Protocols of the Elders of Zion*?"

The *Protocols* is being used as an excuse for fighting Israel, as there can be no peace with a movement that is evil in essence.

Seeing the *Protocols* as a guide to understanding Jewish behavior encourages the PA to demonize virtually every Israeli policy—even those that are manifestly positive. When Israel released four hundred Palestinian prisoners in 2004 in exchange for a kidnapped businessman and the bodies of three Israeli soldiers, the PA found the following *Protocols* spin to demonize the release:

> "We see that Israel is trying to delude the world that one Israeli will be exchanged for 1,000 Palestinians," explained Ahmad Nasser, secretary of the Palestinian Legislative Council. "Israel is interested in planting among the Palestinians, the Arabs or the world the concept of value—the value of a Jew and the value of an Arab."

The interviewer concurred:

> "This concept appears in *The Protocols of the Elders of Zion*, that they [Jews] are superior and the rest are inferior."[4]

Note that the *Protocols* is so deeply incorporated in PA mentality that the journalist cites it quite routinely.

In order to make the *Protocols* seem real, it has to be specific, and the PA goes from the general to the specific; at times the *Protocols* is cited, chapter and verse. One interesting example: The official PA daily, on its "Political-National Education" page, cited precise quotes from Protocols 2 and 12 to explain Israeli policy:

> Moral and psychological manipulation has a significant place in the minds of Jews, and formed a very important source of strength in the Hebrew State. . . .
>
> Disinformation has been one of the bases of psychological manipulation among the Israelis, and propaganda played an important role in the psychological prodding of world political leaders to support Zionism. . . .
>
> *The Protocols of the Elders of Zion* did not ignore the importance of using propaganda to promote the Zionist goals. In the second protocol it is written: "Through the newspapers we will have the means to propel and to influence." In the twelfth protocol: "Our governments will hold the reins of most of the newspapers, and through this plan we will possess the primary power to turn to public opinion."[5]

The PA media have depicted the *Protocols* as an active guidebook, almost as if Israeli leaders were flipping through the pages at cabinet meetings and basing policy on what they discover. Note the following two examples:

> The purpose of the military policy is to impose this situation on the residents and force them to leave their homes, and this is done in the framework of the Protocols of Zion.[6]
>
> *Remember the history, oh Arabs!*
> 1. In 1897 the first Zionist Congress was held in Basel . . .
> 2. In 1907 the actual immigration operation began . . .
> 3. In 1917 the woeful declaration of Balfour was made . . .
> 9. In 1977 the visit which shocked the Arab Nation occurred, the President of Egypt visited Israel . . .
>
> Every ten years, a vital aim is achieved. These are the *Protocols of the Elders of Zion*, of a century, from 1897 till 1997. They have planned and accomplished. Every ten years, another aim was achieved, proving their continuity and their power.[7]

Everything cited until this point is from Fatah political leaders on PA Fatah-controlled TV and newspapers. The Hamas movement agrees with this ideology and even formalizes it by incorporating the *Protocols* into its ideology and citing it in the official Hamas charter:

> "Article Thirty-Two
> Hamas is calling upon the Arab and Islamic peoples to act seriously and tirelessly in order to frustrate that dreadful scheme. . . . Today it is Palestine and tomorrow it may be another country or other countries. For Zionist scheming has no end, and after Palestine they will covet expansion from the Nile to the Euphrates. . . . Their scheme has been laid out in the *Protocols of the Elders of Zion*, and their present [conduct] is the best proof of what is said there."

In order to present the *Protocols* libel as authentic Jewish ideology, the PA educators teach that careful observation of Jewish history shows earlier signs and indications of this libel. Thus, they teach that the *Protocols*, while a relatively new Zionist document, is not a new Jewish ideology but a continuation of the pattern of Jewish thinking and behavior throughout history. According to this view, the *Protocols* is only the apex—the peak of Jewish development.

Here is one example:

Sheikh Attiyeh Sahar, Chairman of the Department of Islamic Research in The Al-Zahar University:

It must be known that this nation, the Jews, are willing of mind soul to alter their religion in order to attain their demands. This is rooted deep in their history. . . . They alienated the God that saved them and willed to worship idols. . . . These things show us that these people, in order to attain their goals, are willing to turn away from their God. . . . We also know that they changed the Bible and replaced it, because it does not serve their purposes, and they drafted the Talmud, as it is known, and came up, finally, with the *Protocols of the Elders of Zion*.[8]

To counter this Jewish threat indicated by the *Protocols*, Palestinian defense bodies undertake "research" to defend against it:

The 65th issue of *The Shahids* (Martyrs) was recently published by the Political Guidance of the Border Patrol. The issue includes many important political, economic and military matters. . . . In addition, there is a chapter about a research paper, entitled "The Jewish Danger: *The Protocols of the Elders of Zion*."[9]

This *Protocols* libel is not limited to the written and spoken word. Palestinian political cartoons reflect the *Protocols* libel of Jews, even when the *Protocols* is not explicitly cited. Some examples:

1. Israel/Jews endanger the world: Cartoon in the official PA daily presents Israel stepping on the entire world. *Al-Hayat Al-Jadida*, May 5, 2005.

2. Israel/Jews endanger the world: Cartoon in the official PA daily, the Star of David, symbol of Israel and Jews, entraps the world. The Arabic text in the cartoon reads "European poll." Al-Hayat Al-Jadida, November 9, 2003.

3. Cartoon in the official PA daily, Jews are the conductor, controlling and dictating policy. Note the bullet holes all over the music notes. The message is that Jews control and dictate the war—music. Al-Hayat Al-Jadida, May 8, 2005.

4. Cartoon in the official PA daily. The text on the desk reads "the Hague court." The Jews are behind it and dictate the actions of the United States, which controls the International Court of Justice. *Al-Hayat Al-Jadida*, February 24, 2005.

5. The Jew attempts world domination. While the world protests, the Jew is putting the entire world under a Jewish skull cap. *Al-Hayat Al-Jadida*, July 4, 2005, repeated on May 8, 2009.

In conclusion, in spite of universal acceptance of the *Protocols* as an anti-Semitic forgery, the representation of *The Protocols of the Elders of Zion* as an authentic book representing a true Jewish conspiracy is part of Palestinian Authority ideology. The PA is using this libel the same way it was used by anti-Semites in the past century: Once it was documented by an "authentic" book that the Jews were part of an international conspiracy to dominate, control, and conquer the world, then fighting them, persecuting them, or even killing them could be presented as legitimate self defense.

The *Protocols* for the Palestinians serves the same purpose as the blood libels and the myths of the poisoned wells: If the Jews are scheming to kill others, then fighting them is legitimate self-defense and even admirable.

The Palestinian Authority successfully used the *Protocols* libel, together with other hate propaganda, to transform the killing of Jews from immoral murder into legitimate self-defense and even a service to humanity. The overwhelming Palestinian popular support for the suicide terror war against Israeli civilians and the transformation of the murderers of Jews into Palestinian heroes and role models for children can be seen as proof of the complete success of the Palestinian Authority's policy of demonizing Jews and Israelis. This revival of the *Protocols* libel was for the Palestinian Authority an important component, as it gave academic support and "authentic" authorization to the intrinsically evil depiction of Jews and Israelis that was so important to the PA, and it made fighting and killing Jews a natural response for Palestinians.

NOTES

Itamar Marcus is founder and director of Palestinian Media Watch (PMW). Barbara Crook is associate director of PMW.

1. *History of the Modern and Contemporary World*, Grade 10 60–61. After world outcry, a later edition of the book removed this reference.

2. Palestinian Authority TV, December 28, 2003.

3. Palestinian Authority TV, May 14, 1999.

4. Palestinian Authority TV, February 6, 2004.

5. *Al-Hayat Al-Jadida*, January 25, 2001.

6. *Al-Hayat Al-Jadida*, November 18, 2001.

7. *Al Quds*, July 10, 2001.

8. Palestinian Authority TV, September 10, 2000.

9. *Al-Hayat Al-Jadida*, December 1, 2003.

PART V

Protocols at the Turn of the Millennium

The Return of the Repressed

—————————————————————————————————— 12 ——

Anti-Semitism from Outer Space

The Protocols *in the UFO Subculture*

——— MICHAEL BARKUN ————————————————————

In the century since the *Protocols* were first published, they have appeared in a variety of guises, but none stranger, perhaps, then a 1991 edition. It begins with a brief, deceptively conventional description of its English translator, Victor Marsden, and its Russian editor, Sergius Nilus, but then it adds this prefatory passage:

> So be it and, again, may ye be given into the hearing and understanding of that which is being given unto you for it is the direct PROTOCOLS as given forth from the ANTI-CHRIST TO HIS PEOPLE FOR THE FINAL TAKING OF PLANET EARTH! IF YE KNOW NOT THINE ENEMY, HOW CAN YE STAND AGAINST HIM? SALU![1]

The phrasing may strike one as a bit odd, even archaic, in style, but the substance is more or less consistent with theological anti-Semitism in its emphasis on the threat posed by Antichrist. Odder than the language, however, is the authorship, for the passage quoted is said to come from a nine-and-a-half-foot-tall extraterrestrial from the Pleiades named Gyeorgos Ceres Hatonn.

His messages from outer space have appeared since 1989 in a series of periodicals with changing names but similar contents, which, for simplicity's sake, I have termed the "Phoenix publications," not after the city but after the name of Hatonn's spaceship.[2] The publications first appeared in Tehachapi, California, but the offices were later transferred to Las Vegas. The communications from Hatonn are not, strictly speaking, examples of channeling but are said to be received as coded radio transmissions by an amanuensis Hatonn identifies as "Dharma" but who in fact is a woman named Doris Ekker of Tehachapi. In addition to numerous brief anti-Semitic references, Hatonn has on at least two occasions "transmitted" the complete text of the *Protocols*, together with his own commentary.[3] In certain respects, Hatonn deals with the *Protocols* in ways that are indistinguishable from those of terrestrial anti-Semites, but in other respects he extends their reach in troubling ways.

Three themes predominate in those portions of the Hatonn materials that deal with *The Protocols of the Elders of Zion*. First, the Hatonn communications treat the *Protocols*, with rare exceptions, as though the forgery issue did not exist. They are largely oblivious to questions of authenticity, and, when they address them at all, they make little attempt to rebut the evidence of forgery. Second, they fold the *Protocols* into what has become a common theme in contemporary anti-Semitic literature, namely that there are false Jews and authentic Jews, and it is only the false Jews who are responsible for the *Protocols*. And, finally, the *Protocols* is treated not merely as a political document but as evidence of a titanic struggle of cosmic significance on which the ultimate fate of the planet rests. This derives not simply from a tendency to see the world as living in the end-times—a propensity widely shared in a millennium-saturated age—but results from the theological influences that created the figure of Hatonn. For Hatonn and his extraterrestrial colleagues are no mere run-of-the-mill aliens. They are, in fact, divinities, exalted spirits in the Ascended Master tradition of Theosophy, who now communicate with humanity from spaceships.

Hatonn ignores the forgery issue most of the time, but, when he does raise it, he manipulates it in order to make it, paradoxically, a sign of authenticity, rather than fraudulence. The argument is not unlike the one suggested in the mid-1920s by Nesta Webster. Webster was an influential British conspiracist whose major work appeared between the two World Wars and who continues to exert a powerful influence on contemporary conspiracy theorists. She claimed to regard the issue of the *Protocols'* authenticity to be "an open question." However, she constructed an elaborate argument to suggest that, even if they were a forgery, the original materials out of which they were constructed came from a genuine revolutionary secret society in which Jews likely played a major role.[4] Therefore, evidence of forgery was irrelevant to the work's validity. Hatonn's view is similar. To the extent that the forgery issue interests him at all, it is in the manner of all conspiracy theorists, for whom nothing is as it seems. If the *Protocols* were forged, then forgery was yet another stratagem of the conspirators. Hatonn, like Webster, sees history as the unfolding of plots, and therefore every untoward event must be the intended effect of a cabal that is its hidden cause. For him, as for her, the rise of Bolshevism ultimately validated the substance of the *Protocols*; the book must be true, no matter who wrote it, under what circumstances.[5] This post hoc argument leads him to conclude, "God always makes sure you get the facts."[6]

The distinction between true and false Jews goes back at least to the late 19th century. As it appears in the Hatonn materials, it takes the form of the so-called Khazar thesis. It is generally uncontested that the leadership of the Black Sea Khazars converted to Judaism in the 7th century. The elite Khazar conversions, however, became the springboard for a far more sweeping theory of Jewish origins, begun by Ernst Renan, who in 1883 suggested that the general Khazar population also converted and became the ancestors of Ashkenazic Jewry. The latter were, therefore, not descendants of Israelites at all but, rather, were deemed to be "Asiatics" with no claim to a biblical inheritance.[7] The most famous recent advocate of this theory was, of course, Arthur Koestler, who, late in life, advanced a version of the Khazar theory in *The Thirteenth Tribe*, duly cited by Hatonn.[8] Although the Khazar theory gets surprisingly little attention in scholarly histories of anti-Semitism, it has been an influential theme among American anti-Semites since the immigration restrictionists of the 1920s, and it figures prominently in Hatonn's analysis of the *Protocols*.

Referring to the authors of the *Protocols*, Hatonn reminds his readers, in his characteristically stilted diction, "Please always be in the remembering at every writing that these are the false 'Jews' often referred to as the imitation Jews of the Khazar choosing."[9] Elsewhere he speaks of the "Zionist Khazars who call themselves Jews."[10] By identifying the *Protocols'* authors as Khazars, Hatonn can claim, first, that he is not really an anti-Semite, and, second, that he is in fact trying to protect the authentic Jews, who have been victimized by the false Jews, the Zionist usurpers.

> The "JEWS" of today are more and more controlled—in ignorance of the fact—by the Zionists. THE JEWS WILL BE THE ONES TO SUFFER THE GREATEST PAIN AT THE HANDS OF THESE UNGODLY MEN.[11]

This takes on a special resonance because of Hatonn's insistence that we live in the end-times. And yet, given the strange provenance of this version of the *Protocols*, one may be sure that it is an apocalyptic vision different from the one that circulates more broadly among fundamentalist Protestant millenarians. Hatonn has a millennial script, but it is not the usual Rapture-and-Tribulation scenario, in which the saved will enjoy Jesus' rescue from end-time chaos.

The clearest picture of this new apocalypse comes in a joint transmission from Hatonn and "Jesus Sananda"—Jesus in his Ascended Master persona—who make clear that the end is near but that it will not follow the scenario laid out in the Book of Revelation. As Jesus Sananda puts it, "There will be no fluffy clouds for a 'Rapture,'"[12] Human sinfulness and environmental corruption will lead to a time of troubles—he does employ the phrase "severe tribulation"—"nuclear war, pestilence, famine, plague, and earth upheaval."[13] The climactic disaster will be a reversal of the poles. This was in fact predicted for May 5, 2000, in a book that circulated widely in the late 1980s.[14] Pole reversal was one among many predicted cataclysms much talked about in New Age circles beginning in the 1970s, under the general rubric of "Earth changes." Other versions emphasized end-time floods that would inundate entire continents, while still others featured earthquakes that would rupture mountain ranges. They all derived from information communicated through such paranormal sources as dreams, channeling, or, as in this case, warnings from benevolent "space brothers."

As Hatonn and Jesus Sananda see it, Jesus will return, but by spaceship for those who believe. Jesus Sananda describes it as "a 'migration' which shall take place as lifting off your orb and into very meticulously prepared shuttle craft into Mother ships for holding in security."[15] Presumably, those who miss the shuttle craft will be doomed to perish on a faltering Earth. Neither Hatonn nor Jesus Sananda explains precisely why such a rescue is necessary, but surely Hatonn's readers know by now that the disasters have been brought about by the evil deeds of Zionist-Khazar controllers.

At one level, the Phoenix-Hatonn materials graft science-fiction elements to the *Protocols*. But, at another level, they draw the *Protocols* into a formidable modern religious tradition, Theosophy and its offshoots. Begun in the late 19th century by Helena Petrovna Blavatsky and Henry Steel Olcott, Theosophy postulates the existence of a group of spiritually evolved beings on a nonmaterial plane of existence, who communicated with worthy Earthly disciples and guided the spiritual course of humanity.[16] The movement was originally centered on the Theosophical Society but subsequently fragmented into numerous, often mutually hostile variants under such figures as Alice Bailey, Guy and Edna Ballard, and Mark and Elizabeth Clare Prophet.[17] Each variant depended on individuals who claimed to have privileged communication with one or more Ascended Masters, whose teachings had divine authority for followers. The first such figures identified by Madame Blavatsky were Indian or Tibetan sages, suggesting the spiritual cachet that attached to Eastern mystics. This may also explain Hatonn's affectation of a kind of broken English that might suggest someone who had acquired it as a second language in the East. Hatonn often addresses his reader as "chela," employing the Indian term adopted by Theosophists to signify "disciple."

Yet, it is not altogether clear exactly where Hatonn fits into a Theosophical scheme. He certainly sounds like an Ascended Master, with his authoritative messages to Earthlings on all matters spiritual and temporal. But Hatonn's precise status in the divine hierarchy has been placed in doubt by one of his more vocal supporters, a figure with the improbable name of Patrick H. Bellringer. Bellringer, who maintains an elaborate website that archives all of the past Phoenix publications, gives Hatonn his formal title, "Commander in Chief of Earth Project Transition." He also calls Hatonn one of the "Higher Spiritual Teachers," which seems to place him clearly among the Ascended Masters.[18] However, in April 2005, Bellringer responded to an e-mail asking, "Is Hatonn like the be-all-end-all god incarnate or is this physical form of God like another lower aspect of God? Any light u [sic] can shed on this matter is greatly appreciated." Bellringer responded by suggesting that "Hatonn" was merely a disguise for the "Creator God 'Aton.'" The Creator God, according to Bellringer, "has chosen to come to us as a nine and one-half foot tall bald-headed Pleiadian Gray and commander of their Star Fleet. So be it! Who am I to question."[19] Who, indeed? To hear Bellringer tell it, then, by implication, the *Protocols* come not merely from an Ascended Master but directly from God.

Theosophy itself developed troubling associations with racial anti-Semitism. There was a racial strain in Theosophy from the beginning. Madame Blavatsky spoke of seven primeval "root races," among which were the Aryans. It was scarcely surprising, therefore, that, while the Theosophical Society itself did not develop into an explicitly racialist organization, racialists quickly developed their own versions of Theosophy. This added to an already overgrown jungle of what some have termed "esoteric Nazism." Those who have mapped it, such as Nicholas Goodrick-Clarke and Joscelyn Godwin, point out that racialists and anti-Semites on both sides of the Atlantic actively incorporated Theosophical motifs.[20]

It is tempting, therefore, to see the Phoenix publications as merely the latest manifestation of an occult anti-Semitism that had circles of adherents in Europe, Latin America, and the United States for many decades. It is also clear that those who have held such occult beliefs have been just as likely to accept the *Protocols* as other anti-Semites. Unfortunately, although the Theosophical connection seems a logical explanation of the Hatonn communications, in the end it fails to do so convincingly. The line of descent seems plausible but in fact breaks down. This is why:

In the first place, the range of reading cited by Hatonn and his colleagues consists for the most part of straight-forward anti-Semitic literature. There is the *Protocols*, of course, and then a few of the "usual suspects"—for example, the aging Ezra Pound acolyte Eustace Mullins and the prolific contemporary British conspiracist David Icke—neither of them in the mold of Nazi esotericism. Whether because his spaceship has a small library or because Hatonn's editors have their own intellectual limitations, there is no sign that either the extraterrestrial Ascended Master or his "ground crew" (as they sometimes call themselves) seems to know much about Theosophy, much less its more recondite Nazi variants. What we actually have is a highly derivative form of Theosophy—bits and pieces of what should really be termed neo-Theosophy, almost certainly lifted from sects that had themselves broken away from the larger Theosophical movement, such as the "I AM" Religious Activity in the 1930s and 1940s or the more recent Church Universal and Triumphant, and that have provided the Hatonn materials with a fragmentary and superficial Theosophical gloss.

The *Protocols* texts I have described sit, therefore, within a setting formed primarily neither by Theosophy nor by occult or esoteric Nazism. Instead, the mixture is much less coherent. The Hatonn materials are an example of what I have elsewhere termed "stigmatized knowledge."[21] By stigmatized knowledge, I mean knowledge claims unrecognized by such validating institutions as universities, the scientific and medical communities, government agencies, and mainstream religious organizations. A wide array of claims is made for knowledge that lacks such recognition, ranging from knowledge said to have been present in the ancient past and forgotten, to knowledge once recognized and superseded or rejected, to knowledge claims that are ignored, to knowledge said to be deliberately suppressed.

The *Protocols* is an obvious form of stigmatized knowledge, since it was published as an authentic document before being unmasked as a forgery, yet many people continue to accept it as authentic—despite the fact that fully ninety one years have passed since the incontrovertible proof of the forgery appeared.

One of the characteristics of believers in stigmatized knowledge is that belief in one form of stigmatized knowledge predisposes acceptance of other forms. And it is this rather simple observation, rather than any complex Theosophical pedigree, that explains the presence of the *Protocols* in the science-fiction setting of Hatonn's spaceship messages.

The Hatonn transmissions have appeared, as I mentioned, in or under the sponsorship of a set of periodicals published under a variety of titles over the past two decades. The most recent Phoenix incarnation is entitled *The Spectrum*, and it is useful to sample the contents of a typical issue. Such sampling will, I think, make clear what I have in mind by stigmatized knowledge and will also suggest the non-anti-Semitic ideas with which the Hatonn's writings cohabit. This issue, published in May 2003, contains one Ascended Master transmission, not from Hatonn but from another similarly revered figure, St. Germain, who warns readers against "agents for the Dark Energies on your planet."[22] But St. Germain's message occupies only 4 of the issue's 108 pages. The rest cover an astonishing range of subjects, drawn together by the thread of stigmatized knowledge.

There is, to be sure, some predictable anti-Semitism, notably in the form of an essay by the aging Eustace Mullins.[23] Then there is a lengthy article on the SARS outbreak, asserting that it is part of a global conspiracy that will eventually lead to the wiping out of half the world's population and in which the Rockefeller family, the UN, and the World Health Organization are said to be key players. The article's author, Dr. Leonard G. Horowitz, a dentist, has become the favored expert on bioterrorism for the antigovernment extreme right.[24] The *Spectrum* issue is also, like many conspiracy publications, filled with ads for bizarre medical devices and panaceas that barely skirt prosecutable claims.

Finally, there is the magazine's lengthy lead article, titled "Our Busy Solar System: What Is NASA Hiding? Get Ready for What's Coming!" As the title suggests, this extended piece, virtually impossible to summarize, has nothing to do with anti-Semitism and does not mention the *Protocols*. Replete with what purports to be corroborating scientific evidence, it claims that extraordinary instabilities in the solar system portend catastrophic events on Earth and that among them is the approach of a mysterious, hitherto unknown planet, referred to as Planet X. There is, indeed, a large "Planet X" literature, mostly in the New Age community, dealing with apocalyptic events that will allegedly occur as the planet approaches in 2012. The general tenor of the article is that a conspiracy exists that involves NASA, the Vatican, and the Jesuits and that aims to suppress this information, because, in some circuitous way, such suppression will advance their nefarious aims, particularly their agenda for One World Government.[25] As this issue of *The Spectrum* suggests, Hatonn's involvement with the *Protocols* is thus defined not only by anti-Semitism and occultism but also by a broader propensity to believe that events of all kinds are the consequences of secret machinations and that received accounts of the world are uniformly false and deceptive.

One's first reaction to such material is to dismiss it as too bizarre to warrant serious attention. But the same might also be said of the *Protocols* themselves, and, unfortunately, all too many people have taken them seriously. There is a subculture of those for whom stigmatized knowledge claims are considered authoritative precisely because they have been stigmatized. To be rejected, to be denied access to university curricula, to respected newspapers, to the pulpits of major religious organizations, to scientific and medical textbooks—for some, it is precisely such rejection that confers the ultimate form of validation. To those already disposed to suspect authority, what could be more persuasive than the cultural products that authority itself rejects? *For them, the* Protocols *is compelling because it has been rejected, not in spite of it.* And if no authority can be trusted, then to believe the *Protocols* may also be consistent with other beliefs, seemingly unrelated to anti-Semitism, such as communications from extraterrestrials, lost teachings from Atlantis, medical miracles no medical school would accept, arguments against the federal income taxes, and a host of other equally marginalized ideas. This leaves us, I am afraid, in the situation of having impeccable arguments against the *Protocols* that will never convince a particular kind of audience, that audience drawn to stigmatized knowledge. I am suggesting, too, that the inability to convince that audience hinges not so much on the intensity of its anti-Semitism (although that may certainly be a factor) as on the *Protocols'* stigmatization, leading to the paradox that *discrediting them is precisely the characteristic that makes them attractive* and that, the more convincing our arguments, the less their power to persuade.

NOTES

1. Gyeorgos Hatonn, *Shrouds of the Seventh Seal: The Anti-Christ Whore of Babylon!* (Las Vegas: Phoenix Source Distributors, 1991), 103, http://fourwinds10.com/journals/four_winds_journals_zip/J024.pdf.

2. Michael Barkun, *A Culture of Conspiracy: Apocalyptic Visions in Contemporary America* (Berkeley: University of California Press, 2003), 151–152.

3. Hatonn, *Shrouds*, 110ff; Hatonn, *Ecstasy to Agony through the Plan 2000* (Las Vegas: Phoenix Source Publishers, 1993), 187ff, http://fourwinds10.com/journals/four_winds_journals_zip/J068.pdf.

4. Nesta H. Webster, *Secret Societies and Subversive Movements* (Christian Book Club, n.d., reprint of the 1924 edition), 408–414.

5. Hatonn, *Shrouds*, 188–189.

6. Ibid., 189.

7. Michael Barkun, *Religion and the Racist Right: The Origins of the Christian Identity Movement* (Chapel Hill: University of North Caroline Press, 1994), 137–142.

8. Hatonn, *Ecstasy to Agony*, 180.

9. Hatonn, *Shrouds*, 191.

10. Ibid., 196.

11. Hatonn, *Ecstasy to Agony*, 178.

12. Hatonn, *Cry of the Phoenix: Death Rattle of Freedom, "The Ceres Plan 2000"* (Las Vegas: Phoenix Source Publishers, 1989), 77.

13. Ibid., 79.

14. Richard W. Noone, *5/5/2000 Ice: The Ultimate Disaster* (New York: Harmony Books, 2003).

15. Hatonn, *Cry of the Phoenix*, 79.

16. Bradley C. Whitsel, *The Church Universal and Triumphant: Elizabeth Clare Prophet's Apocalyptic Movement* (Syracuse: Syracuse University Press, 2003), 19–21.

17. Ibid., 22–38.

18. Patrick H. Bellringer, "Mission Statement," n.d., http://www.fourwinds10.com/fourwinds-info.html.

19. Patrick H. Bellringer, "'Hello, Central' Who Is Gyeorgos Ceres Hatonn/Creator God?" (2005), http://www.fourwinds10.com/news/14-spiritual/K-hello-central/2005/.

20. Joscelyn Godwin, *Arktos: The Polar Myth in Science, Symbolism, and Nazi Survival* (Kempton, IL: Unlimited Press, 1996); Nicholas Goodrick-Clarke, *Black Sun: Aryan, Esoteric Nazism and the Politics of Identity* (New York: New York University Press, 2002).

21. Barkun, *A Culture of Conspiracy*, 26–27.

22. Violinio St. Germain, "What Has Become of the Grand Freedom Experiment Called the United States?" *The Spectrum* 4, no. 11 (2003): 79.

23. Eustace Mullins, "Assault on Iraq: Prelude to World War III," *The Spectrum*, 4, no. 11 (2003): 26–27.

24. Len Horowitz, "Severe Acute Respiratory Syndrome (SARS): A Great Global Scam!" *The Spectrum* 4, no. 11 (2003): 30–37.

25. Rick Martin, "Our *Busy* Solar System: What Is NASA Hiding? Get Ready for What's Coming!" *The Spectrum* 4, no. 11 (2003): 67.

13

The Protocols of the Elders of Zion on the Contemporary American Scene

Historical Artifact or Current Threat?

DEBORAH LIPSTADT

In the fall of 2004, the retailing behemoth Wal-Mart announced that it would begin selling *The Protocols of the Elders of Zion*. Wal-Mart sells only a limited number of books, refuses to sell publications it deems pornographic, and is extremely judicious about any item it puts on its shelves. How had this decision been made? Had Wal-Mart retailing experts done market research and determined that there was a growing demand for the book? And, if so, who was the potential audience? People in rural Idaho and other white supremacist strongholds? Adherents of the Nation of Islam and its leader, Louis Farrakhan? Americans from Muslim and Arab backgrounds whose roots were in countries that actively promulgated the "truth" and accuracy of the *Protocols*? It was possible that this was the act of one employee who wanted this book disseminated on ideological grounds. It was also possible that it was an innocent act by someone who did not really know what the book represented. Wal-Mart never revealed how this decision was made. If it indeed was the result of an "innocent act," this would be a matter of greater concern. It would suggest that the *Protocols* had seeped even further into the mainstream of American life than had been previously imagined.

What happened next was more disturbing than the initial decision. Wal-Mart, facing a barrage of criticism and negative publicity, defended its decision. It declared that, though "some say" this book is a forgery, it had not "seen a clear and convincing version" of the evidence proving that was the case.

What Wal-Mart had seen at that point was unclear. Its next pronouncement on the topic suggests that it had consulted serious scholarly research but that this too had failed to convince the executives of this retailing behemoth. And matters got worse. Wal-Mart, facing even more criticism, justified its decision by warning that "the *Protocols* were taken seriously by the Russians and by people in America like the famed industrialist Henry Ford." This, Wal-Mart proclaimed, "seems to give it validity."

Finally, Wal-Mart observed, in a chilling statement, that if "the *Protocols* are genuine (which can never be proven conclusively), it might cause some of us to keep a wary eye on world affairs."[1] Was this just a very clumsy attempt by Wal-Mart, a corporation known for the attention it pays to the smallest commercial detail, to try to put a putatively positive spin on a bad situation, or was it suggesting that someone should be watching the Jews because of the conspiracies in which they engage?

When the public outcry escalated, Wal-Mart decided to stop sales of the book "for commercial reasons." If I were a Wal-Mart stockholder, I would be pleased that the corporation had corrected a decision that was blatantly stupid at the very best. But "commercial" reasons are not why this book should be removed from the shelves. The reason is that it's a proven forgery that has caused and still has the capacity to cause great harm.

It was striking that Wal-Mart should cite Henry Ford as the basis for its decision to sell the *Protocols*. Ford, more than any other person, was responsible not just for bringing the *Protocols* to the attention of millions of Americans but also for helping to disseminate it in other countries.

In 1918, Henry Ford bought the *Dearborn Independent*, a virtually defunct newspaper. He declared his desire to give the "average citizen a truer and better analysis of matters which now reach him from only one point of view." The paper was an important personal venture for Ford. Each edition carried a page titled "Mr. Ford's Own Page." There is little doubt that Ford was well aware of the views expressed in his name.[2] In May 1920, the paper began a series of articles on the "International Jew." The series was drawn in the main from Werner Sombart's *The Jews and Modern Capitalism* and from the *Protocols* and continued for the next ninety-one issues of the weekly.[3]

The first article warned its readers that:

> There is a race, a part of humanity . . . which has succeeded in raising itself to a power that the proudest Gentile race has never claimed—not even Rome in the days of her proudest power.[4]

The article continued with a description of the Jews' "distinguishing mental and moral traits":

Distaste for hard or violent physical labor, a strong family sense . . . remarkable power to survive in adverse environments, combined with great ability to retain racial solidarity; . . . Shrewdness and astuteness in speculation and money matters generally; an Oriental love of display.

Beginning in July, the paper discussed the *Protocols* itself, emphasizing the Jews' corruption of Christian youth and their pivotal role in Judeo-Bolshevism.[5] Jews were responsible for the assassination of President Lincoln, World War I, the Russian Revolution, and corruption on Wall Street. The paper also blamed Jews for perverting American culture. They were behind the spread of "moron music," such as jazz, and the corruption of baseball.[6] The fad of wearing rolled-down stockings, the plague of rising rents, the deterioration of American literature, and a host of other so-called ills were traced to Jews.

Ford and his colleagues believed that the New York Kehilla, an organization formed by Jews in New York City in order to coordinate charity and educational efforts, was the secret government referred to in the *Protocols*. Presidents Wilson, Taft, and Hoover and Colonel Edward House, President Wilson's personal adviser, were its "willing tools."[7] Jews were responsible for society's ills, particularly the problems that had befallen rural and small-town society. The social dislocation suffered by these "genuine" Americans was the work of an urban plutocratic conspiracy at whose helm were Jews. Jews became the convenient scapegoat for societal changes that had impacted those institutions—farms and small towns—that represented traditional American social values.[8] These were the groups, as Steven Bronner has observed, that felt they were the losers in the modern struggle. Their lifestyle was at risk, and the *Protocols* explained why this had happened and, more important, who was behind it.[9] Readers of the *Dearborn Independent*, learned that "the enemy at home was the same as abroad"— the International Jew who pitted nation against nation and emerged as the only one to profit from the encounter.[10]

Within a short time after the articles began to appear, opposition to them began to coalesce. In December 1920, the Federal Council of Churches of Christ in America, which represented thirty denominations and fifty thousand churches, issued a resolution condemning the articles for "tending to create race prejudice and arouse animosity against our Jewish fellow-citizens and containing charges so preposterous as to be unworthy of credence."[11] A month later, in January 1921, 119 prominent Americans, including Woodrow Wilson and William Howard Taft, signed a petition entitled "The Perils of Racial Prejudice," which protested the introduction into American national

life of a "new and dangerous spirit" and condemned the anti-Semitism promulgated by the *Dearborn Independent* as "subversive of American ideals"
and as "un-American and un-Christian." Not surprisingly, American Jews
responded, as well. Not only did they work behind the scenes to help gal-
vanize the opposition, but also they refused to buy Ford cars. The palpable
anger of the community was exemplified by the announcement, in 1921, of a
parade honoring Chaim Weizmann and Albert Einstein, in Connecticut. The
announcement stipulated that "Positively No Ford Cars permitted in line."[12]

Stung by some of this criticism, Ford defended his reliance on the *Protocols* by arguing that "the Jews are the scavengers of the world. . . . Wherever
there's anything wrong with a country you'll find the Jews on the job there."
Carefully and deftly skirting the issue of whether the *Protocols* was a forgery,
Ford compared the document with what was happening in the world and
contended that the descriptions "fit in with what's going on" and that they
must, therefore, be true.[13] On Christmas day 1920, the paper declared that, if
the *Protocols* is a forgery "let them [the Jews] prove it."[14]

Ford, known as the "Great Simplifier," once wrote that "all the world needs
for the guidance of its life could be written on two pages of a child's copy-
book." Norman Cohn observes in *A Warrant for Genocide*, that a man who
believed that all the world's wisdom could be reduced to two pages was precisely the type of man who could also believe that all the "transformations
and upheavals" of the modern era could have a single explanation as promulgated in the *Protocols*.[15] It is a trait common among conspiracy theorists. (I
have seen it repeatedly among Holocaust deniers.)

Ford apparently anticipated that his attacks would be welcomed by Jews,
since he was addressing the problems associated with "bad" Jews, whom
"good" Jews would be happy to see exposed. So oblivious was he to the
broad nature of his attacks that, when a local rabbi to whom he would send
a new car every year refused to accept the car after the *Dearborn Independent* started the publication of the articles, Ford was perplexed by the rabbi's
rejection of his gift. He asked if he had done anything to insult him.[16]

Ford's anti-Semitism was striking not simply for its "viciousness" but also
for the way, Stephen Watts observes, in which it combined "ignorance, unpredictable absurdity, utter conviction, and naiveté." He would, for example,
instruct his mechanics not to use brass because it was a "Jew" metal. In the
1930s, he propounded the idea that Hitler was supported in his ascendance
to power "by wealthy [German] Jews in order to clean out the less prominent
ones."[17] It is notable that a man who made the automobile something that
was in the reach of the so-called common person and whose hallmark was

the introduction of mass production—the very symbol of industrial modernity—expressed such hostility toward cultural and social modernity.

The *Dearborn Independent* ended its anti-Semitic articles in January 1922. The penultimate article was titled "A Candid Address to Jews on the Jewish Problem." It urged Jews to mend their ways and "bring their misbehavior to an end" and expressed the hope that criticism would "arouse a sense of social responsibility among the Jews." The essay suggested that Jews control their worst instincts before others took the initiative to do so. The concluding essay was addressed to Gentiles. While disavowing violence, it counseled them to be alert to subversion by Jews—including the production of shoddy goods—and urged them to "stop it peacefully but firmly." The series ended with a call for the Church to be "un-Judaized and Christianized" and for the government to be "Americanized."[18]

When published in book form as *The International Jew*, the collected essays would eventually be translated into sixteen languages. By 1928, there were a half-million copies of the book in circulation. Ford also made it widely and very cheaply available in Europe, particularly in Germany. (While visiting a former college friend in Amman, Jordan, in April 1967, I saw a copy prominently displayed on the bookshelf in her living room. Her father, a Jordanian diplomat, had received an autographed copy from Ford himself.)

In the late 1920s, Ford faced a libel suit brought by a Jew, Aaron Shapiro, who had been attacked in the paper. The auto mogul had been warned that his reputation was being seriously compromised because of his involvement with the *Protocols*. After initially trying to fight the libel charge, Ford relented and issued an apology for the harm he had "unintentionally committed" as a result of the publication of the articles. Though the editor of the paper tried to deflect criticism of Ford by claiming that he had written the articles without Ford's knowledge or input, few believed this.[19]

The lawsuit brought against Ford by Shapiro helped reveal the role of Ford's associate Bill Cameron in the issue. Though Cameron claimed at the trial that he alone was responsible for the anti-Semitic material in the *Dearborn Independent*, it is hard to believe that he would have published such controversial stuff without Ford's approval. Subsequently, Cameron tried to blame the anti-Semitism on Edwin G. Pipp, a former editor of the *Detroit News* and an editor of the *Dearborn Independent*, but this makes little sense, since Pipp had resigned before the articles appeared and had issued a public challenge to Ford in his paper, *Pipp's Weekly*. Pipp pointed out that Ford had accepted the *Protocols* as truth without any evidence to support their claims. Pipp had also declared that no honest, sane man could live with the lies promulgated by the *Protocols*.

When interviewed in the 1950s, Cameron refused to declare the *Protocols* a forgery and noted that they had been published by the reputable British publisher Eyre and Spottiswoode, the King's printers. He observed that while they might be fiction when "laid alongside actual happenings in the world, why . . . there was a similarity between what was written in the book and what had occurred here and there." The fact that Cameron would make these comments in the 1950s suggests that his anti-Semitism during his days at the *Dearborn Independent* was deep and unrelenting.

Cameron, as editor of the *Dearborn Independent*, may well have been responsible for one of the more absurd anti-Semitic barbs to appear in the paper. In 1923, an unsigned article argued that, even though the Hebrew Scriptures identify the prophet Jeremiah as a Judean, it was doubtful that he was one because "seldom is a Jew named 'Jerry.'" Cameron can be connected to this absurd comment by a speech he gave in the 1950s in which he observed, "I have never found a Jew named after this great prophet of Judah, Jeremiah."

In examining the history of the *Protocols* in the United States, one cannot underestimate the impact of the concept of the International Jew. Building on centuries of anti-Semitism, it has set the framework for much of the conspiracy theory about Jews in the United States. There were, of course, anti-Semitic conspiracy theories before the *Protocols*, but, of this genre of anti-Semitic literature, the *Protocols*—despite being almost laughable—has had the longest and most active shelf life.

The Protocols *in a Post-Ford World: Theological Adaptations*

In the late 1930s, Father Charles Coughlin began to preach about the *Protocols*. He spoke about them on his radio show and published details of them in his journal, *Social Justice*. Copies of the *Protocols* were sold at his Church of Little Flower with the imprint "Christ Himself sponsored this little leaflet for your protection."

Though Coughlin was a Roman Catholic priest, his perspective on the *Protocols* was more political than theological. In contrast, the British Israelism movement and its American successors, particularly the Christian Identity movement, used the *Protocols* to buttress their preexisting theological view. These far- or hard-right Christian theological movements consider Jews "to be religious imposters who masquerade as a biblical people." Jews, according to their theological worldview, are "dissemblers who presented themselves as a sacred Biblical people [which] they were not and [they are also] participants in a secret organization bent on world conquest."[20] The *Protocols* is not the organizing principle behind these theological movements. However, these movements do link their theological worldview to the *Protocols*. Jews, the descendants of the tribe of Judah, are seen as the mischief-makers of ancient Israel and "its least progressive tribe." Jews, these movements believe, are marked by "darkness and perversity"; they are a people with whom "the rest of their nation could not live." This evil, these movements argue, is "unmasked" by the *Protocols*, the "most perfect plan for the destruction of Christian society ever brought to light."[21]

The Protocols' *American Nuances*

Beginning already with the publication of *The International Jew* and increasingly in the decades thereafter, the *Protocols* took on certain particularly American nuances. The attacks on Freemasonry, so prevalent in the European edition, were of far lesser importance in the United States—possibly because Ford was a Freemason. (There were attacks on Freemasons but not to the same extent as in other places.) On the other hand, in American editions of the *Protocols* and in literature espousing their *Weltanschauung*, the theme of Judeo-Bolshevism was dramatically highlighted. This was particularly true during the 1950s and 1960s, during the height of the Cold War and in the aftermath of the McCarthy era. It was during this period that the connection between Jews and Communism as first portrayed in the *Protocols* gained an American life of its own.

By the 1960s, the *Protocols* was regularly being used to buttress the argument that Jews were behind the threat posed to the United States by international Communism. The situation was apparently serious enough that, in 1963, the Subcommittee on Internal Security of the Senate Committee on the Judiciary decided to investigate the matter. The Subcommittee report observed that the *Protocols* was being used to convince Americans that "international communism is simply a manifestation of a world Jewish conspiracy which seeks to subjugate all the non-Jewish peoples of the world." The Senate report noted that, according to the American version of the *Protocols*, "the real enemy . . . [was] not international communism but 'international Jewry.'"

Even J. Edgar Hoover complained about the time his agency had to devote to dealing with these kinds of charges. Hoover traced the notion that there was a link between communism and Judaism and also between communists and Jews to the Soviet Union itself. According to Hoover, this was one of the way in which the Soviet Union aimed to create "division" and strife in the United States. Richard Helms, then Assistant Director of the CIA, testified before the Subcommittee and charged that contemporary communists were "skillful" in the "production and exploitation" of this forgery. The Senate report pointedly called attention to the ubiquitous nature of the *Protocols* by noting that a similar version of this document was being widely distributed in the Soviet Union but that, in contrast to the American edition, this one equated "international Jewry" with "international capitalism."[22] (One must marvel at the creativity of the anti-Semite.)

It is against this background of the *Protocols'* history in the United States that we can raise certain questions about their contemporary situation in the United States. The *Protocols* and the conspiracy theories they have spawned continue to spread in the United States. In general, however, it is groups on the extreme fringes of the political spectrum that espouse them most whole-heartedly. Some of these groups are so far out of the mainstream that the threat they pose is quite limited. (It is, however, possible for their views to creep into the mainstream. Such may well be the background for the Wal-Mart incident I mentioned at the outset.)

Far-right Christian extremists in America—many of them heirs to British Israelism—continue to rely on ideas propounded by *The International Jew* to argue that America is a Christian country that is threatened by anti-Christian elites that ally themselves with powerful people.[23] They speak of a "Great Conspiracy," a cabal "so far-reaching in scope and so audacious in purpose, that it staggers the imagination of men of good will."[24] Because they espouse not only an extreme form of anti-Semitism but also racism, their impact has been limited. They are, it might be somewhat crudely said, "too" open and overt about their prejudices. This tends to alienate Americans and repulse those who might otherwise intrigued by their ideas.

These groups can, their crude anti-Semitism notwithstanding, cause real harm, as was the case a number of years ago in Chicago, when an adherent of the Christian Identity movement engaged, on the Friday night of the July 4 weekend, in a multistate shooting spree, aiming at people of color and at Jews. The shooter was a follower of Matt Hale, the leader of a white separatist religion and the founder of the World Church of the Creator, who on April 6, 2005 was sentenced to a forty-year prison term for trying to hire someone to kill a federal judge. Both Hale and the shooter adhered to many of the ideas promulgated in *The International Jew*. Similarly, a man who attacked the Jewish Community Center in California's San Fernando Valley in 1999 was an adherent of the Christian Identity movement.

The Nation of Islam and its leader, Louis Farrakhan, have accused Jews of a broad array of conspiracies against African Americans. Among the wrongs the Nation of Islam has accused Jews of committing are infecting blacks with AIDS, conducting the slave trade, and using their enormous wealth to keep African Americans in poverty. Behind these charges stands the *Protocols*, which takes these disparate fictions and folds them into one all-encompassing historical fiction. The various acts may have been different. They may have been committed in different centuries and in different places but they all emanate from the same conspiratorial enterprise.[25]

Some of Farrakhan's charges are so absurd that they would be hilarious were it not for their potential to foment hatred and resentment. In 2000, Farrakhan conducted the following dialogue with a Dallas audience:

> FARRAKHAN: Is the Federal Reserve owned by the government?
> AUDIENCE: No.
> FARRAKHAN: Who owns the Federal Reserve?
> AUDIENCE: Jews.

(One imagines the reaction of both Farrakhan and his followers when President George W. Busy appointed Ben Bernanke as the head of the Federal Reserve. Bernanke's parents kept a kosher home. He learned Hebrew as a child, and his middle name is Shalom Moreover, this man succeeded Alan Greenspan. This is fodder for the conspiracy theorists. It does not get much better.) In a press conference at the National Press Club in 1998, Farrakhan attacked then National Security Adviser Sandy Berger, Secretary of State Madeleine Albright, Treasury Secretary Robert Rubin, and presidential adviser Rahm Emanuel. He told his listeners that "Every Jewish person that is around the president is a dual citizen of Israel and the United States of America. . . . And sometimes, we have to raise the question 'Are you more loyal to the state of Israel than you are to the best interests of the United States of America?'"[26]

The Nation of Islam has also been responsible for what might be called an African American–oriented version of the *Protocols*, *The Secret Relationship between Blacks and Jews*, which essentially holds Jews responsible for all the travails African Americans have encountered.[27] It is unclear how much Farrakhan's adherence to *Protocols*-like conspiracy theories will seep into the African American mainstream. This simple sounding and well integrated explanation, however historically absurd, is the kind of charge that has great viability because it offers a simple explanation for a broad array of problems and tragedies. In short, it makes "sense."

There are, of course, white supremacists, such as David Duke and his cohorts, for whom the ideas in the *Protocols* are virtually organizing principles. Their concept of ZOG, the Zionist Occupying Government, comes directly from the *Protocols*. References to the *Protocols* and charges drawn directly from them permeate the websites of right-wing, White supremacist, Christian identity groups.

There is yet another arena in which the influence of the *Protocols* is evident: Holocaust denial. The *Protocols* have shaped the Holocaust deniers' *Weltanschauung*. At the heart of deniers' arguments is the global conspiratorial view inherent in the *Protocols*. Only a body with the power of those described in the *Protocols* could pull such a hoax. For the deniers to be right, the Jews would have had to have control over the British, American, German, Polish, Soviet, and myriad other governments, as well as the Vatican and the Red Cross. They would have had to be able to plant documents in archives scattered throughout the world, from Washington to the Soviet Union. These documents would have had to be in the proper chronological and bureaucratic sequence and precisely conform to the myriad other documents in a collection, many of which, of course, have nothing to do with the destruction of the Jews.

These documents would also have to have had the correct military markings and have been prepared on the same typewriters and with the same ribbon as the other documents in these files. Jews would have had to convince individual Poles, Russians, Ukrainians, and a host of other nationalities to testify to these lies.

Only a group with the power of the International Jew could accomplish such a feat. The entire notion is so absurd and ludicrous that someone who is beguiled by it is precisely someone who would believe that the *Protocols*, or some aspect of it, is valid. (If, of course, these "Jews" had indeed forged all the evidence for the Holocaust, one is compelled to ask a simple question: Why did not these accomplished forgerss simply prepare the very document that deniers are always demanding—the famed and certainly nonexistent Hitler order for the launching of the Holocaust?)[28]

Currently, however, Holocaust denial in the United States is at its lowest ebb in many years. This is a result, at least in part, of the legal defeat suffered by David Irving, once one of the deniers' leading figures. During my legal battle with him, particularly when he tried to paint me as part of a worldwide Jewish conspiracy dedicated to destroying him, I frequently thought back to the *Protocols*. Without directly mentioning the *Protocols*, David Irving was evoking them when he launched into long attacks on Jews and Jewish organizations, which he collectively labeled "the enemies of truth," and when he described me on his website as "the gold-tipped spearhead of the enemies of truth who hired her . . . to destroy me, my reputation, and my legitimacy as an historian."[29] (He is a misogynist; therefore, I, as a woman, could not control this conspiracy. I, as a woman, could only be lackey of this conspiratorial effort, not someone in a policymaking role—hence, my having been "hired.")

Some of these more extreme fringe groups have engaged in some counterintuitive tactical alliances in their efforts to spread their views. We have seen some strange bedfellows in this regard. Followers of Lyndon LaRouche have worked together with the Nation of Islam staff to promote the claim of a Jewish conspiracy.[30] Certain Black Nationalist groups have aligned themselves with Holocaust denial, despite the fact that most deniers have demonstrated explicitly racist views. David Irving, for instance, talks about feeling queasy when he sees blacks playing for the English cricket team. He complained, in a private speech to his followers, about seeing one of "them" reading "our news to us." (He was clearly referring to people of color, since, in his next sentence, he said, "If I was a chauvinist, I would even say I object even to seeing women reading our news to us." His audience's views and attitudes were reflected, one could argue, in the fact that these statements were met with cheers of "Hear, Hear," applause, and laughter.)[31]

Even stranger alliances have occurred around the war in Iraq. For example, an article by Gore Vidal appeared in the publication published by the right-wing extremist and "father" of American Holocaust denial Willis Carto. Pat Buchanan's publication had Ralph Nader on its cover. These groups and individuals, whose views on everything else are diametrically opposed, seem to agree on the nefarious deeds of Israel and its Jewish supporters worldwide and especially in the United States. They hold Jews responsible for the war in Iraq. The debate over the war opened up a dialogue between these different types of anti-Semites. Though the two sides did not necessarily agree on the nuances of the threat, they agree that that Jews, particularly as embodied in a small cabal of neocons with powerful positions in the Bush administration, had an inordinate role in making this war happen and did it despite knowing that it was contrary to America's best interests.

These groups do not necessarily parrot the same kind of anti-Semitism and global view of Jews power that are propounded by *The International Jew* or the *Protocols*. This is particularly so on the left, who trace the war in Iraq back to Jewish neocons and supporters of Israel. However, those on the left who trace the war back to supporters of Israel tend not to posit that Jews have an all-encompassing control over a broad array of societal institutions.

On some level, this more narrow and tightly focused kind of claim poses a greater danger. Because it is less global, it sounds less paranoid, less conspiratorial, and more plausible. While Americans have been susceptible to conspiracy theories—witness, for example, the debate over JFK's assassination—they tend to shy away from broad, all-encompassing, overarching conspiratorial theories. This more narrowly focused form of *Protocol*-like anti-Semitism is more palatable to many Americans.

The growth of anti-Semitism that we have seen in other countries has not been replicated in the United States. At the same time, we must wonder whether, as the United States becomes a more ethnically diverse society, some of those who come from different lands will bring with them an adherence to *Protocol*-like ideas. This is particularly a matter of concern with regard to the growing Arab and Muslim population in this country; many of these immigrants come from places where the *Protocols* and its conspiracy theories are taken seriously. It is hard to know what will happen as these groups grow in number. It is also hard to predict what will happen if the United States faces another major terrorist incident. In truth, with the growth of the Internet, it is difficult and somewhat anachronistic to speak of national borders. The words of an imam in Cairo or a preacher in Idaho can be heard in real time in Dearborn or Dubai, as well as in an array of other places. .

I end with two cautionary notes. I would argue that, while the conspiracy theories promulgated by the *Protocols* have had but a limited impact in the United States, we who worry about such things must remain alert not so much for the *Protocols* itself as for what Chip Berlet calls their analogs. It is too easy for people to have their *weltanschauung* colored by these myths.

That is one cautionary note. The other is that, even as we are alert to the *Protocols* and to the conspiracy theories they spawn, we must be careful not to become our own worst enemies by aggrandizing the potential of that threat, thereby creating a self-fulfilling prophecy. We who pay attention to the *Protocols* must assiduously avoid giving this century-old forgery an importance and publicity it would otherwise not get. In short, let us—for possibly all the right reasons—not do for the *Protocols* what the American Jewish community did for Mel Gibson's *Passion of the Christ*.

NOTES

1. http://www.tolerance.org/news/article_tol.jsp?id=1070.
2. Steven Watts, *The People's Tycoon: Henry Ford and the American Century* (New York: Knopf, 2005), 377.
3. Ibid.

4. Hadassa Ben-Itto, *The Lie That Wouldn't Die: The Protocols of the Elders of Zion* (London: Vallentine, 2005), 61.

5. Richard S. Levy, "Introduction: The Protocols of the Elders of Zion," *A Lie and a Libel: The History of the Protocols of the Elders of Zion* (Lincoln: University of Nebraska Press, 1995), 26. The paper did not mention the threat of Freemasonry, which played a major role in European editions.

6. *International Jew*, 3:70, 73, 75–76, 83, as quoted in Leo P. Ribuffo, "Henry Ford and The International Jew," *American Jewish History* 68 (1980): 448, 452. See also Robert Singerman, "The American Career of the *Protocols of the Elders of Zion*," *American Jewish History* 71 (1981): 48–78.

7. Watts, *People's Tycoon*, 378–381; Ben Itto, *The Lie*, 63; Norman Cohn, *Warrant for Genocide* (London: Eyre and Spottiswoode, 1967), 163.

8. Michael Barkun, *Religion and the Racist Right: The Origins of the Christian Identity Movement* (Chapel Hill: University of North Carolina Press, 1997), 34.

9. Stephen E. Bronner in this volume.

10. Stephen E. Bronner, *A Rumor about the Jews: Reflections on Anti-Semitism and the Protocols of the Learned Elders of Zion* (New York: St. Martin's Press, 2000), 96.

11. Ben Itto, *The Lie*, 63–64.

12. Ibid.

13. Watts, *People's Tycoon*, 381.

14. Barkun, *Religion and the Racist Right*, 39.

15. Levy, "Introduction," 28; Cohn, *Warrant for Genocide*, 164.

16. Watts, *People's Tycoon*, 390; Ribuffo, "Henry Ford," 473; Barkun, *Religion and the Racist Right*, 34ff, 37, 39.

17. Watts, *People's Tycoon*, 383.

18. Ibid., 380.

19. Ben Itto, *The Lie*, 69. An interesting and revealing postscript to Ford's apology is the fact that, shortly after issuing it, the advertising agencies that handled Ford cars were told to spend about 12 percent of their budget on Yiddish and Anglo-Jewish newspapers.

20. British Israelism and the *Protocols* had already been linked by the *Dearborn Independent* in an article on Christmas Day 1920. It declared that "chosenness is not warranted by the Scriptures themselves." Barkun, *Religion and the Racist Right*, 39; Ribuffo, "Henry Ford," 455.

21. "Gentile Fall Involved in Hope of Jewish Rule,"*Dearborn Independent*, Christmas Day, 1920, pp. 8–9.

22. "*Protocols of the Elders of Zion*: A Fabricated 'Historic' Document," Report Prepared by the Subcommittee to Investigate the Administration of the Internal Security Act to the Committee on the Judiciary, U.S. Senate, 1964, iii.

23. Barkun, *Religion and the Racist Right*, 39; Cohn, *Warrant for Genocide*, 236–238.

24. Barkun, *Religion and the Racist Right*, 143.

25. Levy, "Introduction," 39.

26. This exchange was reported by the *Dallas Observer* online, August 10, 2000. National Press Club, October 19, 1998, http://www.knowledgerush.com/kr/encyclopedia/Nation_of_Islam_anti-semitism.

27. For a critique of *The Secret Relationship between Blacks and Jews*, see Harold Brackman, *Ministry of Lies: The Truth behind the Nation of Islam's "The Secret Relationship between Blacks and Jews"* (New York: Four Walls Eight Windows, 1994), http://www.h-net.msu.edu/~antis/papers/occasional.papers.html.

28. I have been intrigued by the fact that often this simple question, asked of someone who is confused by deniers' arguments and inclined to think that there might be some grounds to them, illustrates the absurdity of the deniers' claims.

29. David Irving, "Action Report," 1999, http://www.fpp.co.uk/Inner/Circle.html.

30. http://www.publiceye.org/tooclose/protocol.html.

31. David Irving, speech to the Clarendon Club, September 19, 1992; *Irving v. Penguin UK and Lipstadt*, K4, Tab. 5, 10–11. This excerpt may also be found at www.hdot.org; see evidence/David Irving:APoliticalSelf-Portrait/2.d.

14

Protocols to the Left, Protocols to the Right

Conspiracism in American Political Discourse at the Turn of the Second Millennium

CHIP BERLET

In the new millennium, conspiracist claims have regularly inserted themselves into public discourse and originated from ideologies ranging across the political spectrum. This is nothing new. Contemporary purveyors included Tea Partiers, 9/11 "Truthers," and armed militia units that feared that President Barack Obama plans to build a global government and impose a "New World Order." What is particularly striking is the way in which conspiracy theories have become a common feature of public discourse and the way in which criticism of Jewish power and Israeli influence in the United States sometimes echoes the calumnies in the forged hoax document known as the *Protocols of the Learned Elders of Zion*. What is depressing is the failure of most societal leaders to confront these destructive tendencies.[1]

President George W. Bush, a conservative Republican, was the target of conspiracy theories from the left and right. Conspiracist critics accused Bush of plotting to create a North American Union that would merge the United States, Mexico, and Canada into a single federated unit similar to the European Union.[2] This claim spread so far and so fast that a reporter raised it in a question at a 2007 press conference where then President Bush was appearing with Prime Minister Harper of Canada and President Calderón of Mexico.[3] The matter became an issue in the 2008 presidential campaign.[4]

Then the conspiracy theorists transferred their targeted scapegoating to President Obama. Was Obama a secret Muslim? Was he born not in Hawaii but in Kenya? Was it possible that Obama was the Antichrist warned about in Christian biblical prophecy.[5] Was he really "the Manchurian president," installed by leftist Democrats, as one book warned?[6]

This chapter argues that all of these conspiracy theories and many more flow out of a history of conspiracist storytelling in the United States.[7] Over time, these story lines have become tropes integrating and adapting the claims made in the *Protocols* as a core yet often obscured source.

Some contemporary conspiracy theorists directly mention the *Protocols* and claim they are a true document. Therefore, it is not surprising to find direct mention of the *Protocols* on ultraright websites, especially those affiliated with neo-Nazis and the racist Christian Identity religious movement. Yet, mentions of the *Protocols* also appear across the political spectrum, as well as in New Age and UFO subcultures.[8]

Others conspiracy theorists make an indirect reference to the *Protocols* in an anti-Semitic context, where the conspiracy theorist suggests that readers or listeners further explore the claims, sometimes with a link to an overtly anti-Semitic explanation of the *Protocols* that assumes their validity.

The appearance of the *Protocols* on the political left occurs mainly on Internet discussions through listserves, on unmoderated websites (such as the various Indymedia sites and its many autonomous city affiliates), and on comments posted to blogs. In many cases, this represents attempts by those on the political right to entice those on the political left to adopt anti-Semitic ideas. However, anti-Semitic conspiracism has become such a problem on the political left that, in 2004, the international progressive magazine *New Internationalist* published a special issue on "Judeophobia," including a refutation of the *Protocols*.[9]

Michael Barkun points out that the "current gambit of many" who cite the *Protocols* is "to claim that they 'really' come from" the minutes of some other secretive group, rather than the Jews.[10] According to Barkun, "It's hard to tell whether they actually believe this or are simply trying to sanitize a discredited text. I don't see that it makes much difference, since they leave the actual, anti-Semitic text unchanged. The result is to give it credibility and circulation when it deserves neither."[11]

The Protocols *as Archetype*

Scholars have documented in this collection and elsewhere that the *Protocols* is a forgery and a hoax document with content plagiarized from earlier texts.[12] There are a number of different versions of the *Protocols*, with different numbered sections, and their authors may have assembled the allegations from a base document that researchers have never found.[13] Nevertheless, the various versions of the *Protocols* tend to have the same general set of allegations:

- Jews are behind a plan for global conquest.
- Jews work through Masonic lodges.
- Jews use liberalism to weaken church and state.
- Jews control the press.
- Jews work through radicals and revolutionaries.
- Jews manipulate the economy, especially through banking monopolies and the power of gold.
- Jews encourage issuing paper currency not tied to the gold standard.
- Jews promote financial speculation and use of credit.
- Jews replace traditional educational curriculum to discourage independent thinking.
- Jews encourage immorality among Christian youth.
- Jews use intellectuals to confuse people.
- Jews control "puppet" governments both through secret allies and by blackmailing elected officials.
- Jews weaken laws through liberal interpretations.
- Jews will suspend civil liberties during an emergency and then make the measures permanent.

The *Protocols* themselves claim that the Freemason fraternal order is part of the conspiracy, with the Jewish elites behind the Freemasons. Another popular variant argues that the secretive Illuminati group infiltrated the Freemasons and continues to control the conspiracy.[14]

Daniel Pipes suggests that the two main branches of contemporary conspiracism (Jews and Freemasons) have "parallel histories" and track back to "conspiracist traditions" that emerged during Christianity's "Crusading era." Pipes dates this to "1096 for the Jews, 1307 for secret societies," and notes that the parallelism extends to "basic themes, mutual influences, shared beliefs, and overlapping culprits."[15]

The Freemason/Illuminati and Jewish conspiracy theories begin as primarily right-wing attempts to defend the status quo. Conspiracists, however, have used similar allegations to attack the status quo. For example, the early-20th-century *Protocols* were derived in part from the late-18th-century conspiracy theories about the Freemasons and Illuminati; yet, between the emergences of these two core genres, there were left-wing populist conspiracy theories in the late 19th century about the "Elite Plutocrats" and the "Financial Octopus." In all cases, however, there is a merger of populist anti-elite rhetoric with fears of subversion and betrayal. These fears propel mobilization and political participation among predominantly middle-class white people who see themselves as the real productive class in American society.[16]

The ease with which conspiracism spreads through the body politic in the United States can be explained to a great extent by giving proper weight to the history of apocalyptic, millennial, and millenarian currents coursing throughout U.S. history.[17] This is especially true when alienated partisans on the right merge dualistic conspiracy theories, demonization, and scapegoating to justify apocalyptic aggression.[18]

The Protocols *and the "Analogs"*

Many conspiracy theories replicate the structure and the essential accusations found in the *Protocols* without directly mentioning them by name. Stephen Bronner calls these conspiracy theories "analogs" of the *Protocols*.[19] Some of these analogs are thinly veiled. For example, there are anti-Semitic claims of a vast conspiracy by Jews that structurally replicate the *Protocols* without mentioning the hoax document. Another way conspiracy theorists try to avoid the label of anti-Semitism is to argue there is a vast conspiracy by the "Rothschild family" or the "Khazars" or some other entity used to suggest that not all Jews are part of the conspiracy or that the conspirators are "not the real Jews." Often purveyors of this line accompany their allegations with claims they are not anti-Semitic.

Coded anti-Semitic claims of a vast conspiracy by "Zionists" or other terms used as stand-in for "Jews" in a conspiracist context are more complicated to unravel. Not all criticisms of Zionism or Israeli government policies are anti-Semitic, but clearly some criticisms are attempts to hide the underlying anti-Semitic conspiracism about Jewish global power or skullduggery. Some in the intended audience, however, are likely to see certain phrases as a clear (if coded) reference to Jews. Phrases such as "international bankers," "banksters," and "cosmopolitan elites" are typical in this genre, and there are many variations.

Some authors seem blithely unaware when their criticism of U.S. policy in the Middle East and the U.S. relationship to Israel veers off into anti-Semitic stereotyping that exaggerates the power and influence of an "Israel lobby." This happens in not only the political left and the political right but also in the center. An example of the latter is the article by two relatively conservative centrist scholars on "the lobby" and U.S. foreign policy that created a furor in 2006.[20] The essay mentions how important it is to avoid anti-Semitic stereotyping, especially given the history of the *Protocols*—and then, some critics observed, the original study replicates in broad strokes the basic tropes of the *Protocols*.[21]

Still, it needs to be stated clearly that conspiracist claims of a vast conspiracy by a named scapegoat other than the Jews, with no conscious (or obvious) attempt to implicate Jews, are the most common form of conspiracist allegation in the new millennium.

Jews as the Puppet Masters

It is easy to locate conspiracy narratives that directly mention the *Protocols* or in which there is a claim that replicates the *Protocols* by asserting a long-standing conspiracy of elite Jews to achieve global control. They appear in forms I divide into analytical categories: "neo-Nazi Judeophobia," "generic anti-Semitism," "the LaRouche network," and the "eclectic, New Age, UFO genre."

Neo-Nazi Judeophobia

The National Alliance is a leading neo-Nazi group that cites the *Protocols*. Its founder, the late William Pierce, stated:

> But Jews seem to have a boom-or-bust mentality. They seem as unable to moderate their behavior as Bill Clinton is unable to keep his zipper up . . . they have moved to tighten their grip on [Russia] by having one of their own installed as prime minister. . . . Amazing, isn't it? It's almost like something right out of the Protocols of the Learned Elders of Zion, this grasping, leering, insatiable greed of theirs.[22]

Other mentions of the *Protocols* are on the website.[23] At various times, the neo-Nazi Christian Identity group Aryan Nations has cited the *Protocols* and has even posted the entire text of the Marsden English-language translation of the Nilus version. A power struggle within Aryan Nations has resulted in two competing factions with websites in 2006, but both cite the *Protocols*.[24]

The August Kreis III faction of Aryan Nations lists as "recommended reading, the 'Protocols of the Learned Elders of Zion' from 1899, minutes of their last century meeting."[25] At various times, the website has carried the full text.[26]

The Jonathan Williams faction of Aryan Nations explains:

> The Protocols were (are) the secret minutes of the First Zionist Congress in Basel, Switzerland in 1897. . . . The Protocols detail a plan for Jewish domination over Gentiles by controlling money and using it to subvert Christian governments. Corrupt, Clinton-like politicians are hired to rule over Gentiles by the Jews. The ultimate goal of such scheming is the establishment of a Jewish-controlled Marxist state. Some say that the Protocols are the blueprint for today's New World Order.[27]

This website also contains excerpts from the German Nazi publication *Der Stürmer*, which mention the *Protocols*, including one 1933 article titled "Secret Plans against Germany Revealed," which charges:

> The non-Jew has no idea of the scope of this struggle. He does not know the Jewish people's secret goals, or the crimes they have committed over four millennia to reach those goals, or the enormous danger it faces if these goals are revealed before they can be realized. The secret goals of the Jewish people are laid out in the "Protocols of the Elders of Zion." The *Stürmer* has written about them more than a hundred times. They contain the Jewish plan for world conquest.[28]

Williams warns that Jews make it clear in "the pages of the 'Protocols' about the need to possess Gold. Their sense of stability comes from their greed. Their exploitation of WHITE History, and their exploitation of the Negro for purposes of entertainment, shows their willingness to serve their Wicked Keeper at all costs."[29]

A number of online bookstores that cater to the extreme right, neo-Nazis, and conspiracists sell print copies of the Marsden translation of the *Protocols*.[30]

Generic Anti-Semitism

Generic anti-Semites leave their feet firmly planted on Mother Earth, but some also use the technique of claiming that most Jews are dupes. The Populists American website explains that the real "enemy of all mankind" is the "Zionist Jews" who are "Not to be confused with other Jews."[31] The website posts the text of the *Protocols* with a disclaimer typical of this genre:

We cannot swear that these PROTOCOLS are the work of Zionist Jews, but as you read these bits and pieces, you can see that everything they say here has come to pass in one way or another. You can also see what they have planned for us in the future. Even if the Zionist did not write them they are following them to the letter.[32]

The website also features the text of the classic anti-Semitic tract "How Jewry Turned England into a Plutocratic State."[33]

The late Eustace Mullins attempted a coded form of anti-Semitism in some of his work, such as *World Order: Our Secret Rulers*, while in other texts his anti-Semitism is vivid, as in *The Biological Jew* and *The Secret Holocaust*.[34] Mullin's *Secrets of the Federal Reserve* should set off warning bells about possible anti-Semitic conspiracism, but it is cited by conspiracists who are shocked when they are accused of using material from an author who writes anti-Semitic material.[35] Some of the claims in Pat Robertson's *The New World Order: It Will Change the Way You Live* track back to classic anti-Semitic texts, including the work of Mullins on the Federal Reserve.[36]

Like Mullins, John Coleman writes in two styles.[37] Coleman wrote pamphlets for the extreme right anti-Semitic Christian Defense League but also wrote the *Conspirators Hierarchy: The Story of the Committee of 300*, which avoids naming Jews as the primary font of the conspiracy.[38] America West published *Conspirators Hierarchy* and publishes material on UFOs and some messages from Commander Hatonn. In *Conspirators Hierarchy*, Coleman has an elaborate flow chart that lists as co-conspirators Royal Families, Zionism, Communism, Fabianism, the CIA, the Mossad, Freemasonry, the Rhodes/Milner Group, the United Nations, the One World Government Church, and "9 Unknown Men."[39]

Dennis King notes that Coleman's work echoes the claims of the Lyndon LaRouche network, especially concerning the role of the British Tavistock Institute. King adds that Mullins interacted cordially with the LaRouche network, and Mullins served as a contributing editor for Coleman's former periodical *World Economic Review*.[40]

The LaRouche Network

In 1978, perennial presidential candidate Lyndon LaRouche stated that there was "a hard kernel of truth" in the *Protocols*.[41] A book issued that same year by his publishing house cited the *Protocols* and stated, "The Order of Zion was simply the Jewish division of the Most Venerable Order of St. John of

Jerusalem, the London-centered chivalric order and secret society." This allegedly linked into the assassination of Lincoln, the Rothschild family, the freemasons, B'nai B'rith, the Ku Klux Klan, and the Mafia.[42]

While the LaRouche network eventually backed away from these obvious and overt anti-Semitic references, it continued to peddle conspiracy theories that implicated not just the Rothschild family but scores of other Jewish political, business, and religious leaders in a grand conspiracy that stretched back to Babylon.[43]

Today, the LaRouche network is one of the world's largest distributors of conspiracist literature based on coded anti-Semitism rooted in the false allegations of the *Protocols*. A recent series of booklets offers good examples of coded rhetoric. The series is titled "Children of Satan" and includes these individual titles: *The "Ignoble Liars" behind Bush's No-Exit War*, *The Beast-Men*, and *The Sexual Congress for Cultural Fascism*.[44] The text of the series links George W. Bush and Dick Cheney with the political faction of neoconservatives in language that discusses the role of Jewish intellectuals and Jewish political advisers in stereotypic ways. The phrases "Children of Satan" and the "Beast-Men" echo the rhetoric of medieval blood libels and accusations that the Jews will be agents of Satan in the Christian end-times. According to the LaRouchites, some 400,000 copies of the first booklet were distributed.[45]

Eclectic, New Age, UFO Genre

On his eclectic "Three World Wars" website, Michael B. Haupt warns of the conspiracy of global elites and highlights the educational value of the *Protocols*:

> The Protocols of the Learned Elders of Zion is a document which should be read by all. No other single document provides us with such a clear understanding of why the world is gradually moving towards a One World Government, controlled by an irreproachable hidden hand. In The Protocols, we are given clear insights as to why so many incomprehensible political decisions are made in both local, national and international politics, which seem to continually work against the favor of the masses and in favor of the vested interests of the banking/industrial cartel—the global power elite.[46]

Haupt sees Republicans, Democrats, and most world leaders, as part of the plot and links to another website where Henry Makow proclaims of the *Pro-*

tocols that "the equation with anti Semitism is really a ploy to divert attention away from this master plan."[47]

On the aptly named Rumor Mill News website, the aspect of the analog is discernable even through the garbled rhetoric. According to Rayelan Allan, the conspiracy actually consists of two factions:

> Faction One is the New World Order, made up of the International bankers, the 300 un-named families who also own our Federal Reserve Banking System. These families are descended ideologically AND biologically from the Rothschild funded Illuminati. Faction One also created the Corporations. . . ." "Corporations were created by the King of England who was owned and controlled by the Rothschilds."
>
> Faction Two is descended from the King of Bavaria, the Knights Templars and the German Abwher. Faction Two was created by men whose countries had been destroyed by the New World Order. . . ." In 1776, the King of Bavaria blew the whistle on the planned take-over of the monarchies of Europe by the Illuminati/Rothschilds. As a result, the NWO, which expected to go "online" in 1776, had to retreat to the shadows and build up their strength for their "next planned world-takeover."[48]

On this site, however, a number of discussions posted by readers cite the *Protocols* directly, including one posted by the indefatigable Henry Makow (mentioned earlier), who runs the *Protocols*-touting website linked to by Haupt.[49] Readers of the Rumor Mill News website debate whether the *Protocols* is a hoax in an online forum.[50]

Conspiracists such as David Icke and the acolytes of the cosmic voyager Commander Hatonn extend the conspiracy into outer space. Michael Barkun examines Hatonn and the *Protocols* in his chapter in this volume.[51] David Icke is worth mentioning for his ability to draw large crowds of New Age devotees to lectures on several continents.[52] According to Icke, space alien lizard reptilians are behind the conspiracy, and, therefore, his website explains:

> Since 1990 David Icke has been on an amazing journey of self and collective discovery to establish the real power behind apparently "random" world events like 9/11 and the "war on terrorism." Here he reveals that a network of interbreeding bloodlines manipulating through their web of interconnecting secret societies have been pursuing an agenda for thousands of years to impose a global centralised fascist state with total control and surveillance of the population.[53]

TABLE 14.1

Scapegoated Villains		Feared Outcomes
Jews	Vatican	One World Government
Freemasons	Jesuits	New World Order
Plutocrats	Muslims	End Times/Armageddon
Secret Elites	Trilateralists	Globalist Corporate Rule
Rockefellers	Bilderbergers	Natural Disaster
Reds	Fascists	Plagues/AIDS
United Nations	People of Color	Nuclear Meltdown
Feminists	Gays and Lesbians	Technical Collapse
Abortionists	Space Aliens	Marshall Law/Repression
Secret Team	Agents of Satan	Economic Collapse

One or more of the "Scapegoated Villains" can be accused of plotting one or more of the "Feared Outcomes."

Icke links this conspiracy to the Illuminati, certain factions of Jews and Freemasons, and the *Protocols*. According to Barkun:

> Icke is certainly the most adroit synthesizer of these ideas. He also tries to position himself as "beyond left and right," as though he was above "mere" politics. He also effects a sympathy for groups he denigrates, claiming, for example, that most Jews and Masons are innocent dupes whom he wants to save from their conniving leaders. This strikes me as, to say the least, disingenuous, but it positions him to claim that he's a victim when, for example, he is charged with anti-Semitism.[54]

Apocalyptic Conspiracism Spreads

Conspiracists modify some of the allegations found in the *Protocols* in order to meet various political needs during the historic epochs in which the authors live. As shown in Table 14.1, the named scapegoats change. The targets of the nefarious conspirators change. The plotline remains the same.

Through a review of published texts, it is possible to identity more than twenty distinct periods in which conspiracism flourished in the public square in the United States:[55]

- 1797–1800 Freemasons/Illuminati (Europe)
- 1798–1802 Freemasons/Illuminati (U.S.)
- 1820–1844 Anti-Masonry (Early Nativism)
- 1834–1860 Catholic Immigrants (Nativism, Know Nothings)
- 1830–1866 Slave Power Conspiracy
- 1873–1905 Plutocrats and Bankers ("The Octopus")
- 1903–1920 Jews (*Protocols*—Russia)
- 1919–1935 The International Jew (*Protocols*—Britain and U.S.)
- 1919–1925 Anarchists and Bolsheviks
- 1932–1946 Bankers, Liberal Collectivists, Reds, and Jews
- 1940–1950 Reds and the End-Times
- 1950–1960 Liberal Internationalists and Reds
- 1958–1968 Civil Rights Conspiracy
- 1960–1970 "Secret Kingmakers"
- 1963–1970 Assassination Conspiracy Theories
- 1960–1980 Sex, Drugs, and Rock and Roll
- 1970–1990 Secret Elites
- 1975– Secular Humanism: Feminists and Homosexuals
- 1986– 1990 "Secret Team"
- 1990– New World Order
- 2001– (Post-9/11) Cheney/Bush Neocon Terror Complicity
- 2001– (Post-9/11) Cheney/Bush Neocon/Mossad/Zionists/Jews Terror Complicity
- 2001– (Post-9/11) Islamic Menace, Cultural Barbarism, "Clash of Civilizations"
- 2006– Bush Building the North American Union
- 2008– Obama and the "Birther" Conspiracy
- 2009– Obama and the Liberal/Communist/Fascist Conspiracy

Variations on a Theme

In Table 14.2, we can see how variations on the basic theme of the *Protocols* emerge through a process of amalgamation and accretion. Each conspiracist blends his own set of conspirators. This illustrates what Kelly calls "fusion paranoia." Barkun refers to an "improvisational style" used by con-

TABLE 14.2. Growth of Analogs and Analogies 1984–2009

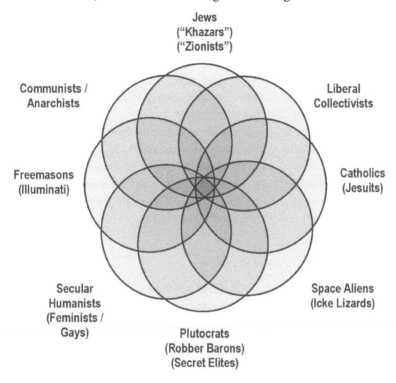

Jews
("Khazars")
("Zionists")

Communists /
Anarchists

Liberal
Collectivists

Freemasons
(Illuminati)

Catholics
(Jesuits)

Secular
Humanists
(Feminists /
Gays)

Space Aliens
(Icke Lizards)

Plutocrats
(Robber Barons)
(Secret Elites)

spiracy theorists to construct their narratives.[56] Table 14.2 lists eight typical scapegoats targeted by conspiracy theorists. Some conspiracists are purists, blaming just Jews or plutocrats for despoiling the ideal community. Others prefer to combine scapegoats on their plate so there is overlap. Jews, Freemasons, and communists are a popular combination. David Icke seems to favor plutocrats, space aliens, and Jews. There are an infinite number of possible scapegoats; thus, there are an infinite number of variations.

In the mid-1980s, a number of conspiracist claims clamored for public attention. Many conspiracy theories that did not mention the *Protocols* or Jews still replicated their basic structure and claims. These are the "analogs" of the *Protocols* according to Bronner.

Neo-Nazis are generally willing to openly cite the *Protocols* and engage in vicious Jew-bashing and to make statements about Israel that far exceed any legitimate criticisms. The ultra-right sometimes does use analog rhetoric about the "Zionists" or the "Mossad," but this is often used as an introductory recruitment device before the real storyline of the *Protocols* is revealed. "We even heard one racist leader suggest that conspiracy theories about Obama and the government are a soft way to get people interested in becoming active in building a white homeland," reported Travis McAdam of the Montana Human Rights Network in 2009.[57]

What about conspiracy theories from other types of groups? They appear in four main demographic subsectors in the United States: right-wing patriots and populists, apocalyptic Christian evangelicals and fundamentalists, the black community, and the Political Left.

In an attempt to limit my already voluminous hate mail intake, I make the following disclaimer: This study does not assert that all people who promote conspiracy theories are anti-Semitic, anti-Catholic, anti-Muslim, racist, on the political right, or on the political left or that they secretly encourage people to believe in the *Protocols*. Nor does it mean to imply these things in a sneaky way. Sometimes an analog is just an analog.

Right-Wing Patriots and Populists

For many years, the John Birch Society (JBS) and other Patriot Movement groups ran bookstores that sold republished editions of the anti-Freemason books by Robison and Barruel, which were published originally in the late 1790s. As late as 2006, the JBS still listed the books online in an "Annotated Bibliography."[58] The outlines of the Patriot view of the conspiracy can be traced with rare economy in the section headings of the JBS bibliography:

- Order of the Illuminati
- French Revolution and Napoleon
- Survival and Continuity of the Illuminati
- Communist Movement: Illuminist Spawn
- Nazism's Illuminist Origins
- World War I and the League of Nations
- The Bolshevik Coup in Russia
- New Deal and Soviet Infiltration of Executive Branch
- Bringing on World War II
- The United Nations and the New World Order,
- Domestic and Foreign Policy Elite
- Maintenance and Expansion of Communist Power since 1917
- Communist Strategy for Conquest
- U.S. Foreign Policy after 1945: Promoting Communism Everywhere
- Glasnost and Perestroika: The KGB's Massive Deception since 1989

It is still a communist plot, but the communists are just one guise of the Illuminati and the secret elites, who also control Wall Street, Barack Obama, Hillary Clinton, and even George W. Bush when he was in office.

Some of the books listed in this JBS resource (especially the work of the prolific anti-Semite Elizabeth Dilling) perpetuate stereotypes about Jews, banking, and global power. In terms of public discourse, however, when the JBS blames the secret elites and plutocrats for the vast conspiracy, the organization is not covertly blaming the Jews.[59] A favorite theme of the JBS is that the liberal globalists are planning a New World Order run by a totalitarian One World Government.

Other books that plow the same field include G. Edward Griffin's *The Creature from Jekyll Island: A Second Look at the Federal Reserve* and Jim Marrs's *Rule by Secrecy: The Hidden History That Connects the Trilateral Commission, the Freemasons, and the Great Pyramids.*[60] Like others in this genre, Marrs claims that he is neither left nor right but that he stands for truth.

In the Patriot Movement analysis, liberals, internationalists, big corporations, and the CIA all conspire together to subvert the proper isolationist and protectionist nationalism envisioned by the founding fathers. This was a subtext of the McCarthy period and a theme of the 1973 book by L. Fletcher Prouty, *The Secret Team: The CIA and Its Allies in Control of the U.S. and the World.*[61]

In 1997, Phyllis Schlafly's Eagle Forum produced a video titled "Global Governance: The Quiet War against American Independence," which spun the basic Patriot Movement theory of the conspiracy. According to the box, the video featured appearances by John Ashcroft, U.S. Senator, Missouri; Jeane Kirkpatrick, former U.S. Ambassador to the United Nations; Jesse Helms, Chairman, Senate Foreign Relations Committee; Helen Chenoweth, U.S. Representative, Idaho; and Patrick Buchanan, syndicated columnist and cohost of the television program *Crossfire*.

Apocalyptic Christian Evangelicals and Fundamentalists

The idea that liberal globalists are planning a New World Order run by a totalitarian One World Government on behalf of Satan is common among certain apocalyptic Christian evangelicals and fundamentalists. Between 1990 and 1997, scores of books on the subject appeared on the shelves of Christian bookstores.[62]

Here are some titles: Donald S. McAlvany, *Toward a New World Order*; Dave Hunt, *Global Peace and the Rise of Antichrist*; William T. Still, *New World Order: The Ancient Plan of Secret Societies*; John F. Walvoord, *Arma-*

geddon, Oil and the Middle East Crisis; Pat Robertson, *The New World Order*; Gary H. Kah, *En Route to Global Occupation*; Peter LaLonde, *One World under Antichrist: Globalism, Seducing Spirits and Secrets of the New World Order*; Peter Lalonde and Paul Lalonde, [*Racing toward*] *The Mark of the Beast*; Michael D. Evans, *Jerusalem Betrayed: Ancient Prophecy and Modern Conspiracy Collide in the Holy City*.[63]

Tim LaHaye and Jerry B. Jenkins, in the Left Behind fictional book series, pursue the same end-times conspiracy theories. More than 70 million copies of the books have been sold.[64] Gershom Gorenberg has castigated the authors for the anti-Semitism threaded through the books. Gorenberg writes:

> Nor is contempt for Judaism the books' only disturbing message. They promote conspiracy theories; they demonize proponents of arms control, ecumenicalism, abortion rights and everyone else disliked by the Christian right; and they justify assassination as a political tool. Their anti-Jewishness is exceeded by their anti-Catholicism. Most basically, they reject the very idea of open, democratic debate.[65]

Apocalyptic Christian Zionists with conspiracist narratives have also produced books that reflect the themes of the Left Behind series. In 2003, Charles H. Dyer updated his 1991 book *The Rise of Babylon: Is Iraq at the Center of the Final Drama?* That year also brought the publication of Michael D. Evans's book *Beyond Iraq: The Next Move (Ancient Prophecy and Modern Conspiracy Collide)*.[66]

The Black Community

In the black community, the comedian and political activist Dick Gregory has been propounding assassination conspiracy theories for decades.[67] The prevalence of conspiracy theories in the black community follows a unique route through folklore accounts that reflect a history of repressive racism, according to Patricia A. Turner, and, as such, they function as "tools of resistance."[68] Nonetheless, some black conspiracy theorists pick up standard conspiracy dishes from the collective *smörgåsbord*. For example, the journalist and television commentator Tony Brown, in *Empower the People: Overthrow the Conspiracy That Is Stealing Your Money and Freedom*, cites two books on the Freemason/Illuminati conspiracy, as well as the Lyndon LaRouche network publication *Dope, Inc.* and books by Eustace Mullins, E. C. Knuth, and others who suggest that powerful Jews are behind the conspiracy.[69]

Some members of the Nation of Islam adopt conspiracy theories, including the anti-Semitic variety.[70] These sometimes come from Muslim tracts on the Jewish/Freemason conspiracy or from the LaRouche network. At the same time, LaRouche network speakers join NOI organizers for tours of traditionally black college campuses; the program focuses on the vast conspiracy run by the Anti-Defamation League and Jewish/Zionist elites.[71]

Conspiracy books are popular in many African American bookstores and book carts, and, in March 2006, I purchased three books from such a cart at the corner of Sixth Avenue and 32nd Street, a block from Penn Station in New York City. In *Al-Islam, Christianity, and Freemasonry*, Mustafa El-Amin cites a discussion of how the *Protocols* reveals the plan of subversives to infiltrate Freemasonry, but Jews are mentioned obliquely.[72] El-Amin, however, cites *Freemasonry* (a book originally published in Arabic by the Muslim World League), which directly links Jews, Zionism, and Freemasons.[73] El-Amin also cites the overtly anti-Semitic *Secret Societies and Subversive Movements*, by Nesta Webster.[74]

Vicomte Léon de Poncins, in *Freemasonry and Judaism: Secret Powers behind Revolution* and *Freemasonry and the Vatican: A Struggle for Recognition*, links Jews, Freemasonry, Satanism, the French Revolution, and the Bolshevik Revolution. De Poncins writes that the *Protocols* is hard to authenticate but that this is irrelevant because there is so much other evidence verifying the basic plot.[75]

The Political Left

On the political left, fascination with conspiracy theories grew after the assassination of President John F. Kennedy, in 1963. The left-wing attorney Mark Lane harvested this in 1966 with *Rush to Judgment*, the first of several of his books claiming that elaborate conspiracies were behind the assassination.[76] Conspiracism on the left increased again after the assassinations, in 1968, of the Rev. Dr. Martin Luther King Jr. and Robert F. Kennedy.

Conspiracism percolated at the margins of the political left through the mid-1980s.[77] This was especially true in the work of popular left conspiracists such as Mae Brussel, David Emory, and John Judge. In 1986, the liberal Christic Institute filed a lawsuit, *Avirgan v. Hull*, that unwittingly helped pull at the seam of what would soon unravel into the Iran-Contra scandal.[78] Known in the popular press as the La Penca bombing case, the charges originally concerned a series of allegations of CIA misconduct involving covert action and gunrunning in Central America in an effort to support the overthrow of the socialist Sandinista government in Nicaragua. Christic's leader, the attorney Daniel Sheehan, soon wrapped the case in bubbles of conspiracism floating back to the Vietnam War.

The La Penca case intersected with two other claims of government misconduct that took the flotsam and jetsam of miscellaneous facts and assembled them into a heroic sculpture of conspiracist allegation. One was the claim that the government, through the Federal Emergency Management Administration (FEMA), had set up a series of concentration camps for dissidents under the rubric "Rex 84." The other was the claim of an "October Surprise" involving an arms-for-hostages trade to influence the 1980 presidential election in the United States—a claim that was reheated in the atmosphere of Iran-Contra in the late 1980s.[79] All of these claims eventually unraveled, and a federal judge fined Christic more than $1 million for bringing a frivolous and unsubstantiated case to court. Nonetheless, these conspiracist claims became *causes célèbres* in a significant portion of the political left.[80]

When the U.S. government initiated the Gulf War, in 1991, conspiracy theories swept the political left, especially on alternative radio stations and on computerized information networks (including the still-novel Internet). After this died down somewhat, the conspiracy theories circulated in small leftist subcultures, which provided the seed bank from which the 9/11 "Truth" movement emerged after the terror attacks in September 2001.

How Did the Scapegoats Cross Political Boundaries?

Prior to the early 1990s, New World Order conspiracism was limited to two subcultures, primarily the militantly antigovernment right, and secondarily Christian fundamentalists concerned with end-time emergence of the Antichrist.[81]

From the vantage point of the year 2011, conspiracy theories about secret plans for global domination clearly are coming from both the left and the right. A variety of more diffuse conspiracy beliefs are held by an alarming number of folks across the political spectrum according to numerous public polling studies. Barkun notes that this is a shift and writes:

By "militantly antigovernment right" I mean those who consider governmental institutions, policies, and/or officials as illegitimate and tyrannical. They may, for example, claim that the federal courts have no jurisdiction over most Americans, or that there is no legal basis for the income tax.

These views are often accompanied by pedantically elaborate pseudo-legal or pseudo-historical arguments. "Christian fundamentalists" may have many of the same policy preferences, but are far more likely to base them on end-time ideas and scriptural references, such as the rise of Antichrist."[82]

There developed what Kelly calls a broad constituency for "fusion paranoia" about plots by powerful secret forces in league with government officials.[83] What united the disparate subcultures was a distrust of the current government leadership, whether controlled by Democrats or Republicans. Barkun notes that these "stigmatized knowledge ideas don't break down neatly along left-right lines."

How do we track the trajectory of conspiracy theories from right to left? Table 14.3 starts with the premise that there are three main threads of conspiracist scapegoating that trace back to the Freemasons, the plutocrats, and the *Protocols*. Note that individuals and groups in a specific thematic category may not be directly connected. For example, Fletcher Prouty apparently was not in the John Birch Society, even though his work was thematically similar to work by JBS members.[84]

Building on alliances and cross-fertilization forged through assassination research that spanned political boundaries beginning in the 1960s, three trigger events facilitated sharing of scapegoats and narratives from right to left beginning in the 1980s:

- The Iran-Contra Scandal
- The first Gulf War and George H. W. Bush's use of the term "New World Order" in a speech
- The terror attacks on 9/11, followed by the invasions of Afghanistan and Iraq

For many years after World War II and the Nazi genocide, there were attempts to isolate naked anti-Semitism as outside the boundaries of acceptable political debate. Because of this, while still seeing Jews as the main scapegoat, some overt anti-Semites such as neo-Nazis (and practitioners of the racist version of Christian Identity) softened their rhetoric for the purposes of initial recruitment. This was certainly true with groups such as Willis Carto's Liberty Lobby and the LaRouche network, both of which became adept at hiding the underlying anti-Semitism of their conspiracy theories.

As stated before, not all criticisms of Zionism or the state of Israel are anti-Semitic or linked to the conspiracism of the *Protocols*, but an increasing number of such criticisms do step over the line into bigoted conspiracist stereotyping of Jews. In Table 14.3, the term "Zionism" in quotes refers to the use of the term as a form of coded anti-Semitism, whether or not the group or individual is aware of (or even denies) the anti-Semitism.

In the mid-1970s, the right-wing networks run by Carto wove references to "dual loyalists" and "Zionists" into anti-CIA conspiracy theories. In this case, the terms were clearly code phrases for "Jews," an easy assessment to make since, at the time, Carto also controlled the Institute for Historical Review, which published Holocaust denial literature.

In the mid-1980s, Daniel Sheehan of the Christic Institute praised the work of the right-wing populist L. Fletcher Prouty and adopted not only the analysis but also the title of Prouty's book, *Secret Team*, as a slogan for the La Penca bombing case. Behind the scenes at the ostensibly left-wing Christic Institute, Sheehan and his investigators had secretly opened up a back channel to right-wing groups with a history of purveying anti-Semitic conspiracy theories.[85] This included material passed into the case that originated with Willis Carto's Liberty Lobby and its *Spotlight* newspaper and material originating with the Lyndon LaRouche network.[86]

From the Secret Team, attention turned to the conspiracy theories of Danny Casolaro and his quest for the head of the "Octopus" that he alleged was behind the plot to rule the world. The Gulf War launched by George H. W. Bush in 1991 spurred another round of conspiracy theories, this time on the political left, in which some activists increasingly portrayed the Secret Team in terms that at best showed insensitivity to historic anti-Semitism. The Lyndon LaRouche network sent organizers into progressive antiwar marches and events in at least thirty cities across the country.[87] Some on the left heralded key figures in the right-wing Patriot movement, such as Bo Gritz, for their alleged knowledge of CIA covert action and foreign policy machinations.[88]

From podiums at antiwar events came rhetoric in which criticism of U.S. foreign policy in the Middle East began to move from careful criticism of Israeli policies and Zionist ideology into outlandish and bigoted claims about Jewish global power: The Mossad controlled the CIA; the "Israeli Lobby" had made a puppet of Bush; "Zionists" dictated U.S. foreign policy and global affairs.[89] It is unclear how much of this was latent anti-Semitism among leftists and how much was picked up from the right-wing groups that used the Gulf War to recruit from the left, but this period opened up new vistas for right-left synergy, especially around anti-Semitic conspiracy theories.

TABLE 14.3. Cross-Movement Trajectory of Scapegoats, 1984–2006

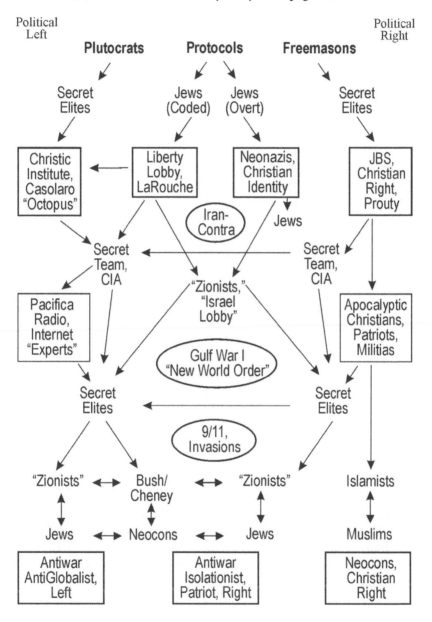

The terror attacks on September 11, 2001, moved conspiracy theory to center stage. Within weeks, progressives were circulating claims that government officials were "Guilty for 9-11."[90] This has turned into a "9/11 Truth movement," where conspiracists debate whether Bush and Cheney allowed the attacks to happen to gain political advantage or actually planted explosives to collapse the World Trade Center and sent a missile into the Pentagon. One promotional blurb for the book America's "War on Terrorism" proclaims that author "Michel Chossudovsky blows away the smokescreen, put up by the mainstream media, that 9/11 was an 'intelligence failure.' Through meticulous research, the author uncovers a military-intelligence plot behind the September 11 attacks, and the cover-up and complicity of key members of the Bush Administration."[91]

The attacks created a number of other conspiracist celebrities. Despite that fact that Michael C. Ruppert has been excoriated by a number of liberal and left authors, his "From the Wilderness" website remains immensely popular, and he packs thousands into auditoriums for rambling speeches.[92] Ruppert's Crossing the Rubicon: The Decline of the American Empire at the End of the Age of Oil was published by the progressive New Society Publishers in 2004.[93] The progressive theologian David Ray Griffin became a key figure in the 9/11 "Truth" movement.[94]

Almost immediately after 9/11, some in the political left began to criticize Bush and Cheney in ways that conflated the neoconservatives, Zionists, and Jews. This tendency also began to emerge in certain hard-right political sectors and among some libertarians. In some cases, this tracked back to a genre of 9/11 conspiracy books by Jim Marrs, former LaRouche analyst Webster Griffin Tarpley, and others who echoed the apocalyptic trope of the Protocols.[95]

A number of progressive commentators criticized this trend.[96] The issue of anti-Semitism seeping into the antiglobalization movement also gained attention within the political left.[97] Naomi Klein complained that "every time I log onto activist news sites like indymedia.org, which practice 'open publishing,' I'm confronted with a string of Jewish conspiracy theories about September 11 and excerpts from The Protocols of the Elders of Zion." Klein argued that the antiglobalization movement was not anti-Semitic but that "it just hasn't fully confronted the implications of diving into the Middle East conflict."[98]

Apocalyptic Christians, on the other hand, found themselves in a strange alliance with neoconservatives in which scapegoating of Islam became com-

206 | CHIP BERLET

monplace.[99] Christian conspiracism about the Middle East and Muslims has been covered in a previous section, but here I note that Hal Lindsey, who helped ignite the fuse of apocalyptic expectation with *The Late Great Planet Earth*, has added fuel to the fire with *The Everlasting Hatred: The Roots of Jihad*.[100] Secularized conspiracism in the countersubversive tradition is well represented by Paul Sperry's *Infiltration: How Muslim Spies and Subversives Have Penetrated Washington*.[101] Conspiracist interpretations of Islam and Muslims, however, should not be confused with the work of a number of scrupulous and careful authors across the political spectrum who have detailed the very real threats posed by certain forms of militant Islamic fundamentalism.

Conclusions

All conspiracist theories start with a grain of truth embedded in preexisting myths and prejudices, which movement leaders then hyperbolize. People who believe conspiracist allegations sometimes act on those irrational beliefs, and this has concrete consequences in the real world. Conspiracist thinking and scapegoating on a mass scale are symptoms, not causes, of underlying societal frictions. Nonetheless, the spread of conspiracy theories across a society is perilous to ignore because scapegoating and conspiracist allegations are toxic to democratic civil society and are tools used by cynical demagogic leaders to mobilize a bigoted mass base.

In addition, some racial supremacist and fascist organizers use conspiracist theories that do not appear to have anti-Semitic themes as a relatively unthreatening entry point in making contact with potential recruits. Even when conspiracist theories do not center on Jews, people of color, or other scapegoated groups, however, they create an environment where racism, anti-Semitism, and other forms of prejudice, bigotry, and oppression can flourish.

When analyzing the analogs of the *Protocols* in a scholarly fashion, it is easy to forget that there are real-world consequences. Jeremiah Duggan was a young man from England studying in France when he learned of an international conference, in March 2003, to oppose the U.S. invasions of Afghanistan and Iraq.[102] It turned out that Jeremiah was actually attending a conference held by the LaRouchite Schiller Institute in Wiesbaden, Germany.

Jeremiah learned about the *Protocols* as a child growing up in a Jewish family. He knew that what he was hearing at the conference involved anti-

Semitic conspiracy theories. He wrote in his notes a summary of the arguments from the podium: "Jewish lead to Fascism leads to Cheney."[103] Jeremiah stood up at the LaRouche network conference and objected to the anti-Semitic conspiracy theories he was hearing. What happened next is unclear. A few hours later, Jeremiah was dead, struck by cars as he was running away from the conference. A British coroner's inquest ruled that there was insufficient evidence for suicide and that Jeremiah was in a "state of terror" when he fled the conference and died.[104] German authorities refused to re-open the case, but a British court ordered a new forensic analysis to pursue allegations that Duggan's death was not a suicide. The LaRouche network has a long history of intimidating people who disagree with its members.[105] We should not dismiss or ignore the coded anti-Semitic conspiracism of groups such as the LaRouche network, which uses the anti-Semitic conspiracy theories derived from the *Protocols* as a tool to gain recruits.

History demonstrates that conspiracism cuts across political, social, economic, and intellectual boundaries. We need to teach each generation about the dangers of apocalyptic dualism, demonization, scapegoating, and conspiracism. Most studies of anti-Semitic scapegoating do not sufficiently examine the role of dualistic versions of apocalyptic aggression in the production of a violent response to alleged conspiracies of Jews or other scapegoats cast in the role of the "Other."

Dualism or Manichaeism is the idea that the world is divided into the forces of good and evil. Dualism as a broad concept is another metaframe, and it exists in many societies, including the United States, where it is especially prevalent among the subcultures of Christian evangelicalism and fundamentalism. Hofstadter noted that the "fundamentalist mind . . . is essentially Manichean."[106] While this is perhaps overly simplistic, Dick Anthony and Thomas Robbins use the phrase "exemplary dualism" to refer to the most hyperbolic form of dualism whereby "contemporary sociopolitical or socioreligious forces are transmogrified into absolute contrast categories embodying moral, eschatological, and cosmic polarities upon which hinge the millennial destiny of humankind."[107] This is found in "totalist" religious and ideological movements "with highly dualistic worldviews" and "an absolutist apocalyptic outlook" where members cast a "projection of negativity and rejected elements of self onto ideologically designated scapegoats."[108]

The forgery of the *Protocols* needs to be a centerpiece of educational curricula. We must never forget that dualism and demonization can create social movements that use conspiracist scapegoating to rationalize and justify apocalyptic aggression that can lead to genocide as a final solution.

1. Portions of this chapter were adapted from previously published magazine and journal articles and other text by the author, cited as appropriate here in the endnotes.

2. Chip Berlet, "Fears of Fédéralisme in the United States: The Case of the 'North American Union' Conspiracy Theory," *Fédéralisme Régionalisme* 9, no. 1 (2009); "Le fédéralisme américain," http://popups.ulg.ac.be/federalisme/document.php?id=786.

3. Office of the Press Secretary, The White House, "President Bush Participates in Joint Press Availability with Prime Minister Harper of Canada, and President Calderón of Mexico, Fairmont Le Chateau Montebello, Montebello, Canada," August 21, 2007, http://www.whitehouse.gov/news/releases/2007/08/20070821-3.html (accessed November 26, 2007)

4. Berlet, "Fears of Fédéralisme."

5. Chip Berlet, "'The Manchurian President': Chicago's Commie Liberal Puppet: The Paranoid Style of American Politics Is Alive and Well," *In These Times* (September), http://www.inthesetimes.com/article/6336 (accessed February 26, 2010).

6. Aaron Klein with Brenda J. Elliott, *The Manchurian President: Barack Obama's Ties to Communists, Socialists and Other Anti-American Extremists* (Washington, DC, 2010).

7. Richard Hofstadter, "The Paranoid Style in American Politics," in *The Paranoid Style in American Politics and Other Essays*, ed. Hofstadter (New York, 1965); David Brion Davis, ed., *The Fear of Conspiracy: Images of Un-American Subversion from the Revolution to the Present* (Ithaca, NY, 1972); Richard O. Curry and Thomas M. Brown, eds., *Conspiracy: The Fear of Subversion in American History* (New York, 1972); George Johnson, *Architects of Fear: Conspiracy Theories and Paranoia in American Politics* (Los Angeles, 1983); Frank P. Mintz, *The Liberty Lobby and the American Right: Race, Conspiracy, and Culture* (Westport, CT, 1985); David H. Bennett, *The Party of Fear: The American Far Right from Nativism to the Militia Movement*, rev. ed. (New York, [1988] 1995); George E. Marcus, ed., *Paranoia within Reason: A Casebook on Conspiracy as Explanation* (Chicago, 1991); Patricia A. Turner, *I Heard It through the Grapevine: Rumor in African-American Culture* (Berkeley, CA, 1993); Joel Kovel, *Red Hunting in the Promised Land: Anticommunism and the Making of America* (New York, 1994); Daniel Pipes, *Conspiracy: How the Paranoid Style Flourishes, and Where It Comes From* (New York, 1997); Mark Fenster, *Conspiracy Theories: Secrecy and Power in American Culture* (Minneapolis, 1999); Nancy Lusignan Schultz, ed., *Fear Itself: Enemies Real and Imagined in American Culture* (West Lafayette, 1999); Chip Berlet and Matthew N. Lyons, *Right-Wing Populism in America: Too Close for Comfort* (New York, 2000); Robert Alan Goldberg, *Enemies Within: The Culture of Conspiracy in Modern America* (New Haven, 2001); Michael Barkun, *A Culture of Conspiracy: Apocalyptic Visions in Contemporary America* (Berkeley, CA, 2003); Chip Berlet, *Toxic to Democracy: Conspiracy Theories, Demonization, and Scapegoating* (Somerville, MA, 2009).

8. It is not difficult to find the full text of the *Protocols* on the Web by using a search engine. Usually the text is the Marsden translation of the Nilus version. For example, in 2006, a search pulled up this site as the top hit for the *Protocols*: http://www.biblebelievers.org.au/przion1.htm#TABLE%20OF%20CONTENTS (accessed March 2, 2006).

9. *New Internationalist* (London), Special Issue on Judeophobia, no. 372 (October 2004), http://www.newint.org/issues/2004/10/01/ (accessed February 26, 2010).

10. Transcript of interview with Michael Barkun, conducted by author for Chip Berlet, "Zog Ate My Brains," *New Internationalist* (London), Special Issue on Judeophobia, no. 372 (October 2004); interview at http://www.publiceye.org/antisemitism/nw_barkun.html (accessed February 26, 2010).

11. Ibid.

12. For details, see Norman Cohn, *Warrant for Genocide: The Myth of the Jewish World Conspiracy and the Protocols of the Elders of Zion* (London, [1967] 1996). Note that two related works by Cohn link in the idea of apocalyptic millenarianism: *The Pursuit of the Millennium: Revolutionary Millenarians and Mystical Anarchists of the Middle Ages*, rev. and expanded (New York, [1957] 1970), with the original subtitle *Revolutionary Messianism in Medieval and Reformation Europe and Its Bearing on Modern Totalitarian Movements*; and *Cosmos, Chaos and the World to Come: The Ancient Roots of Apocalyptic Faith*, rev. ed. (New Haven, [1993] 2001).

13. Cesare G. De Michelis, *The Non-Existent Manuscript: A Study of the Protocols of the Sages of Zion*, trans. Richard Newhouse, English ed., rev. and exp. (Lincoln, 2004).

14. Chip Berlet, "Anti-Masonic Conspiracy Theories: A Narrative Form of Demonization and Scapegoating," in *Freemasonry in Context: History, Ritual, Controversy*, ed. Arturo de Hoyos and S. Brent Morris (Lanham, MD, 2004), 273–300.

15. Pipes, *Conspiracy*, 131.

16. Berlet and Lyons, *Right-Wing Populism in America*, 1–18.

17. Frances FitzGerald, "The American Millennium," *The New Yorker*, November 11, 1985, 105–196; Paul Boyer, *When Time Shall Be No More: Prophecy Belief in Modern American Culture* (Cambridge, 1992); Charles B. Strozier, *Apocalypse: On the Psychology of Fundamentalism in America* (Boston, 1994); Stephen D. O'Leary, *Arguing the Apocalypse: A Theory of Millennial Rhetoric* (New York, 1994); Robert Fuller, *Naming the Antichrist: The History of an American Obsession* (New York, 1995); Philip Lamy, *Millennium Rage: Survivalists, White Supremacists, and the Doomsday Prophecy* (New York, 1996); Damian Thompson, *The End of Time: Faith and Fear in the Shadow of the Millennium* (Hanover, [1996] 1998); Richard K. Fenn, *The End of Time: Religion, Ritual, and the Forging of the Soul* (Cleveland, 1997).

18. Chip Berlet, "Dances with Devils: How Apocalyptic and Millennialist Themes Influence Right-Wing Scapegoating and Conspiracism," *The Public Eye* 12, nos. 2 and 3 (Fall 1998): 1, 3–22; Berlet, "Mapping the Political Right: Gender and Race Oppression in Right-Wing Movements," in *Home-Grown Hate: Gender and Organized Racism*, ed. Abby Ferber (New York, 2004), 19–47; Berlet, "When Alienation Turns Right: Populist Conspiracism, the Apocalyptic Style, and Neofascist Movements," in *Trauma, Promise, and the Millennium: The Evolution of Alienation*, ed. Lauren Langman and Devorah Kalekin Fishman (Lanham, MD, 2005), 115–144; Berlet, "The New Political Right in the United States: Reaction, Rollback, and Resentment," in *Confronting the New Conservatism. The Rise of the Right in America*, ed. Michael Thompson (New York, 2007), 71–108; Berlet, "The United States: Messianism, Apocalypticism, and Political Religion," in *The Sacred in Twentieth-Century Politics: Essays in Honour of Professor Stanley G. Payne*, eds. Roger Griffin, Robert Mallett, and John Tortorice (Basingstoke, UK: Palgrave/MacMillan, 2008), 221–257.

19. Stephen Eric Bronner used the term "analogs" to discuss conspiracy theories that replicated the claims in the *Protocols* at the conference "Reconsidering 'The Protocols of the Elders of Zion': 100 Years after the Forgery," The Elie Wiesel Center for Judaic Studies, Boston University, October 30–31, 2005.

20. John Mearsheimer and Stephen Walt, "The Israel Lobby," *London Review of Books* 28, no. 26 (March 23, 2006), http://www.lrb.co.uk/v28/n06/mear01_.html (accessed April 7, 2006); the website carries several critical letters. See also the unedited version, listed as a .pdf file available at http://ksgnotes1.harvard.edu/Research/wpaper.nsf (accessed April 7, 2006).

21. For a roundup of criticisms, see Charles A. Radin, "'Israel Lobby' Critique Roils Academe," *Boston Globe*, March 29, 2006, 1, 7.

22. William Pierce, "A Confluence of Crises," transcript of radio broadcast, American Dissident Voices, September 19, 1998, http://www.natvan.com/pub/1998/091998.txt (accessed March 4, 2006).

23. Survey of mentions of *Protocols* at National Alliance website, http://www.natvan.com (accessed March 4, 2006).

24. August Kreis III faction: http://www.aryan-nations.org; Jonathan Williams faction: http://www.twelvearyannations.com (both accessed March 4, 2006).

25. http://www.aryan-nations.org/holyorder/A%20Study%20from%20Thessalonians.htm (accessed March 4, 2006).

26. The text was introduced and provided on separate pages for each numbered "protocol"; for example, aryan-nations.org/dagon/protocolmenu.htm; aryan-nations.org/dagon/ProtocalIntro.htm; aryan-nations.org/dagon/protocol1.htm (all accessed March 4, 2006).

27. Twelve Aryan Nations, http://www.twelvearyannations.com/hitler/julius.html (accessed March 4, 2006).

28. Cited on website to "Secret Plans against Germany Revealed," *Der Stürmer*, no. 34 (July 1933), http://www.twelvearyannations.com/hitler/secret_plans.html (accessed March 4, 2006).

29. Jonathan Williams, "Jews Are Burning America," http://www.twelvearyannations.com/id40.htm (accessed March 4, 2006).

30. See, for example, the Christian Defense League, http://www.cdlreport.com/patrioticbooks2.htm (accessed March 4, 2006).

31. The Populists American, http://www.gnrevival.com/HOME%20PAGE.htm (accessed March 4, 2006).

32. Thomas Jefferson Jackson, "The Protocols," The Populists American, http://www.gnrevival.com/new_page_37.htm (accessed March 4, 2006).

33. World Service, "How Jewry Turned England into a Plutocratic State," Frankfurt, Germany, 1940, reprinted online, The Populists American, http://www.gnrevival.com/new_page_31.htm (accessed March 4, 2006).

34. Eustace Mullins, *The World Order: Our Secret Rulers,* 2nd ed. (Staunton, VA.: Ezra Pound Institute of Civilization, 1992); Eustace Mullins, *The Biological Jew* (Staunton, VA: Faith and Service Books, International Institute of Jewish Studies, c. 1968); Eustace Mullins, *The Secret Holocaust* (self-published, possibly Damon, VA: 1983), reprinted by several groups, including Sons of Liberty (Metairie, LA, 1984).

35. Eustace Mullins, *Secrets of the Federal Reserve: The London Connection* (Staunton, VA, 1984). On naïve ignorance, see errata page for Don Paul and Jim Hoffman, *Waking up from Our Nightmare: The 9/11/01 Crimes in New York City* (San Francisco, 2004), http://www.wtc7.net/store/books/wakingup/errata.html (accessed March 4, 2006).

36. Pat Robertson, *The New World Order: It Will Change the Way You Live* (Dallas, 1991); Jacob Heilbrunn, "On Pat Robertson: His Anti-Semitic Sources," *New York Review of Books*, April 20, 1995, 68–70; see also Michael Lind, "Rev. Robertson's Grand International Conspiracy Theory," *New York Review of Books*, February 2, 1995, 21–25.

37. Dennis King, *Lyndon LaRouche and the New American Fascism* (New York, 1989), 283.

38. John Coleman, *Conspirators Hierarchy: The Story of the Committee of 300* (Carson City, NV, 1992).

39. Ibid, 254.

40. King, *Lyndon LaRouche*, 283.

41. Lyndon LaRouche, "New Pamphlet to Document Cult Origins of Zionism," *New Solidarity*, December 8, 1978, cited by King, *Lyndon LaRouche*, 275, see also 174, 274–285.

42. U.S. Labor Party Investigating Team (Kostandinos Kalimtgis, David Goldman, Jeffrey Steinberg), *Dope, Inc.: Britain's Opium War against the U.S.* (New York, 1978), 25–37, quote from 31–32; on the *Protocols*, see 31–33; on the Rothschilds, see the chart on 154–155 or consult index for more than twenty pages of entries on the Rothschilds.

43. King, *Lyndon LaRouche*, 174, 274–285; Chip Berlet and Joel Bellman, *Lyndon LaRouche: Fascism Wrapped in an American Flag*, report (Somerville, MA, 1989); Berlet and Lyons, *Right-Wing Populism in America*, 273–276.

44. LaRouche, "Children of Satan: The 'Ignoble Liars' behind Bush's No-Exit War," http://larouchein2004.net/pdfs/pamphletcos.pdf; "Children of Satan II: The Beast-Men," http://larouchein2004.net/pdfs/pamphlet0401cos2.pdf; "Children of Satan III: The Sexual Congress for Cultural Fascism," http://larouchein2004.net/pdfs/040614beast3.pdf; all published in Leesburg, Virginia, by the author (all accessed February 17, 2006).

45. Jeffrey Steinberg, "LaRouche Exposé of Straussian 'Children of Satan' Draws Blood," *Executive Intelligence Review* 30, no. 19 (May 16, 2003), http://www.larouchepub.com/other/2003/3019lar_expose_strauss.html (accessed April 1, 2006).

46. Michael B. Haupt, Three World Wars website, http://www.threeworldwars.com/protocols.htm, October 21, 2005 (accessed March 4, 2006).

47. Henry Makow, "*Protocols* Forgery Argument Is Flawed," http://www.savethemales.ca/000298.html (accessed March 4, 2006).

48. Rayelan Allan, "What Do I Mean When I Talk about the Two Factions?" Rumor Mill News, http://www.rumormillnews.com/cgi-bin/archive.cgi?read=41807 (accessed March 4, 2006).

49. Henry Makow, "'Protocols of Zion' Is the Illuminati Blueprint *PIC*," http://www.rumormillnews.com/cgi-bin/archive.cgi?read=36210 (accessed March 4, 2006).

50. See, for example, "Hoax Origins of the 'Protocols of Zion,'" http://www.rumormillnews.com/cgi-bin/archive.cgi?read=14413 (accessed March 4, 2006).

51. For a taste of Hatonn, visit "Phoenix Journal 26," http://www.fourwinds10.com/journals/J26-50.html (accessed March 4, 2006).

52. David Icke website homepage, http://www.davidicke.com (accessed March 4, 2006).

53. "Reptilian Agenda," http://www.reptilianagenda.com/index.html (accessed March 4, 2006).

54. Transcript of author interview with Barkun. See also discussion of Icke in Barkun, *A Culture of Conspiracy*, 103–109.

55. Berlet, *Toxic to Democracy*, in which each epoch is documented with citations to specific publications: http://www.publiceye.org/conspire/toxic2democracy/; the dates are approximations. This chapter began life as a slide show illustrating the continuity of texts replicating in some way the claims made in the *Protocols*. The show is online at http://www.publiceye.org/conspire/paradigm/protocols-2005.html.

56. Michael Kelly, "The Road to Paranoia," *The New Yorker*, June 19, 1995, 60–70; Barkun, *A Culture of Conspiracy.*

57. Chip Berlet, "Taking Tea Partiers Seriously," *The Progressive* (February 2010): 24–27, http://www.progressive.org/berleto210c.html (accessed February 24, 2010).

58. William H. McIlhany, "An Annotated Bibliography," September 16, 1996, http://www.jbs.org/artman/publish/article_41.shtml (accessed April 1, 2006).

59. For a more nuanced discussion of the JBS and anti-Semitism in the Patriot Movement, see Berlet and Lyons, *Right-Wing Populism in America*, 175–198.

60. G. Edward Griffin, *The Creature from Jekyll Island: A Second Look at the Federal Reserve*, 4th ed. (Westlake Village, CA, 2002); Jim Marrs, *Rule by Secrecy: The Hidden History That Connects the Trilateral Commission, the Freemasons, and the Great Pyramids* (New York, 2000).

61. L. Fletcher Prouty, *The Secret Team: The CIA and Its Allies in Control of the U.S. and the World* (Englewood Cliffs, 1973).

62. Based on author's visits to these bookstores.

63. Donald S. McAlvany, *Toward a New World Order, The Countdown to Armageddon* (Oklahoma City, 1990); Dave Hunt, *Global Peace and the Rise of Antichrist* (Eugene, OR, 1990); William T. Still, *New World Order: The Ancient Plan of Secret Societies* (Lafayette, LA, 1990); *John F. Walvoord, Armageddon, Oil and the Middle East Crisis: What the Bible Says about the Future of the Middle East and the End of Western Civilization* (Grand Rapids, MI, 1990); Pat Robertson, *The New World Order: It Will Change the Way You Live* (Dallas, 1991); Gary H. Kah, *En Route to Global Occupation* (Lafayette, 1991); Peter LaLonde, *One World under Antichrist: Globalism, Seducing Spirits and Secrets of the New World Order* (Eugene, OR, 1991); Peter Lalonde and Paul Lalonde, *[Racing toward] The Mark of the Beast: Your Money, Computers, and the End of the World* (Eugene, OR, 1994); Michael D. Evans, *Jerusalem Betrayed: Ancient Prophecy and Modern Conspiracy Collide in the Holy City* (Dallas, 1997).

64. Tim LaHaye and Jerry B. Jenkins, *Left Behind: A Novel of the Earth's Last Days*, Left Behind Series, Vol. 1 (Wheaton, IL, 1995); Tim LaHaye and Jerry B. Jenkins, *Tribulation Force: The Continuing Drama of Those Left Behind*, Vol. 2 (Wheaton, IL, 1997). The original series runs through to: Tim LaHaye and Jerry B. Jenkins, *Glorious Appearing: The End of Days*, Vol. 12 (Wheaton, IL, 2004).

65. Gershom Gorenberg, "Intolerance: The Bestseller," book review of Left Behind series by LaHaye and Jenkins, *American Prospect*, September 23, 2002, http://www.prospect.org/print/V13/17/gorenberg-g.html, (accessed February 17, 2006).

66. Charles H. Dyer, *The Rise of Babylon: Is Iraq at the Center of the Final Drama?* (Chicago, [1991] 2003); Michael D. Evans, *Beyond Iraq: The Next Move (Ancient Prophecy and Modern Conspiracy Collide)* (Lakeland, FL, 2003).

67. Mark Lane and Dick Gregory, *Code Name "Zorro": The Murder of Martin Luther King, Jr.* (Englewood Cliffs, NJ, 1977). See references to Gregory in Turner, *I Heard It through the Grapevine*, 124–125, 147–148, 188.

68. Turner, *I Heard It through the Grapevine*, xvi.

69. Tony Brown, *Empower the People: Overthrow the Conspiracy That Is Stealing Your Money and Freedom* (New York, 1998), 333–337.

70. Goldberg, *Enemies Within*, 150–188.

71. Anti-Defamation League, *The LaRouche Cult and the Nation of Islam* (New York, 1994).

72. Mustafa El-Amin, *Al-Islam, Christianity, and Freemasonry* (Jersey City, NJ, [1985] 1990), 106–122, esp. 107.

73. Muhammad Safwat al-Saqqa Amini and Sa'di Abu Habib, *Freemasonry*, Arabic version, (Makkah al-Mukarramah, 1980); English version (New York, 1982); cited in El-Amin, *Al-Islam, Christianity, and Freemasonry*, 106.

74. Webster, *Secret Societies and Subversive Movements*; cited in El-Amin, *Al-Islam, Christianity, and Freemasonry*, 107, 120.

75. Vicomte Léon de Poncins, *Freemasonry and Judaism: Secret Powers behind Revolution* (Brooklyn, NY, 2000), reprint of 1929 English translation (with title and subtitle reversed), which was itself reprinted in 1969 by the Christian Book Club of America; see Robert Singerman, *Antisemitic Propaganda: An Annotated Bibliography and Research Guide* (New York: Garland Publishing, 1982), 53, entry 0198; Vicomte Léon de Poncins, *Freemasonry and the Vatican: A Struggle for Recognition*, (Brooklyn, NY, n.d., circa 2000), apparently a reprint of a work originally titled *Judaism and the Vatican: An Attempt at Spiritual Subversion*; see Singerman, *Antisemitic Propaganda*, 267, entry 1175.

76. Mark Lane, *Rush to Judgment*. See also Lane and Gregory, *Code Name "Zorro": The Murder of Martin Luther King, Jr.*; Mark Lane, *Plausible Denial: Was the CIA Involved in the Assassination of JFK?* (New York, 1991).

77. This section is based in part on Chip Berlet, *Right Woos Left: Populist Party, LaRouchian, and Other Neo-fascist Overtures to Progressives and Why They Must Be Rejected*, rev. and updated (Cambridge, MA, [1991] 1994), http://www.publiceye.org/rightwoo/Rwooz. html; and Berlet, "Big Stories, Spooky Sources," *Columbia Journalism Review* (May-June 1993), http://archives.cjr.org/year/93/3/spooky.asp (both accessed April 1, 2006).

78. "What Is the Christic Institute?," http://www.skepticfiles.org/socialis/christic.htm (accessed April 2, 2006).

79. Daniel Pipes, "The 'October Surprise' Theory," in *Conspiracy Theories in American History: An Encyclopedia* (Santa Barbara, CA, 2003), 2:547–550, http://www.danielpipes. org/article/1654 (accessed April 2, 2006).

80. Berlet, *Right Woos Left*.

81. Barkun, *Culture of Conspiracy*, 179.

82. Author interview with Barkun.

83. Kelly, "The Road to Paranoia."

84. Suleiman Al-Nkidan, (no title given), *Al-Sharq Al-Awsat* (London) (October 25, 2001); cited in "Terror in America (21): Saudi Columnists Condemn Conspiracy Theories and Anti-U.S. Sentiment in the Arab World," Special Dispatch Series, no. 294, The Middle East Media Research Institute (MEMRI), October 31, 2001, http://memri.org/bin/articles. cgi?Page=archives&Area=sd&ID=SP29401 (accessed April 2, 2006).

85. Berlet, *Right Woos Left*.

86. Ibid.

87. Chip Berlet, "Right-wing Conspiracists Make Inroads into Left," *The Guardian* (NY) (September 11, 1991), 3; Berlet, *Right Woos Left*.

88. Berlet, *Right Woos Left*.

89. Ibid.

90. Illarion Bykov and Jared Israel, "Guilty for 9-11: Bush, Rumsfeld, Myers," originally posted November, 14, 2001, on the website http://www.emperors-clothes.com, now available at The Emperor's New Clothes, http://www.tenc.net/indict/indict-1.htm (accessed April 2, 2006).

91. http://www.globalresearch.ca/globaloutlook/truth911.html (accessed April 2, 2006).

92. David Corn, "When 9/11 Conspiracy Theories Go Bad," AlterNet, March 1, 2002, http://www.alternet.org/story/12536/; David Corn, "The September 11 X-Files," *The Nation*, May 30, 2002, http://www.thenation.com/blogs/capitalgames?bid=3&pid=66; Norman Solomon, memo to Philip Maldari, March 7, 2002, http://www.publiceye.org/conspire/Post911/Solomon1.html; Norman Solomon, response to a statement written by Michael Ruppert, April 4, 2002, http://www.publiceye.org/conspire/Post911/Solomon2.html (all accessed April 2, 2006).

93. Michael C. Ruppert, *Crossing the Rubicon: The Decline of the American Empire at the End of the Age of Oil* (Gabriola Island, BC, Canada, 2004).

94. David Ray Griffin, *The New Pearl Harbor: Disturbing Questions about the Bush Administration and 9/11* (Northampton, MA, 2004); David Ray Griffin, *The 9/11 Commission Report: Omissions and Distortions* (Northampton, MA, 2005). See also Chip Berlet, Review of Griffin, *New Pearl Harbor*, in *Public Eye* magazine, 18, no. 2 (Summer 2004): 18–21; an expanded version of this review is online at http://www.publiceye.org/conspire/Post911/dubious_claims.html. There is also a response by Griffin at http://www.publiceye.org/conspire/Post911/Griffin1.html; (all accessed April 2, 2006).

95. Jim Marrs, *Inside Job: Unmasking the 9/11 Conspiracies* (San Rafael, CA, 2004); Webster Griffin Tarpley, *9/11 Synthetic Terror: Made in USA* (Joshua Tree, CA, 2005).

96. Stephen R. Shalom and Michael Albert, "Conspiracies or Institutions: 9-11 and Beyond," Z-Net, June 2, 2002, http://www.zmag.org/content/Instructionals/shalalbcon.cfm; Michael Albert, "Conspiracy Theory," Z-Net, http://www.zmag.org/parecon/conspiracy.htm (both accessed April 2, 2006).

97. Naomi Klein, "Sharon's Best Weapon: The Left Must Confront Anti-Semitism Head-On," *In These Times*, May 27, 2002, http://www.inthesetimes.com/issue/26/13/feature2.shtml. Earlier examples of warnings can be found in Berlet and Lyons, *Right-Wing Populism in America*, 342–343; and Pressebüro Savanne, "Right-Left—A Dangerous Flirt," http://www.savanne.ch/right-left.html (both accessed April 2, 2006).

98. Klein, "Sharon's Best Weapon."

99. Michael Northcott, *An Angel Directs The Storm: Apocalyptic Religion and American Empire* (London, 2004); Hugh Urban, "Bush, the Neocons and Evangelical Christian Fiction: America, 'Left Behind,'" *Journal of Religion and Society* 8 (2006), http://moses.creighton.edu/JRS/2006/2006-2.html (accessed February 17, 2006). See also R. J. Lifton, *Superpower Syndrome: America's Apocalyptic Confrontation with the World* (New York, 2003), and Richard A. Horsley, *Jesus and Empire: The Kingdom of God and the New World Disorder* (Minneapolis, 2002).

100. Hal Lindsey, *The Everlasting Hatred: The Roots of Jihad* (Murrieta, CA, 2002).

101. Paul Sperry, *Infiltration: How Muslim Spies and Subversives Have Penetrated Washington* (Nashville, TN, 2005).

102. For the details of the story, visit the Justice for Jeremiah website, http://justiceforjeremiah.com (accessed March 15, 2006).

103. Copies of notes supplied to author by Jeremiah's mother, Mrs. Erica Duggan, on file at Political Research Associates.

104. Hugh Muir, "British Student Did Not Commit Suicide, Says Coroner: German Verdict on Death Dismissed at UK Inquest," *The Guardian*, November 5, 2003, http://www.guardian.co.uk/antiwar/story/0,12809,1077921,00.html (accessed April 5, 2006).

105. Chip Berlet, "The LaRouche Network: A History of Intimidation," a research paper prepared at the request of Erica Duggan, for submission to a coroner inquiry, November 2, 2003, http://justiceforjeremiah.com/chip_his.html (accessed April 5, 2006).

106. Richard Hofstadter, *Anti-Intellectualism in American Life* (New York, 1963), 135.

107. Dick Anthony and Thomas Robbins, "Religious Totalism, Exemplary Dualism, and the Waco Tragedy," in *Millennium, Messiahs, and Mayhem: Contemporary Apocalyptic Movements*, ed. Thomas Robbins and Susan J. Palmer (New York, 1997), 261–284, quote from 267. See also Dick Anthony and Thomas Robbins, "Religious Totalism, Violence and Exemplary Dualism: Beyond the Extrinsic Model," in *Millennialism and Violence*, Cass Series on Political Violence, ed. Michael Barkun (London, 1996).

108. Anthony and Robbins, "Religious Totalism," 264, 269.

PART VI

Quo Vadis?

How to Respond to the Return of the Protocols

15

Conspiracy Then and Now

History, Politics, and the Anti-Semitic Imagination

STEPHEN ERIC BRONNER

Anti-Semitism has a long history, and countless bigoted tracts have been written, but no other work has gripped the popular imagination like the *Protocols*.[1] The tract originally had very little impact beyond sparking a few pogroms in Russia. Between the two world wars, however, it emerged as the most widely read of anti-Semitic texts. Without too much exaggeration, the distinguished historian Henri Rollin noted that this pamphlet, with its fictitious vision of a Jewish world conspiracy, had been read more than any other work in the Western world except the Bible. In the aftermath of 9/11, it has gained new popularity, especially in the Middle East. There and elsewhere, rumors circulate that "the Jews" were responsible for the attack on the World Trade Center and other sites and that only Jewish control of the media prevents the world from knowing that Jews stayed home on that terrible day and that not one Jew was killed.

What does it matter whether this assertion is true? It fits the stereotype, and it is useful to mark the scapegoat. The thinking behind the *Protocols* still retains its appeal. *The Matzah of Zion*, published in 2003 by Mustafa Tlas, the former Syrian minister of defense, is now in its eighth edition. This book offers an Arab version of the undying myth about how Jews use the blood of Christian children to bake their matzah for Passover. Then, too, there is the forty-one-part soap opera *Horse without a Horseman* (2002), which aired on Egyptian television; the program offered a history of the Middle East from 1855 through 1917 and devoted an important episode to the supposed Jewish conspiracy and scenes of the "Elders of Zion" melodramatically plotting their strategy.

The new anti-Semitism is not really very different from the old in its assumptions or its theory. Whether the new anti-Semitism has shifted from the Occident to the Orient, whether its context or function has changed, it still employs the same method of justification. For the anti-Semite, it has never been the pedantic matter of whether any particular claim is empirically verifiable or whether a supposedly seminal tract like the *Protocols* is authentic. None of this has any impact on a belief born of prejudice. What is crucial is the knowledge born of "experience" or "feeling" of the anti-Semite. This can never be contradicted, and, for that very reason, it is sufficient. Even though the language employed at the first Zionist Congress was German and the *Protocols* was fabricated in French, the anti-Semite could *believe* that the former flowed from the latter "conspiracy"—and that is enough.

Anyone can enter the discussion when irrational criteria for argumentation are employed, and, in this sense, the first insight into the appeal of a work like the *Protocols* becomes apparent: It turns the ignoramus into a sage in his own eyes and in the eyes of those with a prior disposition to believe what he says. But there is more to its appeal. Appearing in Imperial Russia in 1905, amid a democratic revolution that was sweeping the country, the *Protocols* provided a way for the aristocracy to shift blame for the uprising from its own policies and practices to an "alien" group opposed to the national complex of premodern traditions and existential social definitions associated with "throne and altar."[2] Or, to put it another way, from the standpoint of the *Protocols*, the Revolution of 1905 was provoked not by a cruel and authoritarian theocracy ruling an economically underdeveloped land that had just been quickly defeated in the Russo-Japanese War but by an alien entity that despised Christian civilization: That alien entity was "the Jews."

Arguing in this way leads to a view of anti-Semitism as more than a mere prejudice. It instead becomes an explanatory device with a social function and a political purpose. It therefore makes sense that the *Protocols* should basically have disappeared from view once the Revolution of 1905 came to end. It also makes sense that the popularity of the work should have risen once again in the immediate aftermath of World War I. The end of that war brought about the collapse of four empires that had seemingly existed since time immemorial: the Russian, the German, the Austro-Hungarian, and the Ottoman. The *ancien regime* had finally been demolished, and its mass base among the peasantry and the petty bourgeoisie no less than its elites was panicked and disoriented. These remnants of feudalism shared nothing in common with the proletariat and the bourgeoisie or the socialist and the liberal worldviews born of the Enlightenment. The pillars of the past were fundamentally irrelevant to the modern production process and the secular democracies of interwar Europe that rested upon the new classes.[3] They needed not merely an explanation for World War I, which would naturally preserve them from all guilt and blame, but also a way of thinking that would existentially justify their continued salience.

The *Protocols* provided that explanation and that existential self-justifi-cation: Anti-Semitism became a worldview with special appeal for "the los-ers" in the development of modernity. There should be no misunderstand-ing: Not every opponent of the Enlightenment legacy became a Nazi, and not every peasant, petty bourgeois, or aristocrat became an anti-Semite. But there existed what Max Weber called an "elective affinity (*Wahlverwand-schaft*) between Counter-Enlightenment thought and a rising fascist-Nazi movement, as well as between premodern groups, threatened by modernity, and anti-Semitism. In the worldview of this right-wing revolutionary move-ment, which would seemingly always have these premodern groups as its mass base, the primary issue was the threat to Christian—or Aryan[4]—civi-lization posed by an anti-Christian or "alien" segment of society identified with rationalism and modernity. This alien entity could only be the Jews, who had not merely rejected but had murdered the Savior and whose nefari-ous plans were made plain in the *Protocols*. Its agents manipulated the pro-letariat *and* the bourgeoisie, propagated socialism *and* liberalism, fostered social justice *and* civil liberties, while introducing Bolshevik dictatorship *and* parliamentary democracy.[5] The *Protocols*, indeed, had the virtue of crystalliz-ing every opponent of the political right into a single enemy.

Rediscovered and used by the "whites" against the "reds" during the civil war that immediately followed the Russian Revolution of 1917, it was brought to the capitals of Europe by reactionary émigrés; Alfred Rosenberg, who introduced the *Protocols* to the young Nazi movement and later became its court philosopher,[6] was among them. The pamphlet peddled by him and by other reactionaries like him had particular salience for the Germans, who had experienced the destruction of their empire apparently without warning since news from the battlefields was severely censored. By 1918, the old elites were already promulgating the myth that the army was never defeated at the front. Germany had been "stabbed in the back," and it was clear from the *Protocols* who had held the knife. The German defeat was part of the defeat suffered by traditional society, and this defeat was the culmination of a con-flict that had actually been taking place since time immemorial.

Such an explanation profoundly changed the terms in which World War I could be understood. Not only were the prewar elites preserved from responsibility for bringing about the catastrophe, but also the basis was cre-ated for an alignment between them and the new proponents of the "con-servative revolution," or the burgeoning fascist right, with its militant ideals deriving from what Ernst Juenger called "the brotherhood of the trenches." The *Protocols* linked the old romantic nationalism of the 19th century with the neo-Romantic and, ultimately, racist brand of the 20th century. The pamphlet provided what Georges Sorel termed a "myth": a sense of peril, a motivation for action, a justification for violence, and, perhaps above all, a heroic self-understanding for these two wings of an *international* reactionary movement united by a resistance to the heirs of the Enlightenment and the harbingers of modernity.

There is, indeed, nothing mysterious about the popularity enjoyed by the *Protocols* during the interwar period. Anti-Semitism was socially acceptable almost everywhere in Europe: *Volksunde,* or the equivalent, was taught in schools, the higher reaches of society were closed to Jews, and most nations exhibited resentment of the manner in which they were entering the public sphere. Virtually every continental nation faced the same conflicts over modernity between the advocates of liberalism and socialism on one side and the reactionaries of the old and the new right on the other. Usually forgotten because of the extreme nationalism preached by movements like the various right-wing groups in German, the *action française,* and the Spanish *Falange* and *Opus dei,* as well as the fascist groups in Hungary, Romania, and elsewhere, is the cooperation between them. International publishing consortiums, often supported by important industrialists like Hugo Stinnes, linked them no less than other various publishing enterprises linked the socialists and the communists. The popularity of the *Protocols,* then, was that it met the needs of an international situation in which the traditional right and the new fascist right were facing conditions roughly similar throughout the continent.

To be sure, the *Protocols* provided no economic, political, or organizational views that might bind traditional conservatism with revolutionary fascism. But it did insist upon the need for what Ernst Cassirer termed a "mytho-poetic," rather than a rational or scientific, way of understanding social reality. The tract drew a line in the sand between the supporters of the Enlightenment legacy and its critics. The *Protocols* insisted that, like the Indian god Vishnu with his countless tentacles, "the Jew" controlled all the institutions, parties, and media associated with what merely *appeared* to be the contradictory forces of modernity. The pamphlet claimed that, in reality, modernity was unified. A single alien agency was at work, but it lurked in the shadows. Anti-Semites would make the most of these claims during the interwar years, when Walther Rathenau, the Jewish industrialist and foreign minister of Germany during the Weimar Republic, stated (critically) the phrase that became a famous slogan: "Three hundred men control the future of Europe." Empirical investigation was therefore insufficient to discover the "hidden hand" manipulating events. Intuition and experience were required for gleaning the alien agent of social destruction, and these qualities belong to only the most *irrationally conscious* representatives of the Christian—or, ultimately, Aryan—"community" (*Volksgemeinshaft*).[7]

Anticipating the future, the *Protocols* make clear that all things are possible: world war and world domination. It was the Jews who had brought about the catastrophe that was faced by the European public in the 1920s and 1930s, and, given the intelligence of their enemy, anti-Semites would have to react with the same degree of ruthlessness, the same insistence upon ethnic loyalty, the same stealth, and the same forms of manipulation of media and the public sphere. Resistance against "the Jew" would therefore be justified by psychological projection. The violence, lying, and manipulation in which the Jews are supposedly engaged became, through a combination of myth and prejudice, exactly the activities in which anti-Semites actually engaged. The lie thus became the truth content of the *Protocols*, and Heinrich Himmler put the matter well when he noted that this was "a book that explains everything and that tells us whom we should fight the next time."

It is somewhat of an exaggeration to suggest in the most obvious terms that the *Protocols* offered "a warrant for genocide."[8] The issue of genocide was not broached in the tract, and even those like Richard Wagner, who embraced the most extreme anti-Semitism, had no sense of the implications that their theoretical ravings might produce in practice. The Holocaust can only be considered sui generis. No movement and no writer, with the possible exception of Kafka, anticipated anything like Auschwitz. What the *Protocols* did offer, however, was an articulated understanding of what I have termed the "chameleon effect." What this means is that the Jew changes shape to fit whatever enemy of society is required: The Jew *is* the liberal, the socialist, the communist, the avant-gardist, the homosexual, and so on. Just as the Jew can take any form, any Jew can be a member of the conspiracy, and, since the conspiracy is invisible, even the most innocent Jew must be presumed guilty. The extent to which the chameleon effect is in operation is the extent to which anti-Semitism informs a reactionary worldview. In Germany, where for complex reasons its articulation was most radical, there was ultimately—using the phrase of Hannah Arendt—no "place" for any Jew in society, and, in this sense, genocide became a logical necessity.

Hegel liked to speak about the ruthlessness of history, its "cunning," whereby consequences transform intentions and intentions turn into their opposite. Anti-Semitism is a case in point. Its power is no longer what it once was, and seeking to understand it in terms of the 1930s is self-defeating. Anti-Semitism is no longer socially acceptable. Once the dimensions of the Holocaust became public, which is precisely why modern bigots place such stress on its denial, the connection between anti-Semitic theory and its hideous implications for practice appeared inescapable. Anti-Semitism is no longer taught in schools, it lacks a new literature, it is bereft of an articulated chameleon effect, and it lacks a secure mass base. In the Western democracies, at least, there is no longer a single party or organization with the hint of a chance at real power that embraces anti-Semitism as its dominant ideology. To deny the difference between the ways anti-Semitism was practiced in the interwar period and the way it appears today leaves the individual wandering in, to use another phrase of Hegel, "the night in which all cows are black."

Without a sense of context, indeed, combating the contemporary bigot becomes that much more difficult. "The Jew" was the victim in the 1920s and 1930s, just as the Jew had been the victim throughout the preceding centuries. Jews were subjugated within a Christian world, much of which remained enthralled with the feudal traditions of throne and altar. Tolerance often remained less a matter of law than of whimsy, and they lived in fear of reactionary institutions and paranoid religious beliefs. Jews were fragmented and seen as unified, ostracized and seen as invasive, powerless and seen as omnipotent. The conspiratorial fears of Jewish world conquest, in short, lacked any trace of empirical justification, and the anti-Semitic portrait of "the Jew" had nothing to do with living, breathing Jews. Today, however, the situation has changed. No longer is it the case that Jews lack their own state, lobbyists capable of representing their interests, or a fundamental unity. In all the Western democracies, interest groups are working on issues of concern to a Jewish constituency, and Jews are entrenched in modern society. Terrible things still occur. A cemetery is still desecrated here and there, now and then a Jew is still beaten up on his way home from synagogue, and some crackpot or other denies the Holocaust. But the police are usually on the case, and grievances are generally addressed. Anti-Semitic utterances are instantly condemned by most of the international community, and, in Western nations, even "salon" anti-Semitism is considered a vulgar holdover from times past.

Anti-Semitism is no longer what it was. The old ideology is now most prevalent in the Middle East, the site of the Israeli-Palestinian conflict. In this regard, Jews can view themselves as the victim of history. But Israel cannot. It has among the ten largest armies in the world. It is clearly the strongest military power in the Middle East; and, aside from dozens of favorable arms sales, it was accorded $90 billion in foreign aid and other grants between 1949 and 2000.[9] Israel has unsurprisingly proven victorious on the battlefield; it has expelled inhabitants living in what are today known as the "occupied territories"; it oversees 5.5 million Palestinians living in fifty-nine refugee camps; and it is making the most of borders that remain arbitrarily imposed and not clearly defined. There is something profoundly disingenuous in comparing anti-Semitism today with what existed in times past. Embracing such comparisons undermines critical thinking, fosters a reverse racism, paves the way for political manipulation, and—perhaps above all— insults the memory of people who paid the highest price for their beliefs and truly suffered under the yoke of anti-Semitism.

This is not to deny that anti-Semitism still exists, only to state that it exists in a new and very different context. Anti-Semitism has become interwoven with the barbarous treatment of the Palestinians, the attempts by right-wing Zionists and religious zealots to create a "greater Israel," the willingness of the Israeli state to align itself with reactionary regimes in world affairs and to uncritically embrace policies of the United States in the Middle East.[10] For all the talk about peace and security, Israel has been creating ever more settlements on the West Bank—populated primarily by fanatical Zionists and religious zealots—and implementing policies akin to apartheid with respect to its own growing Arab citizenry. The Middle East provides a very different context for this bigoted ideology, and imbues it with a different set of symbolic meanings than it had in Europe.

It is important to remember the way the *Protocols* set up an unqualified conflict between Jews and non-Jews without reference to context or conditions. This tract had less use for rational argumentation and empirical evidence than for intuition and myth. It was, in the first instance, an attempt to clamp down on discourse, and, precisely because writings like the *Protocols* arbitrarily identify the enemy of "civilization" with nothing more than a set of stereotypes, there is a sense in which anti-Semitic thinking can actually be embraced by Jews themselves.[11] Little wonder, then, that Israeli advocacy organizations attempt to portray every new mention of the *Protocols* as a step toward the emergence of a new Hitler and, often with the same hysterical paranoia as the bigot, every criticism of Israeli policy as an expression of anti-Semitism. Enough of these Jewish zealots see a conflict stemming from time immemorial between the Jews and the *goyim*; often enough, although usually in private, it is said that the anti-Semites have dominated us for two thousand years and, now that "we" have power, there is no reason to give an inch. The retreat into "racial" or tribal thinking becomes a logical consequence.

Jews thereby become defined by what they should oppose. What results is not merely a form of anti-Semitic "blowback"[12] but a more subtle resentment against the need for "permission to narrate" events in the Middle East from any perspective other than those acceptable to professional supporters of the Israeli state.[13] Such a stance is self-defeating. It calls upon them to embrace untenable myths and assumptions and thereby impairs their ability to understand the criticisms directed against them. New research suggests that the once firmly held belief that Israel was the product of a "people without a land [finding] a land without a people" was a myth from the beginning; it is the same with the old notions of a national founding in which the original settlers were peacefully removed from their land and a subsequent war in which an overwhelming Arab force united by its bigotry was valiantly confronted by the "miracle" of Jewish nationalism.[14] Finally, less and less persuasive today is the attempt to invoke the memory of the Holocaust in order to justify every reactionary twist and turn of Israeli policy, if only because the Palestinians played no role in its enactment. As the world grows larger, as other atrocities take center stage, and as the survivors pass on, the philosophical and historical meaning and symbolism of the Holocaust will need to change even while established patterns of thinking and plain ethnocentric prejudices inhibit the emergence of a new discussion.[15]

Dealing with ongoing anti-Semitic beliefs in a Jewish plan for world conquest, in the first instance, is possible only if we admit that Jews are no longer in the ghetto or an oppressed minority. It calls for recognizing that anti-Semitism is entangled in a genuine political crisis made more difficult by the way in which Palestinians can be considered, using a phrase from Edward Said, "the victim of a victim." Disentangling genuine prejudice from legitimate critique of Israeli imperialist ambitions should be the aim of all progressive inquiry into the problem of anti-Jewish bigotry. It would, in this regard, be naïve to expect that anti-Jewish prejudice would disappear even if a new Palestinian state were created and if the United States were to withdraw support from corrupt regimes like that in Saudi Arabia and change its policies in the Middle East. Conquering prejudice is not a mechanical exercise, and its success is not a foregone conclusion. The suffering endured by generations of Palestinians, by those who experienced the Israeli invasion of Lebanon in 1982, and by others in the Middle East will leave an arguably ineradicable residue. Nevertheless, it makes sense to believe that an anti-Semitism that has only grown with the success of Israeli imperialist policy will diminish with a change in that policy.

Works like the *Protocols*, of course, undermine any such effort. The seemingly immutable struggle between Christian and Jew becomes extrapolated into a new context as the struggle between Arab and Jew—to the detriment of both. Prejudice inhibits the ability to differentiate between progressive and regressive tendencies within the Jewish community and the Israeli state. By the same token, it enables Jews to avoid choosing between the imperatives of a democratic nonimperialist state and the current regime. Anti-Semitism thereby subverts the ability to develop a sensible politics even as it renders any form of reconciliation impossible. Works like the *Protocols*—now one hundred years old—thus still play into the hands of the most reactionary elements in both Israeli and Arab society, thereby guaranteeing only a further downward spiral. They remain the crutch for what is most dangerous in politics: intellectual laziness and ideological fanaticism.

NOTES

1. For a more complete analysis, and for a set of selections from the *Protocols*, see my *A Rumor about the Jews: Anti-Semitism, Conspiracy, and the Protocols of Zion* (New York: Oxford University Press, 2004).

2. On the dynamic between centralizing forms of group identity, which strengthen existential feelings of superiority, and the "differentiating" impact of groups that seemingly threaten those feelings, see the now forgotten work from 1927 by Arnold Zweig, *Caliban oder Politik und Leidenschaft Versuch ueber die menschlichen Gruppenleidenschaften dargetan am Antisemitismus* (Berlin: Aufbau, 1993)

3. The continental empires all witnessed the withdrawal of the political withdrawal of the bourgeoisie during the 19th century and the transformation of liberalism into the ideology of an economic elite. The mass base for the republican vision was, instead, the proletariat that was inspired by "orthodox Marxism" and organized in the huge social democratic parties of what was known as the Second International. Interesting is the fact that the labor movement found its recruits in nations that were nondemocratic and that it had the most problems finding support in nations that already retained a republican system. See John H. Kautsky, *Social Democracy and the Aristocracy: Why Socialist Labor Movements Developed in Some Industrial Countries and Not in Others* (New Brunswick, NJ: Transaction, 2002).

4. The Nazis merely replaced Christian with "Aryan" in the ongoing historical battle with "the Jew." Cf. Adolf Hitler, *Mein Kampf*, tr. Ralph Mannheim (Boston: Houghton Mifflin, 1943), 300ff, *passim*.

5. To be sure, the situation was more complicated in what remained of the Ottoman Empire, where an indigenous bourgeoisie and a proletariat were lacking. But this simply shifted the source for the destruction of the old world in a slightly different direction. Even British Intelligence believed that the leaders of the new regime, "the Young Turks," were part of a conspiracy led by the Jews and buttressed by Germany that that controlled the Bolshevik regime. See David Fromkin, *A Peace to End All Peace: The Fall of the Ottoman Empire and the Creation of the Modern Middle East* (New York: Henry Holt, 1989), 480.

6. Ernst Piper, *Alfred Rosenberg: Hitler's Chefideologe* (Munich: Karl Blessing Verlag, 2005).

7. Note the insightful essay by George L. Mosse, "Community in the Thought of Nationalism, Fascism, and the Radical Right," in *Confronting the Nation: Jewish and Western Nationalism* , ed. Mosse (Hanover, NH: University Press of New England, 1993), 41ff.

8. Cf. Norman Cohn, *Warrant for Genocide: The Myth of the Jewish World-Conspiracy and the Protocols of the Elders of Zion* (London: Eyre and Spottiswoode, 1967).

9. Carl Boggs, *Imperial Delusions: American Militarism and Endless War* (Lanham, MD: Rowman and Littlefield, 2005), 186.

10. On the American view of Israel, see Lawrence Davidson, *America's Palestine: Popular and Official Perceptions from Balfour to Israeli Statehood* (Gainesville: University Press of Florida, 2001).

11. Bronner, *A Rumor about the Jews*, 129ff.

12. "The term 'blowback,' which officials of the Central Intelligence Agency first invented for their own internal use, is starting to circulate among students of international relations. It refers to the unintended consequences of policies that were kept secret from the American people. What the daily press reports as the malign acts of 'terrorists' or 'drug lords' or 'rogue states' or 'illegal arms merchants' often turn out to be blowback from earlier American operations." Chalmers Johnson, *Blowback: The Costs and Consequences of American Empire* (New York: Henry Holt, 2001).

13. Edward W. Said, *The Politics of Dispossession: The Struggle for Palestinian Self-Determination, 1969–1994* (New York: Vintage, 1995), 247ff.

14. It is interesting that there is very little disagreement over the facts of the Arab expulsion, or (*nakba*), by the two most famous Israeli "revisionist" historians, who, incidentally, have radically different political beliefs: cf. Ilan Pappe, *A History of Modern Palestine: One Land, Two Peoples* (Cambridge: Cambridge University Press, 2003); Benny Morris, *The Birth of the Palestinian Refugee Problem Revisited* (Cambridge: Cambridge University Press, 2003).

15. For a more elaborated argument, see Stephen Eric Bronner, "Making Sense of Hell: Three Meditations on the Holocaust," in *Political Studies* 47, no. 2 (June 1999): 314–328.

16

Jewish Self-Criticism, Progressive Moral *Schadenfreude*, and the Suicide of Reason

Reflections on The Protocols of the Elders of Zion *in the "Postmodern" Era*

RICHARD LANDES

We are in what some call the "postmodern" era. I prefer to con-sider it yet another stage of modernity, indeed yet another crisis/challenge in modernity's turbulent development. When it comes to the Arab-Israeli con-flict and role played by *The Protocols of the Elders of Zion*, this new configu-ration produces a peculiar dynamic: on the one hand we find a premodern Arab political culture reacting violently to the demands of modernity and eagerly adopting and adapting both the *Protocols* and the murderous behav-ior to which that text gives its warrant. On the other hand, within Western culture we have a hypermodern strain that, when it does not actually adopt the apocalyptic madness of the *Protocols*, embraces its "analogs" and engages in the inflated rhetoric of catastrophe and conspiracy that inflames those ten-dencies: the Mossad and Bush did 9/11 to bring fascism to the United States, Israel is a Nazi apartheid state, America and Israel are the axis of evil and the greatest threat to global peace.

It is hard to explain why there is such a tremendous appetite for nega-tive narratives about Jews (and especially Israelis) in the early 21st century. The easiest response invokes the *Deus ex machina* of anti-Semitism: "Esau hates Jacob." Historians, however, even if they invoke anti-Semitism as an "organic" factor, nonetheless need to identify its well-springs: Why does Esau hate Jacob? And, in this current case why, after almost two generations of its having lain dormant, do we suddenly find that hatred returning again, and this time anomalously—at least as far as anti-Semitism's traditional cultural matrix in Europe is concerned—from the "left" and not the "right"?

Apocalyptic Conspiracy, Moral Failure, and the Crises of Modernity

Here one point of connection with the Melian Dialogue suggests itself.[1] One commonly hears the complaint about Israel from the "left": "Alas, I'm afraid that the Jews are like everyone else . . . no sooner do they escape the pain of oppression than they turn around and do it to others."[2] Recent work in his archives reveals that Harry Truman expressed similar sentiments in 1947, presumably echoing a broader (British) discourse.[3] Today it is a common progressive complaint, often accompanied with avowals of (disappointed) affection for Israel.

Why would the "left" find this discourse so attractive, particularly when, on the one hand, the Israeli "occupation" of the territories conquered in 1967 differs so radically from the Nazi occupation of Jewish-populated areas in Europe from 1940 to 1945,[4] and, on the other hand, the Arabs openly express the ardent desire to finish Hitler's job and the Palestinians offer a textbook case of a movement that cannot wait to gain power in order to oppress both its enemies and its own people?[5]

One would sooner expect people sensitive to this enormous moral dilemma of the impact of power on people's moral behavior to worry about how Palestinians will behave once they get power than to insist, on the one hand, that giving the Palestinians a state will "solve" the problem and bring peace and, on the other, that Israel's behavior resembles that of the Nazis. This historically inappropriate but apparently enormously attractive discourse, now reaching exceptional levels of irrationality in places like England, demands explanation.[6]

At one level, I think we might understand this as the working of a kind of "moral *Schadenfreude.*" For some reason, the "left"—especially the radical "left"—takes great pleasure in belittling Israel's moral struggle. Like so much of the zero-sum thinking that characterizes the mentality of "rule or be ruled," those who adopt this discourse can make themselves look bigger by making others (here the Zionists) look smaller. And, for reasons that need close examination, since 2000 this eagerness to demean Israel morally, has, in conjunction with a virulent turn in Arab and Muslim paranoia, become a veritable landslide of demonization.[7]

This peculiar attraction of moral *Schadenfreude* on the "left" is particularly ironic, since it was precisely the behavior of radical "left-wing" revolutionary movements like the Jacobins and the Bolsheviks that "proved" to many observers that the *Protocols* spoke truth about the evil agenda of the self-styled egalitarians. Indeed, the rapid shift from a discourse of justice and equality to a totalitarian terror that crushed the very "people" it claimed to liberate marked the Russian Revolution's dynamic from the start—exactly as the *Protocols* had predicted. Who could not see a plan in the way revolutionary demagogues duped "the people" into overthrowing the imperial aristocracy and then instituted a still more oppressive slavery? This rapid ideological betrayal did much to convince impartial observers that, whatever its dubious empirical origins, the *Protocols* articulated a profound political and historical truth. Nietzsche had already pointed out this "lust to power" lurking behind the egalitarian "slave morality," that drove so many "losers" to oppose the dominion of the "blond beast."[8]

In light of its own checkered past, the radical left's lust to demean Israel makes some sense as an attempt on its part to cover its own terrible shame. For in *almost* every case where a radical egalitarian movement took power by violence, a fortiori when it then found itself attacked by external reactionary regimes (France 1789, Russia 1917, China 1949, Israel, 1948, Egypt, 1952, Syria, 1960, Iraq 1962, Cambodia, 1975, for example), the "left" turned rapidly to authoritarianism and imperialism (if not totalitarianism). In this set of historical examples, where no "leftist" regime sustained democratic features—real choice in elections, freedom of dissent, a free press, rule of public law—for more than a few years, Israel's sixty years of democratic culture under the most difficult of conditions—constant threat, against not merely the "revolution" but also the entire people—stands out as exceptional, if not unique.

This observation may help us understand the unhinged quality of the progressive assault on Israel: It derives from the resentment of "bad conscience." In order to keep the discussion away from the dramatic failures and betrayals of the "left" historically—by both the totalitarians and their fellow travelers, including brilliant men like George Bernard Shaw, Bertrand Russell, Jean-Paul Sartre, and Noam Chomsky[9]—current anti-Zionist discourse, in which Israel is an imperialist, racist, *right-wing*, messianic-colonialist-apartheid state, operates as a means to make the painfully obvious unspeakable. To defend Israel as a progressive movement that stayed faithful to its own principles more than any other such movement, *under still more trying conditions*, provokes voluble scorn. Indeed, critics of Israel dismiss out of hand such arguments as "entirely to the defense of the State of Israel with nary a suggestion that any of its policies might be misguided."[10] And, through the back door, this progressive combination of unwillingness to self-criticize and eagerness to criticize Israel, opens the door to scapegoating and demonization that lead, via analogs, to the *Protocols*.[11]

Since 2000, in particular, this powerful appetite for moral *Schadenfreude* among "progressives" has driven a shrill activism of moral anger against Israel on the "left." From the stunning enthusiasm with which progressives (especially European) welcomed the Intifada and the wave of suicide terror it unleashed,[12] through Durban's demopathic orgy of anti-Zionism,[13] to the feeding frenzy about the "Jenin Massacre,"[14] to current movements to boycott and divest from Israel, the equation of Israel with the Nazis has dominated much of public discourse from international conferences, to academic podia, to "peace" movements opposing the war in Iraq. If it were merely a sad lament, such a trope (or meme) might not be so terrible. But the move from moral *Schadenfreude*—"Alas, you're just like (i.e., as bad as) everyone else"—to moral sadism—"Israel is just like (or worse than) the Nazis"—has proven surprisingly easy for many.

And, along with that slide from moral lament to moral assault, we find the appearance among the "left" of increasingly pervasive conspiracy thinking about the Bush administration, with all the axiomatic assumptions of dastardly malevolence among "the [near] enemy" that underlie such speculations. At this point, a strong current of "progressive" discourse, at least as it expresses itself on the Internet,[15] has adopted the language, the logic, and the aggressive and often anti-Semitic certainties of conspiracy theorists.[16] And as a result, we come full circle. By using totalistic apocalyptic rhetoric, conspiracy theories harden lines where they should be softened (democratic left vs. right) and soften lines that should be hardened (democracy vs. jihadi Islamism).

The Jews, Self-Criticism, and the Left-Islamist Alliance

The current situation poses agonizing dilemmas for Jewish intellectuals. On the one hand, many of them find themselves part of this "progressive community" that grows increasingly virulent in its anti-Zionism,[17] and some of them find that a "prophetic" self-criticism compels them to denounce what they see as Israel's sins. On the other, the slippery slope from anti-Zionism to anti-Semitism has spread its pall over the young 21st century with alarming rapidity, reintroducing the *Protocols* and its analogs into a rhetoric that threatens to engulf leftist discourse.[18] This has led many Zionist Jews to call for a circling of the wagons.[19]

So what should Jewish intellectuals do about this alarming turn of events? In particular, should Jews denounce other Jews whose criticism of Israel has crossed over some invisible line of legitimacy and may enable consuming and paranoid hatreds? Or, on the contrary, should progressive Jews denounce those Jews who circle the wagons as a tribal show of "my side, right or wrong"?

This brings us to a particularly knotty problem in Jewish thought at the beginning of the 21st century (or, for us medievalists, the beginning of the third millennium). The questions that this volume raises revolve around the astonishing perdurability of the *Protocols*, their revival in the early 21st century in ways few anticipated—their spread, via analogs, to progressive groups that one normally associates with ideologies profoundly opposed to the prejudice and racism of the text. So we—both Jews and Gentiles—need to ask ourselves two fundamental questions: What makes this text so appealing? And how do we deal with it when reason fails, as, alas, it so often does in these matters?

Among Jewish intellectuals, two paradigms compete. They are basically mutually exclusive (despite the best-intended efforts of those who seek the middle ground). On the one hand, we find "progressive" school, articulated in this volume by Stephen Bronner. This approach wants Israel and its Jewish supporters to self-criticize: to question its own myths, to listen to the Palestinian narrative, to hold Israel accountable for the suffering with which it has afflicted the Palestinians (and Lebanese) with its imperialist policies. For those who feel that hatred of Israel is an understandable response to Israeli aggression, leaving an "ineradicable residue" of hostility, the return of the *Protocols* has muddied the waters. Its prominence among Arabs, Muslims, and now even the "left" allows Zionists who refuse to self-criticize to reject Palestinian criticism as driven by irrational anti-Semitism. For this school, anti-Semitism is not the main problem in the Middle East conflict; Israeli policies are.

The contrary paradigm takes the anti-Semitic tendencies of Israel's critics seriously. Rather than adopting Palestinian narratives *in place of* the Israeli narratives, it submits them to the same historical and empirical critiques, filtering out their myths and fantasies. For example, it argues, to use language like "imperialism" in reference to Israeli policies and not pay attention to the imperialist tendencies among the Arab enemies of Israel has far less to do with a real critique of imperialism[20] than with the adoption of Palestinian rhetoric, itself based on *Protocols*-inspired fantasies about secret Jewish imperialism.[21]

According to a widespread Arab myth, for example, the Israeli flag's two blue stripes symbolize the Nile and the Euphrates—the real borders of the Jewish state's ambition.[22] Such mythology has much more to do with Arabs' projections of their own imperialism, which dates back to the 7th century[23] and now, at least in fantasy, flourishes in the 21st century, than with Jews' invocation of some biblical passages. In a televised sermon, Sheikh Ibrahim Mudeiris, an employee of the Palestinian Authority, linked the imperialist ambitions of the Muslims to their genocidal attitude toward the Jews:

> We have ruled the world before, and by Allah, the day will come when we will rule the entire world again. The day will come when we will rule America. The day will come when we will rule Britain and the entire world—except for the Jews. The Jews will not enjoy a life of tranquility under our rule, because they are treacherous by nature, as they have been throughout history. The day will come when everything will be relieved of the Jews—even the stones and trees which were harmed by them. Listen to the Prophet Muhammad, who tells you about the evil end that awaits Jews. The stones and trees will want the Muslims to finish off every Jew.[24]

And, since the Arab paranoid fantasy about the Israelis as Elders of Zion serves as a major justification of Arab aggression against Israel, it seems imprudent for progressive Jews to affirm it with remarks about Israeli imperialism, however generously and progressively they intend that affirmation. Indeed, one might argue, these "admissions" further justify aggression and encourage the worst kind of that very imperialism that, in principle, they oppose.

In 1975, the UN passed a resolution condemning Zionism as "racism." The following year, Muhamar Qaddafi hosted a UN conference in in Tripoli that addressed the issue of Zionism and racism. One of the Libyan delegates declared,

> Zionism, with its ethnic, racist, inhuman, principles, with its diabolic projects which create chaos the world over, with its dangerous plan of domination . . . and with its tentacles that play a virtually decisive role in the direction of the politics of the greatest countries in the world, cannot be considered as a menace for this region alone, but for the whole world.[25]

Such statements channeling the *Protocols* may not be surprising from a Libyan intellectual. Attending the conference and contributing to its volume of articles, however, was Edward Saïd, who, three years before *Orientalism* appeared, was already laying out the principles of his "postcolonial" discourse:

Zionism and imperialism feed each other. . . . The struggle against imperialism and racism in modern Europe is a civilizational struggle and we cannot successfully carry it out unless we understand the ideas of the enemy and the origin of these ideas. . . . In theory as in practice, Zionism is a degraded replication of European imperialism.

Such an analysis, however valuable the rhetoric for the Palestinian cause, makes short shrift of historical nuances. One might even argue that postcolonial discourse, with its obsession with Western imperialism in every form, no matter how disguised by capitalism, consumerism, or Zionism, and that discourse's complementary inability to register raw imperialism from the "Third World," represents a *Protocols* analog—the same fevered anger over a plot in which one's own frustrated desire for world domination gets projected onto the Jews.[26] Nietzsche could not ask for a better terrain in which to examine the *ressentiment* of frustrated millennial longings.

It is one thing for highly "progressive" Jews to bewail the "imperialistic" tendencies of their brethren with the inflated "prophetic" rhetoric with which they hope to whip their fellow Jews and Israelis into the right path.[27] But such self-appointed "prophets" need to consider the serious consequences of how this rhetoric plays out in public. Outsiders may not understand—one might argue cannot understand—how little this moral rhetoric has to do with empirical reality. Indeed, from a more impartial perspective that takes into account the historical context of how other nations have operated and continue to operate, such an overheated moral discourse often gives voice to a description that actually *inverts* reality.[28]

What people, an outside observer might ask, would willingly take responsibility for things for which they are only partially responsible? Doesn't everyone avoid blame as much as possible? Haven't those forced to admit crimes probably done far worse things they're still hiding? For the sake of these outsiders trying to understand the Arab-Israeli conflict, Jews need to be clear that the standards to which they hold their fellow Jews should not in any way obscure the fact that a far more noxious imperialism—one that genuinely seeks and brutally exercises dominion over as many subject people as possible (including their own commoners and women)—operates among Israel's enemies.

This alternative approach does not consider a focus on the longstanding popularity of *The Protocols of the Elders of Zion* among Arabs and Palestinians (and its recent spread to Western "progressive" thinking) as muddying the waters of—and therefore inhibiting—Jewish self-criticism; rather, it views the *Protocols'* popularity among Arabs as an integral part of their political culture's hostility to modernity and democracy and as a major contributor to the kind of hatreds and fears they express toward the Israelis (i.e., the Jews who have inexcusably thrown off the *Dhimma*). From this perspective, to take at face value Palestinian claims that they are the "victims of the victims"—with its easy slide into comparisons of Israelis with Nazis—and then to internalize them may constitute a serious misjudgment that harms everyone, not least the Palestinians. To put it in postmodern terminology, why should the Jews/Israelis allow the scapegoating Palestinian narrative to establish hegemony in their discourse, to colonize their own minds? Should responsible progressives not oppose an unholy marriage between premodern sadism and postmodern masochism?

For example, those who dismiss the invocation of the Holocaust in explaining the dynamics of the Arab-Israeli conflict "because the Palestinians played no role in its [the Holocaust's] enactment"[29] adopt a Palestinian narrative of dubious historical validity. On the contrary, the Mufti of Jerusalem enthusiastically embraced both Hitler and the Nazi project of Jewish extermination.[30] Nazi ideology—in particular, the *Protocols*—helped to define Arab attitudes toward Israel.[31] And today, Hitler's *Mein Kampf* is a Palestinian bestseller. The Arab nations were the only ones in the world after the Holocaust—only three years later—to openly declare their desire to "finish Hitler's job," a sentiment that has issued forth from their political and military leaders repeatedly ever since.

Arab Palestinians may wish to paint themselves as the innocent victims of Israeli aggression, to claim the mantle of the "Jew" to the Israeli "Nazi." But there is no reason why Israelis and Jews—or any fair-minded observer—should adopt that "narrative." And if a moralist wishes to emphasize the innocence of the Palestinian commoner (who knew little of any of this) and his suffering, at least he or she should acknowledge the significant contribution of Arab and Palestinian leadership to that suffering and the role of this demonizing narrative in that leadership's ability to control its people and subject them to that suffering.

Whereas the aggressively self-critical Israeli/Jewish "progressive" discourse makes the Palestinians (and their Arab allies) into victims of an unwarranted Israeli imperialist assault, a more plainly straightforward perspective (based not on analogous thinking but on direct words and deeds) views Palestinian leaders as frustrated heirs to *Protocols*-inspired Nazi genocidal plans.[32] In other words, to critique the "Zionist" narrative as fictive and adopt a "Palestinian" narrative confounds epistemological procedures. It defines Israel through the eye of the hostile "other," with no counterbalance.[33] In a sense, it adopts and validates a *Protocols*-driven perception of the world, a projective inversion of the blood libels.[34]

We could all agree to differ. But the problem cuts much deeper because the approach to the evidence that one adopts has an impact far beyond an academic "difference of opinion." How one proceeds and the intended and unintended consequences of proceeding according to the varying perspectives carry great weight.

For example, proponents of the "progressive approach" sometimes justify their epistemological inconsistency in adopting Palestinian narratives in place of the Israeli on the basis of a kind of "therapeutic" approach: "If we bend over backward far enough, Palestinians and other Arabs will respond in kind."[35] The withdrawal to the 1967 borders, based on an acceptance of (one of the more "moderate") Palestinian narratives that blames the "Occupation" for the conflict, operates in the same moral universe. An Israeli or Jew might reason: "They" want peace and national autonomy just as "we" do, and if "we" make major concessions, acknowledge the Palestinians as the "other" whose hostility to Israel is the result of "our" having denied "their" existence, if "we" cease "our" imperial policies, then Arab hostility "will likely diminish with a change in that policy."[36] Such moves are gambles, to be sure, proponents of this approach argue, but should we not take risks for "the peace of the brave"?

The opposing paradigm argues, however, that such a policy will backfire because it misidentifies the source of the hostility. The deep wellsprings of aggressive paranoia, whose presence we can most readily detect in how the *Protocols* and its attendant demonizing of Israelis permeate Palestinian culture, suggest just the opposite: Concessions to Palestinians at this point will far more likely bring on further aggression, as have the Oslo Process, the retreat from Lebanon, and the withdrawal from Gaza—all moves that the adherents to the progressive paradigm greeted with great enthusiasm as major steps toward "peace." Rather than seeing the Palestinian "other" as a projection of our own (liberal) cognitive egocentrism, this approach argues, we must see him as part of an autonomous culture with its own cultural imperatives. (This approach does have the advantage of treating "others" with enough respect to consider them autonomous agents, rather than as mere clones of the liberal West, acting solely "in reaction" to Israeli actions.)

Nor is this only a matter of Israeli foreign policy, over which Jewish intellectuals have a limited impact. How intellectuals judge the conflict has direct impact on a much larger issue—the sudden, (for most) astonishing, and continuing spread of Judeophobia around the world, above all in the Muslim world but also in Europe and among the American "left" in the new century.[37] Progressives tend to minimize this threat, presumably in order to insist that, with the new situation of Jewish "empowerment," the sins of Israel outweigh the dangers of paranoid anti-Semitism. Notes Bronner in this volume:

> Terrible things still occur. A cemetery is still desecrated here and there, now and then a Jew is still beaten up on his way home from synagogue, and some crackpot or other denies the Holocaust. But the police are usually on the case, and grievances are generally addressed. Even anti-Semitic utterances are instantly condemned by most of the international community, and, in Western nations, even "salon" anti-Semitism is considered a vulgar holdover from times past.

Such a statement suggests a strange lack of familiarity with the state of European attitudes towards Jews in the 21st century. In particular, it seems to dismiss one of the most astonishing and disturbing phenomena of the early years of the century—the widespread failure of European governments (and cultural elites) to acknowledge or reprove a wave of Muslim violence against Jews in the wake of the Intifada's outbreak in October 2000.[38]

As a result, any attempt to sound the alarm gets dismissed in a moral equivalence that dissolves rather than distinguishes shades of grey.

> Little wonder, then, that Israeli advocacy organizations attempt to portray *every* new mention of the *Protocols* as a step toward the emergence of a new Hitler and, often with the same hysterical paranoia as the bigot, *every* criticism of Israeli policy as an expression of anti-Semitism.[39]

Thus, efforts to mark off *certain* particularly virulent forms of *Protocols* use, of especially vituperative criticism of Israel as problematic, get buried in the banality of "every" and "any." For example, when Alvin Rosenfeld criticized the most extreme examples of Jewish attacks on Israel—such as comparisons of Israel to the Nazis and calls for the dismantling of the State of Israel—as feeding this "new anti-Semitism," progressives counterattacked by accusing him of trying to shut down debate by tarring *anyone* critical of Israel for *anything* with the brush of anti-Semitism.[40]

The debate needs to occur and to address precisely the problem Bronner identifies: "Disentangling genuine prejudice from legitimate critique of Israel should be the aim of all progressive inquiry into the problem of anti-Jewish bigotry." But if, in such an effort, the eagerness of progressive Jews to down-play the anti-Semitism and the morphing spread of conspiracism among the "left" leads them to dismiss *any* warnings as "right-wing Zionist propaganda" and to attack those whose sound a warning about excessive Jewish self-criti-cism as "enemies of free speech," then we are in serious danger of losing our bearings.[41] And such disarray comes at a crisis in Western culture's (progres-sive) experiment with freedom.

Dangerous Jews: The Humiliations of Modernity and Apocalyptic Paranoia

This subject of self-criticism brings us, then, full circle to the remarkable par-adoxes of the *Protocols*. As Mehlman points out in his essay on France during the Dreyfus Affair, there is something disingenuous about the "modernist" stance in which the Jews are "innocent" victims.

> Here we encounter the danger of a certain philo-Semitic strand of thought: In wanting to demonstrate the inexistence of a "Jewish threat," one risks reducing the Jews to being innocuous.

Precisely. And, whatever else they may be, the Jews are definitely not innocu-ous. On the contrary, Jews play a significant role in those cultures where they are taken most seriously (e.g., Latin Christianity) and contribute a great deal to economic and democratic development where they were given the most "rights"—especially in the case of modern Anglophone and Francophone Christianity and post-Christianity. In a sense, the *Protocols* have a point: Jews play a powerful role in the emergence of modernity.

One of the great surprises of the 19th century came precisely to those philo-Judaic enlightenment figures who condescended to "freeing" the fos-silized, superstitious Jews so that they could become upright citizens. Few if any, even among the Jews, expected Jews to become so successful, so perva-sive in the elite echelons of modern civic democracies.[42] Indeed, Jews' suc-cess was so great that it earned them the dubious honor of having much of the world believe the message of the *Protocols*: that they were manipulating the entire (anarchic) modernist project (Darwin and Nietzsche, their dupes), that they rule the world entirely by dint of their intelligence and will.

And therein lies the terrifying problem: what if Jews *do* play a critical, even a central role in the emergence of modern democratic culture? How to assess it without alarm? Modern "secular" scholars focus on Greece and

Rome as the source of modern political thought and consider the Jews as fortunate beneficiaries of, rather than major contributors to, democracy. (Try to find a survey of political philosophy that begins with the Bible as a source of egalitarian thought and legislation—the *isonomia* of the Ten Command- ments, for example—rather than with Plato and Aristotle.)[43] No recognition, no alarm.

Ironically, however, like other psychotics, the paranoid believers in the *Protocols* perceive something that the sane and sober academics do not—the centrality of the Jews to the entire project of modernity. Unlike the mod- ernist "scholars," with their preference for the secular, the unsuperstitious, the objective, these deeply frightened believers intuit something crucial: The Jews are at the origins of this drive for a legislation of freedom.[44] The French revolutionaries acknowledged as much by framing the text of their Univer- sal Declaration of the Rights of Man with the two stone tablets of the Ten Commandments.[45]

Modernity, however, is an acquired taste, and going through the transfor- mations it demands can be a very painful experience. To those alpha males who cannot imagine a world where the rules of the jungle do not apply, the demands of civil society can seem like death and annihilation. Free speech and press alone mean the constant fear of public humiliation without the right to defend one's manhood with blood; gender equality permits women an unthinkable level of defiance. Once one enters the world of permissive- ness and uncertainty that freedom brings, one is never the same. The Chris- tianity that accepts the division of church and state on which democracy is built is not the same as the more assertive, inquisitorial one that pressed its theocratic powers to throttle dissent (heresy) in the Middle Ages.

Similarly, the Islam that emerges from the passage to modernity will not be the same as the "virile" one that today dreams of conquering the whole world and responds to perceived insults—including the charge that Islam is a violent religion—with violent rioting. A modern Islam will have to learn the self-restraint that Catholics showed in vociferously but peacefully protesting Andres Serrano's Christ in urine, that fundamentalist Christians showed in protesting the removal of the tablets of the law from an Alabama courtroom, or that Jews showed in protesting a political cartoon of Ariel Sharon mod- eled on Goya's Saturn, devouring not his own but Palestinian children.[46] So free societies demand.

In this sense, the Jews have long learned these restraints. Without them, they could not have both survived in the diaspora as the "humiliated rem- nant/*dhimmi*"—an astonishing act of sustained psychological resilience[47]—

and, when no longer humiliated in principle and in public, flourished in civil societies. My guess is that, once we remove the blinders of Christian and post-Christian (secular) supersessionism, the scholarly consensus will find the Jewish contribution to modern freedom much closer to that of the paranoids' estimation than that of secular scholars, who think it secondary at best.

The paranoids make their mistake, then, not in believing that the Jews played a central, even a primary role in modernity. The paranoids' mistake comes from their attribution of motive. In their own form of cognitive ego-centrism, they project their *libido dominandi* onto the Jews. They assume that the Jews, in their prominence among the elites, are doing what they themselves would do were they to hold such positions—namely planning to enslave the world.

The idea of a malevolent Jewish "guiding hand" lies at the core of the *Protocols* toxic power, and that projection is mistaken precisely where the Jews derive their greatest influence: their sincerity. Jews, especially ones who engage the modern world, really do believe in what they say. Many Jews, and especially the most passionate ones, are the opposite of demopaths. Indeed, most of the severe self-criticism that Jews engage in publicly constitutes a heroic effort not only to avoid being demopaths but to avoid even giving the impression that they are.

Thus, the very gauge of that sincerity lies in the knot of self-criticism that constitutes one of Judaism's most pronounced features. Every aspect of modernity draws strength from the ability to give and take criticism, *toch-achah*—science, democratic politics, technology, education for commoners, free media, academia, social legislation, progressive morality, and justice. The Jews' commitment to self-criticism, their readiness to admit publicly to things that many individuals and peoples would find too humiliating to bear, makes them at once major contributors to the modernist project and major threats to a manhood that would sooner die than "lose face." Rather than a fierce patriotism, many Jews show an iconoclastic "allergy to an all too comfortable—or melodramatic—vision of us virtuous victims and those dastardly villains," which may often lead to inaccurate or exaggerated confessions of fault, sometimes just "out of disgust with the self-satisfaction of the virtue-trippers among the ranks."[48]

The problem, of course, is that sincere Jews thereby contribute to an epistemological crisis. Outsiders, not realizing how pervasive and *rhetorical* Jewish self-criticism is and how often Jews engage in it to prove their sincerity, end up taking these admissions of guilt as accurate. They take them as reliable information about the "real world," rather than as a window onto the overheated moral perfectionism of the "prophetic" calling.[49] When NPR did a survey of the Palestinian refugee problem, it interviewed Palestinians who said it's all the Israelis' fault and Israelis who said "we're at least half to blame."[50] An evenhanded listener, uninformed about the radical differential between self-critical Israeli narratives and scapegoating Palestinian ones,[51] could easily come away thinking, "Well, then it's probably about 75 percent Israel's fault. I can understand why Palestinians are upset."[52] The virulent anti-Zionism that so easily spills over into the new anti-Semitism of the 21st century[53] illustrates, to paraphrase the joke,[54] how people become anti-Semitic because they take seriously a tenth of the "sins" to which Jews—in their prophetic enthusiasm—confess.

At its simplest, shorn of its demonizing and masochistic narratives, modernity is a battle of manhoods between *real* men who conquer others and real *Menschen* who "conquer themselves," between men who crush and intimidate criticism and those who listen and assess feedback, between those who become men by killing other men and those who become men by letting others—including women—have the same freedoms they want . . . a moral battle between scapegoating and shouldering responsibility.

And so the irony comes full circle: The very trait that marks the Jews as sincere modernizers makes them dangerous. The pervasive language of honor and humiliation that comes from the most delirious believers in the *Protocols*—especially the Nazis and the Jihadis—reflects the genuine danger to manhood that Jews pose to alpha males from authoritarian cultures.[55] Modernity prunes back aristocratic privilege—above all, the privilege to commit violence.

So these threatened men, in their defense, use Jewish self-criticism to blame, indeed, to demonize the Jews. For those who fear freedom, Jewish admissions of guilt—for having justifiably provoked the wrath of the Palestinians, the Arabs, the Muslims, the Christians, the aristocrats, the atheists, the postmoderns, the Gentiles, the world—are proof not of Jewish sincerity but of the accuracy of the accusations. And if Jews, in their eagerness to prove their sincerity, redouble their self-criticism, they will, whether they like it or not, feed the hungry beast. At this point—not at all points, but definitely at this one—Jewish angelism, with its generous admissions of guilt, makes things worse.

And while it feeds the hungry beast of Islamist imperialism, it also corrupts the "progressive" left, which, by taking Jewish self-criticism seriously and using it to affirm Palestinian scapegoating narratives, essentially abdicates the progressive project. In so doing, perfectly sincere progressives accede to the totalistic demands of a dishonest "victim" narrative: "We victims" need not self-criticize; "we" have a legitimate right to our narrative (questioning it insults us) . . . "you" must allow "us" to hope and work for the day when these paranoid narratives produce their embedded atrocities against the Israelis and Jews, atrocities that will restore "our" lost Arab and Muslim honor. Then we will dance in your streets. Who cares about the cost in Arab lives and holy sites? As the editor of a major Arabic daily in London commented: "If the Iranian nuclear missiles strike Israel [and, obviously, Palestinian areas], by Allah, I will go to Trafalgar Square and dance with delight."[56]

When the "progressive left" acquiesces to these demands, it fails the basic test of a free society: It rewards the violent and punishes the restrained. Thus, the British Editorial Cartoonist Society responded to the Jews' civil protest against the Goya Sharon-eating-Palestinian-babies cartoon by giving Dave Brown its award for "Cartoon of the Year" (2003); at the ceremony, Brown thanked the Jewish protesters for making his cartoon so famous.[57] When an interviewer asked why British cartoonists do not give Arafat similar treatment, the head of the Society, Peter Benson, replied: "Jews don't issue fatwas [i.e., don't threaten those who criticize them—no matter how viciously—with violence]."[58]

It is magnanimous to be self-critical and to take responsibility for failures, even though, in the larger scale of things, one could easily point the finger at people far more (ir)responsible, *in situations where you know that others have a great deal of respect in return*. But if others—including those to whom you are giving a break by taking the blame—express contempt and hostility and jump on your generosity to demean you, then it's time to stand up for yourself and call others to task. As Ehad Ha-Am once put it: "It is extremely dangerous for an individual, or a people, to confess to sins which they have not committed."[59]

"Postmodern" may signal the end of a comforting and productive hypothesis that "objective" truth can be recorded in language. It may signal a demand that we listen to many narratives and not subordinate them all to a single grand one. But it does not signal an end to the use of false and misleading information and the need to judge the quality of the narratives to which we lend our ears. Scapegoating and paranoid narratives—with their imbedded calls to violence—flourish when listeners fail to distinguish between honesty and dishonesty, no matter how well intentioned their motivations.

1. On the Melian Dialogue and its relationship to the *Protocols*, see Landes, chapter 2, in this volume.

2. Take, for example, the following comment, dated June 16, 2003, at a site maintained by the *Journal of Mimetics* which invokes the *Nazion* thesis (i.e., equating Zionists with Nazis).

> The *Nazion* thesis is intended to explain why the *state of Israel is engaged in a Nazi-like persecution* of a *helpless minority group*. Jews were traumatized from European persecution, culminating in the holocaust, and without realizing what was happening, the evil that had been done to them was per-petuated onto others. In a broader sense, this is roughly the thesis of C. Fred Alford's, *What Evil Means to Us* [Ithaca: Cornell University Press, 1997]. Alford presents what might be known as the "hot potato" theory of evil. The evil we do is largely the result of evil done to us. We are made to suffer, and we find relief in imposing our suffering onto others. So, for instance, your boss chews you out; you come home and yell at your wife; she unfairly pun-ishes your kid; he makes vicious fun of the kid who lives around the corner, and on and on it goes. Connecting postwar Zionism to Nazism is a way of making sense of Israeli persecution of Palestinians without having to resort to racist notions of inherent Jewish evil. Now *that* would be a hate-inspired belief." (http://cfpm.org/~majordom/memetics/2000/15638.html)

Note that in comparing the Israelis to the Nazis on the basis of this "do onto others" meme, the author believes he is specifically *not* anti-Semitic. Note also the "empirical" data [in italics—ed.] that underlie his "scientific" analysis.

3. "The Jews, I find, are very, very selfish. They care not how many Estonians, Latvians, Finns, Poles, Yugoslavs or Greeks get murdered or mistreated as Displaced Persons as long as the Jews get special treatment. Yet when they have power, physical, financial or political neither Hitler nor Stalin has anything on them for cruelty or mistreatment to the underdog. Put an underdog on top and it makes no difference whether his name is Russian, Jewish, Negro, Management, Labor, Mormon, Baptist he goes haywire. I've found very, very few who remember their past condition when prosperity comes." Harry Truman, *1947 Diary*, July 21, http://www.trumanlibrary.org/diary/page21.htm. Note the similarity with Foreign Secretary Ernest Bevin's remark about the pushy Jews who "want to get too much to the head of the queue," which itself echoes a comment Prime Minister Clement Attlee had made in a cable to Truman in 1946 (see David Cesarani, "Anti-Zionism in Britain, 1922–2002: Continuities and Discontinuities," *Journal of Israeli History* 25, no. 1 [2006]: 143).

4. Up until the first "Intifada," in 1987, the "occupied territories" were among the fastest-growing economies in the world, with a rising birth rate and increasing life expec-tancy (*Developing the Occupied Territories: An Investment in Peace*, by World Bank Staff [World Bank Publications, 1993], 16, http://books.google.com/books?id=8XFkA5REmN EC&pg=PA16&lpg=PA16&dq=gaza+%2B%22ten+fastest+growing+economies%22&sou rce=web&ots=w6-DX7-LlO&sig=3vyssFFY7IgI7ojCRC889klfRmo&hl=en#PPA16,M1), hardly what one would think to compare with the Nazi occupation of regions with large Jewish populations.

5. See chapter 11. For those who have not visited sites that translate from the original languages, what Palestinians and other Muslims say about Israel and the Jews, it would seem important to become familiar with the contents of both Palestinian Media Watch (http://www.palwatch.org/) and MEMRI (http://www.memri.org).

6. On the alarming report of the British parliamentary commission of inquiry into anti-Semitism, see John Mann, *Report on the All-Party Parliamentary Inquiry into Anti-Semitism* (September 2006), http://thepcaa.org/Report.pdf. On the irrationality involved, see the experience of the Druze Amir Hanifes, who tried to address the UCU boycott of Israeli academics and found them impervious to empirical evidence: "Ignored by the Brits: Druze PhD student defends Israel, but British academicians uninterested," *Ynet News*, June 6, 2007, http://www.ynetnews.com/articles/0,7340,L-3408890,00.html. See Anthony Julius, *Trials of the Diaspora: A History of Anti-Semitism in England* (Oxford: Oxford University Press, 2010), especially chap. 7. For one explanation that focuses on the resentments of the British and European "left"—anti-Americanism and anti-Zionism— see Nick Cohen, *What's Left?* (London: Fourth Estate, 2007); Andreij Markovitz, *Uncouth Nation: Why Europe Dislikes America* (Princeton: Princeton University Press, 2007), esp. chap. 5.

7. For an interesting reflection on the trivializing of the Holocaust as a form of rhetorical inflation, see Theodore Dalrymple, "Trivializing the Holocaust II: Auschwitz Isn't a Metaphor," *City Journal*, April 2002, http://www.city-journal.org/html/eon_4_12_02td. html. For a broader discussion of the "left's" attraction to the comparison of Zionism with Nazism, see Pierre-André Taguieff's *La nouvelle judéophobie* (Paris: Mille et une nuits, 2002); English translation: *Rising from the Muck: The New Anti-Semitism in Europe* (New York: Ivan R. Dee, 2004). On the wave of Judeophobia in the global community since 2000, see Robert Wistrich, *A Lethal Obsession: Anti-Semitism from Antiquity to the Global Jihad* (New York: Random House, 2010).

8. Friedrich Nietzsche, *Genealogy of Morals*, Essay I, 13–17, ed. Walter Kaufmann (New York: Vintage Books, 1989), 44–56.

9. Paul Hollander, *Political Pilgrims: Western Intellectuals in Search of the Good Society* (New York: Transactions Publishers, 1997). On Chomsky's handling of the Cambodian "killing fields," see Leopold Labedz, "Under Western Eyes: Chomsky Revisited," *Encounter* (1982): 28–35.

10. Reader's report. There is ample room for criticism in my analysis, indeed, as later, I argue that self-criticism represents one of the salient features of both Jewish and Israeli culture. Dismissing the argument that "criticism, especially criticism from Jews, gives aid and comfort to the enemy" (same reader's report), without distinguishing between the totalistic language comparing Israel with apartheid and Nazism on the one hand and legitimate criticism (that presumably maintains some measure of consistency by being applied to "both sides") ignores the main point. See later discussion of the Alvin Rosenfeld controversy (nn. 19, 40–41).

11. On the problem of conspiracy theory and the culture wars between right and left, see R. Landes, "Jews as Contested Ground in Post-Modern Conspiracy Theory," *Jewish Political Studies Review* 19, nos. 3-4 (2007): 9–34.

12. Oriana Fallaci, "On Jew-Hatred in Europe," *Panorama* magazine, April 17, 2002 (in Italian; for an English translation, see http://www.imra.org.il/story.php3?id=11611).

13. On the *World Conference against Racism, Racial Discrimination, Xenophobia and Related Intolerance*, held at Durban in September 2001, see the discussion and links at NGO Monitor, http://ngo-monitor.org/article/ngo_forum_at_durban_conference_ and Anne Bayefsky's reflections on the longer-range consequences: "Terrorism and Racism: The Aftermath of Durban," *Jerusalem Letter/Viewpoints* No. 468 (5762/2001), http://www.jcpa.org/jl/vp468.htm. For a discussion of demopathy, see Landes, "Self-Criticism and Identifying Demopaths: A Pressing Agendum for the Humanities in the 21st Century," http://www.theaugeanstables.com/2008/04/18/self-criticism-and-identifying-demopaths-a-pressing-agendum-for-the-humanities-in-the-21st-century/.

14. See Martin Seiff, "The Jenin 'Massacre'" (UPI), Part I: "Documenting the Myth," http://www.upi.com/inc/view.php?StoryID=20052002-032952-3644r; and Part II, "Why the Europeans bought the Jenin Myth," http://www.upi.com/inc/view.php?StoryID=21052002-123835-3473r.

15. See "Antisemitism on the Internet: An Overview" (2004), http://www.inach.net/content/INACH%20-%20Antisemitism%20on%20the%20Internet.pdf; Andre Oboler, "Online Antisemitism 2.0: 'Social Anti-Semitism' on the 'Social Web'" (2008), http://www.jcpa.org/JCPA/Templates/ShowPage.asp?DBID=1&LNGID=1&TMID=111&FID=381&PID=470&IID=2235. For one of many examples of the left's anti-Semitism online, see the critique of the *Guardian*'s "Comment Is Free" at CiFWatch, http://cifwatch.com/.

16. On leftist conspiracy mongering, see Berlet in this volume.

17. This was the situation in which Michael Lerner found himself in 2003, when International ANSWER rejected his participation in an "antiwar" rally because he was "pro-Israel" (see the May-June 2003 issue of *Tikkun*, which is dedicated to the dispute and to which I contributed).

18. Perhaps the first of these was Taguieff, *Rising from the Muck*. See also Phyllis Chesler, *The New Anti-Semitism: The Current Crisis and What We Must Do about It* (New York: Jossey Bass, 2003); Abraham Foxman, *Never Again? The Threat of the New Anti-Semitism* (San Francisco: HarperCollins, 2003); *A New Anti-Semitism? Debating Judeophobia in 21st-Century Britain*, ed. Paul Iganski and Barry Kosmin (London: Profile Books, 2003); *Europe's Crumbling Myths: The Post-Holocaust Origins of Today's Anti-Semitism*, ed. Manfred Gerstenfeld (Jerusalem: Jerusalem Center for Public Affairs, 2003); Gabriel Schonfeld, *The Return of Antisemitism* (New York: Encounter Books, 2004); Paul Giniewski, *Antisionisme: le nouvel antisémitisme* (Angers: Cheminements, 2005); Fiamma Nierenstein, *Terror: The New Anti-Semitism and the War against the West* (Hanover, NH: Smith and Kraus, 2005); *Old Demons, New Debates: Anti-Semitism in the West*, ed. David Kerzer (Teaneck, NJ: Holmes and Meier, 2005). Two massive tomes appeared in 2010: Wistrich, *Lethal Obsession*; and Julius, *Trials of the Diaspora*. Every book and virtually every essay acknowledges that the current wave dates to October 2000 and the impact of the Second Intifada.

19. Alvin Rosenfeld, "'Progressive' Jewish Thought and the New Anti-Semitism," American Jewish Committee Publications, 2006, http://tinyurl.com/ygnw2q. For an introduction to the controversy with good bibliography, see the Wikipedia entry "Progressive Thought and the New Anti-Semitism," http://en.wikipedia.org/wiki/Progressive_Jewish_Thought_and_the_New_Anti-Semitism. For one of the more thoughtful responses from someone who self-identifies as a progressive, see Gershom Gorenberg, "Shotgun Blast: An essay attacking "progressive Jews," *The American Prospect*, February 6, 2007, http://prospect.org/cs/articles?articleId=12439.

20. Any other nation in recorded history nation—Greece, Rome, Britain, France—that had the immense military superiority that Israel has over its Arab neighbors would have conquered the "resource-rich" regions around its borders as quickly as possible. Even the movement for "Greater Israel," no matter how unjust or inappropriate one might deem it, has exceptionally limited territorial ambitions compared with real imperialism. If there's a dangerous and genuine imperialism in the Middle East, it's Arab and Muslim: Ephraim Karsh, *Islamic Imperialism: A History* (New Haven: Yale University Press, 2006).

21. See Marcus and Crook in this volume.

22. Daniel Pipes, "Imperial Israel: The Nile-to-Euphrates Calumny," *Middle East Quarterly*, March 1994, http://www.danielpipes.org/article/247 http://www.danielpipes.org/article/247. More recently, Itamar Marcus and Barbara Crook have documented Palestinian use of this myth: "From the Nile to the Euphrates: PA Continuous Libel (1997–2007) about Secret Plan to Conquer Arab Nation," June 12, 2007, Paltinian Media Watch, http://pmw.org.il/bulletins_jun2007.htm#b100607.

23. Karsh, *Islamic Imperialism*.

24. Friday sermon, PA TV, May 13, 2005, http://memri.org/bin/articles.cgi?Page=archives&Area=sd&ID=SP90805. The reference at the end is to an early apocalyptic Hadith that states that, at the end of time, the Muslims will rise up and kill the Jews, and who will take shelter behind rocks and trees, and those very rocks and trees will call out, "Oh Muslim, oh servant of Allah, there is a Jew behind me, come kill him." The Hadith has wide circulation right now in the Muslim world; Hamas has it enshrined in its charter (article 7).

25. Abdullah Sharafuddin, "Introduction," *Zionism and Racism*, Proceedings of an International Symposium, Tripoli, 1977, 16.

26. See the various articles in *Postcolonial Theory and the Arab-Israel Conflict*, ed. Philip Carl Salzman and Donna Robinson Divine (New York: Routledge, 2007).

27. Julius calls these hypercritics "scourges": *Trials of the Diaspora*, 546–559.

28. The Jenin Massacre, which triggered much of the most virulent anti-Zionist discourse, stands as a good example of inversion: One of the most self-sacrificing military expeditions in the history of such operations (infantry going door to door, rather than bombing from the air), becomes a vicious massacre. On Jenin, see two documentaries: Pierre Rehov, *The Road to Jenin* (2003), and Martin Himel, *Jenin: Massacring the Truth* (2005). The 2002 "documentary" by Mohammed Bakri, *Jenin, Jenin* was banned by an Israeli court for its dishonesty, a decision overturned by the Supreme Court, which argued that "The fact that the film includes lies is not enough to justify a ban" ("Israeli Court Lifts Jenin Film Ban," http://news.bbc.co.uk/2/hi/middle_east/3262325.stm). For a systematic critique of Bakri's movie, see eyewitness Dr. David Zangen, "Seven Lies about Jenin: David Zangen Views the Film *Jenin, Jenin* and Is Horrified," http://www.mfa.gov.il/MFA/Archive/Articles/2002/Seven%20Lies%20About%20Jenin-%20David%20Zangen%20views%20the%20ofil.

29. Bronner in this volume.

30. Christopher R. Browning, *The Origins of the Final Solution: The Evolution of Nazi Jewish Policy, September 1939–March 1942* (Omaha: University of Nebraska Press, 2004), 406; David Dalin and John Rothmann, *Icon of Evil: Hitler's Mufti and the Rise of Radical Islam* (New York: Random House, 2008).

31. For the links between Haj Amin al Husseini (Arafat's uncle) and the Nazis, see Maurice Pearlman, *Mufti of Jerusalem: The Story of Haj Amin el Husseini* (London: Gollancz, 1947), and Jeffrey Herf, "Convergence: The Classic Case, Nazi Germany, Anti-Semitism and Anti-Zionism during World War II," *Journal of Israeli History* 25, no. 1(March 2006); and Herf, *Nazi Propaganda for the Arab World* (New Haven: Yale University Press, 2009). On the tendency of scholarship to ignore or even deny the link, see Yigal Carmon, "Was ist arabischer Antisemitismus?" in *Neu-alter Judenhass: Antisemitismus, arabisch-israelischer Konflikt und europäische Politik*, ed. Klaus Faber, Julius H. Schoeps, and Sacha Stawski (Berlin: Verlag für Berlin-Brandenburg, 2006), 209–210; on the anti-Semitic links between Nazism and Islamism, see Matthias Küntzel, *Jihad und Judenhass: Über den neuen antijuedischen Krieg* (Freiburg: Ca Ira, 2002). On the key link in terms of propaganda, see Joel Fishman, "The Big Lie and the Media War against Israel: From Inversion of the Truth to Inversion of Reality," *Jewish Political Studies Review* 19, no. 1–2 (Spring 2007), http://www.jcpa.org/JCPA/Templates/ShowPage.asp?DRIT=3&DBID=1&LNGID=1&TMID=111&FID=253&PID=0&IID=1704&TTL=The_Big_Lie_and_the_Media_War_Against_Israel:_From_Inversion_of_the_Truth_to_Inversion_of_Reality.

32. Bronner makes only a quick allusion to the role of the *Protocols* in what he terms the "Israeli-Palestinian" conflict and no mention of the genocidal rage that dominates the public sphere in both Palestinian culture and, more broadly, Arab and Muslim culture.

33. *Les Alter-juifs*, ed. Shmuel Trigano, special issue of *Controverses* 4 (2007); R. Landes, "When Cain Is the 'Other': On the 'Other' in the Arab-Israeli Conflict," http://www.theaugeanstables.com/2008/12/22when-cain-is-the-other-on-the-other-in-the-arab-israeli-conflict/.

34. See Alan Dundes, "The Ritual Murder of Blood Libel Legend: A Study of Anti-Semitic Victimization through Projective Inversion," in *Blood Libel Legend: A Casebook in Anti-Semitic Folklore*, ed. Alan Dundes (Madison: University of Wisconsin Press, 1991), 336–366.

35. Ephraim Karsh, "Amos Oz's *Nostra Culpa*," *Contentions* (May 16, 2007), http://www.commentarymagazine.com/contentions/index.php/karsh/443.

36. Bronner in this volume.

37. See n. 11.

38. Bronner's statement might have been written in the 1990s, a time when the disappearance of anti-Semitism brought on the Sartrean anticipation that perhaps Judaism might also disappear (Alan Dershowitz, *The Vanishing American Jew* [New York: Touchstone, 1997]). For an analysis of this tendency to dismiss alarms about anti-Semitism, which permeated the discourse of French anti-Israeli Jews for the first years of the 21st century, see Muriel Darmon, "Du paradoxe identitaire au paradoxe dialectique: genèse d'un nouveau culte," in Trigano, *Les Alter-juifs*, 17–23. See Parliamentary report (n. 6).

39. Bronner in this volume. Italics mine. See n. 10.

40. "It is no surprise Alvin Rosenfeld's article is creating a furor. The casualties of his onslaughts are rational dissent and language itself. If you're a Jew who has *ever* said or written *anything* critical of Israel, then you may be contributing to an 'intellectual and political climate that helps to foster' hostility toward the Jewish state and exacerbates hatred against Jews." Letti Pogrebin, "Who Dares Criticize Israel?" *Moment* Magazine, April 2007 (italics mine), http://www.momentmag.com/Exclusive/2007/2007-04/200704-Opinion-Pogrebin.html. See n. 19 on the Rosenfeld essay, n. 10, on the rhetoric of "any criticism. . . ."

41. See Alvin Rosenfeld's essay on what he identifies as a "dialectical scam": "Rhetorical Violence and the Jews. Critical Distance," *New Republic*, November 28, 2007, http://www.spme.net/cgi-bin/articles.cgi?ID=1884; further discussed by Bruce Bawer, *Surrender: Appeasing Islam, Sacrificing Freedom* (New York: Anchor Books, 2010), 22–30.

42. For the sake of a shorthand definition here, modern civic democracies are political experiments based on a constitution that implements the principle of "equality before the law" (Greek *isonomia*).

43. On this problem, see the work of Yoram Hazony, for example, his preface to Aaron Wildavsky, *Moses as Leader* (Jerusalem: Shalem Center, 2005); more recently, Joshua Berman, *Created Equal: How the Bible Broke with Ancient Political Thought* (New York: Oxford University Press, 2008).

44. Eric Nelson, *The Hebrew Republic: Jewish Sources and the Transformation of European Political Thought* (Cambridge, MA: Harvard University Press, 2010).

45. Jonathan P. Ribner, *Broken Tablets: The Cult of the Law in French Art from David to Delacroix* (Berkeley: University of California Press, 1993), 11.

46. See discussion of the Alabama court in Lee Harris, *The Suicide of Reason: Radical Islam's Threat to the West* (New York: Basic Books, 2007), 209. On Dave Brown and the Goya-Sharon, see n. 57.

47. See Friedrich Nietzsche, *Daybreak*, ¶205, ed. Maudemarie Clark and Brian Leiter (Cambridge: University of Cambridge Press, 1997), 24.

48. Mehlman, this volume. Jeffrey Mehlman makes these remarks in partial explanation of his interest in the Scholem thesis about "antinomian Jewish messianism" as a possible legitimate source for the kinds of fears the *Protocols* articulates. Confusing the personal antinomianism of a Shabbetai Zvi or Jacob Frank with the ruthless imperialism of the Elders of Zion, however, may not be a particularly accurate way to elucidate the issues at play.

49. On the arrogation of "prophetic" claims by "progressive" Jews, see Seth Farber, *Radicals, Rabbis and Peacemakers: Conversations with Jewish Critics of Israel* (Monroe, ME: Common Courage Press, 2005); for a critique, see Rosenfeld, "'Progressive' Jewish Thought," 20–24; Julius, *Trials of the Diaspora*, 546–559.

50. Mike Shuster, "The Mideast: A Century of Conflict.Part 3: Partition, War and Independence," *Morning Edition*, October 2, 2002, transcript at http://www.npr.org/news/specials/mideast/history/transcripts/part-three.partition-20021002.html.

51. Imagine a ferociously self-critical volume titled *Radicals, Imams and Peacemakers: Conversations with Muslim Critics of Palestine.*

52. For a critique of the skew in interviews, see the referenced "CAMERA Critiques NPR Series," http://www.camera.org/index.asp?x_context=6&x_article=357; for an analysis of the issue raised in the Mishna about two men disputing ownership of a Talit, see Daniel Gordis, "Back to the Mishnah," *Shalem Center Newsletter*, January 2, 2008, http://rs6.net/tn.jsp?e=001Be_GNeUEsgPhkhaFjuNYOjemq5sqjv4g4N9Xb9b1bqf7O-sZTQlOt-fwNePFoTdN4fZLkq6pMEe32KAw5sUWsrcyVxPFFDWPzg_pXfcasmyZp3DBPB_iOjB-vDl4JnmMgnhWla93F4VHeO5odeblMlRobhW9WhBu2f.

53. See n. 19.

54. An anti-Semite is someone who takes seriously a tenth of the jokes the Jews tell about themselves.

55. Christopher Forth, *The Dreyfus Affair and the Crisis of French Manhood* (Baltimore: Johns Hopkins University Press, 2004).

56. Abd Al-Bari Atwan, editor-in-chief of *Al-Quds Al-Arabi* newspaper, on ANB Lebanese television, June 27, 2007.

57. For both the Goya original and the Dave Brown cartoon of January 2003, see http:// backspin.typepad.com/backspin/2003/11/evolution_of_an.html. On protests, see Richard Allen Greene, "Israeli Embassy Protests Anti-Sharon Cartoon in British Newspaper," *Jewish Telegraphic Agency*, February 26, 2003, http://www.jta.org/page_view_story.asp?strweb head=Israel+protests+London+newspaper+cartoon&intcategoryid=2.

58. Interview in Martin Himel, *Jenin: Massacring the Truth*, http://www.aish.com/ jewishissues/mediaobjectivity/Jenin_Massacring_Truth.asp; transcription and discussion at Daimnation, "The Society of British *Dhimmi* Cartoonists," http://damianpenny. wordpress.com/2004/04/28/the-society-of-british-dhimmi-cartoonists/ . Note that in his self-defense, Brown seems incapable of distinguishing the crucial difference (to Benson's calculus) between the nonviolence of the Jewish protest and the violence of the Muslim objections to the Danish cartoons: "They [the Jews] started a campaign, and by the end people who hadn't even seen the cartoon were outraged. It's the same problem as this Danish thing—there's a text and phone campaign among Muslims which is having the same effect." Dave Brown, "Drawn into the Row," *The Independent*, February 6, 2003.

59. Cited by David Mamet, *The Wicked Son: Anti-Semitism, Self-Hatred, and the Jews* (New York: Random House, 2009), 48.

About the Contributors

MICHAEL BARKUN is Professor Emeritus of Political Science at the Maxwell School of Syracuse University. His numerous books include *Chasing Phantoms: Reality, Imagination, and Homeland Security since 9/11*; *A Culture of Conspiracy: Apocalyptic Visions in Contemporary America*; and *Religion and the Racist Right: The Origins of the Chirstian Identity Movement*.

CHIP BERLET, a senior analyst at Political Research Associates, is the coauthor (with Matthew N. Lyons) of *Right-Wing Populism in America: Too Close for Comfort*.

STEPHEN ERIC BRONNER is Distinguished Professor (II) of Political Science at Rutgers University and Director of Global Relations at its Center for the Study of Genocide, Conflict Resolution, and Human Rights. His books include *Critical Theory: A Very Short Introduction*; *A Rumor about the Jews: Anti-Semitism, Conspiracy, and the 'Protocols of Zion'*; *Reclaiming the Enlightenment: Toward a Politics of Radical Engagement*; and *Peace Out of Reach: Middle Eastern Travels and the Search for Reconciliation*.

BARBARA CROOK is associate director of Palestinian Media Watch.

DAVID G. GOODMAN is Professor of Japanese Literature, Jewish Studies, and Theatre at the University of Illinois at Urbana-Champaign. His books include *Jews in the Japanese Mind: The History and Uses of a Cultural Stereotype* (coauthored with Masanori Miyazawa); *After Apocalypse: Four Japanese Plays of Hiroshima and Nagasaki*; *The Return of the Gods: Japanese Drama and Culture in the 1960s*; and *Angura: Posters of the Japanese Avant-Garde*.

MICHAEL HAGEMEISTER is Professor of East European History at Ludwig Maximilian University, Munich. He is the author of *Nikolaj Fedorov: Studien zu Leben, Werk und Wirkung* and editor, with Boris Groys, of *Die Neue Menschheit. Biopolitische Utopien in Russland zu Beginn des 20. Jahrhunderts*.

JOHANNES HEIL is First Vice-Rector and Ignatz-Bubis-Chair in the Department of Religion at Hochschule für Jüdische Studien in Heidelberg, Germany. He is the author of *Gottesfeinde—Menschenfeinde. Die Vorstellung von jüdischer Weltverschwörung.*

STEVEN T. KATZ is Slater Professor of Jewish and Holocaust Studies and Director of the Elie Wiesel Center for Judaic Studies at Boston University. His many publications include four edited volumes on comparative mysticism, four volumes on post-Holocaust theology, and the multivolume *Holocaust in Historical Context.*

RICHARD LANDES is Professor of History at Boston University and was Director and Co-Founder of its Center for Millennial Studies.. His publications include *The Apocalyptic Year 1000: Studies in the Mutation of European Culture; Encyclopedia of Millennialism and Millennial Movements; Relics, Apocalypse, and the Deceits of History: Ademar of Chabannes (989–1034);* and *Heaven on Earth: The Varieties of the Millennial Experience.*

DEBORAH E. LIPSTADT is Dorot Professor of Modern Jewish and Holocaust Studies at Emory University. She is the author of several books, including *History on Trial: My Day in Court with a Holocaust Denier* and *The Eichmann Trial.*

ITAMAR MARCUS is the founder and director of Palestinian Media Watch, an Israeli NGO that studies Palestinian society and especially the messages conveyed by Palestinian leaders through the broad range of institutions and infrastructures they control. He was appointed by the Israeli government to represent Israel in negotiations with the Palestinian Authority on incitement.

JEFFREY MEHLMAN is University Professor and Professor of French Literature at Boston University. He is the author of nine books, most recently *Adventures in the French Trade: Fragments toward a Life* and *Émigré New York: French Intellectuals in Wartime Paris, 1940–1944.*

DAVID REDLES is Associate Professor of History at Cuyahoga Community College in Cleveland. He is author of *Hitler's Millennial Reich: Apocalyptic Belief and the Search for Salvation.*

CHARLES B. STROZIER is Professor of History at John Jay College and the Graduate Center, CUNY, and a training and supervising psychoanalyst at the Training and Research Institute for Self Psychology (TRISP). His books include *Apocalypse: On the Psychology of Fundamentalism in America*; *The Year 2000: Essays on the End*; and his latest, *9/11 and New York City in the Words and Experiences of Survivors and Witnesses*.

JEFFREY R. WOOLF is Senior Lecturer in the Talmud Department at Bar Ilan University. The author of more than thirty-five scholarly articles, he recently published *Sacred Community in Medieval Ashkenaz: The World of the Qehillah Qedoshah*.

PAUL ZAWADZKI is Senior Lecturer in the Department of Political Sciences at the Université de Paris 1, Panthéon Sorbonne. He is the editor of *Malaise dans la temporalité*.

Index

Ademar of Chabannes, 59, 62, 71. *See also* conspiracy stories

Adso of Montier-en-Der, 65, 71

African Americans: and conspiracy theories, 180, 200–201. *See also* Nation of Islam

Al Aqsa Intifada, 14

al Aqsa Mosque, 9, 85

Al-Astal, Riad, 154

Albright, Madeleine, 180

Al-Farah, Attallah Abu, 154

Allan, Rayelan, 194

Amakusa Shirō, 139

America (Baudrillard), 51

America West, 192

analogs to *Protocols*: defined, 2, 15, 189, 210n19; emergence of, 2–3, 197, 229; real-world consequences of, 207–208; in UFOlogy, 15–16, 187. *See also* conspiracy theories; stereotypes of Jews

Anthony, Dick, 208

Antichrist: birth of, 90n26; Jews as agents of, 6, 7, 65, 66, 81–82, 83–84, 89n21, 129n27, 138; and *katéchon*, 8, 83, 89n15; in mainstream discourse, 66; modern Russian prophecies of, 8–9, 85–87, 115

Anti-Defamation League of B'nai B'rith, 150n40

anti-Judaism. *See* Christian anti-Judaism; conspiracy stories

anti-Semitism: contrasting with Christian anti-Judaism, 50, 87, 89n20; and modernity, 1–2, 49, 219–227; and true vs. false Jews, 164, 165. *See also* apocalyptic paranoia; Christian anti-Judaism; conspiracy stories; conspiracy theories; Dreyfus Affair; *Protocols of the Elders of Zion*; stereotypes of Jews

apocalyptic paranoia: cultural examples of, 40, 91n31; moving from passive to, 29–31; and nuclear weapons, 41–43; objectification of other in, 5; redemptive possibilities in, 40–41; scapegoating in, 17, 195–198, 202–207; and violence, 6, 35, 39. *See also* Arabs; Aum Shinrikyō; fundamentalism/fundamentalists; Hitler, Adolf; Islam/Muslims; Japan; Nazism/Nazis; Nilus, Sergei; paranoia/paranoid mindset; Russia

Arab-Israeli conflict, 229. *See also* Israeli-Palestinian conflict

Arabs: apocalyptic paranoia, 19, 230, 233–237, 247n20; conspiracism of, 13, 229; embrace of *Protocols*, 3, 183, 219, 229, 235–236; imperialist ambitions, 233–234, 235; Six-Day War, 13, 109. *See also* Palestinians/Palestinian Authority

Arafat, Yasser, 17

Arendt, Hannah, 94, 223

Ariosophy, 113, 129n24

Aron, Raymond, 100, 102, 104, 105–106

Aryan-Jewish eschaton, 11–12, 120–127

Aryan Nations groups, 190–191

Aryans: mythology of, 127n2; in Theosophy, 167. *See also* Aryan-Jewish eschaton

Asahara Shōko, 147

Athenians to the Melians (dialogue), 3, 24, 25, 28, 230

Augustine, 24, 51, 53

Aum Shinrikyō: apocalyptic paranoia of, 6, 13, 39, 42; genocidal hatred toward Jews, 14, 146–147, 151n54; terrorist atrocities, 13, 146

Balashov, Dmitrii, 86

barbarianism, 108

Drumont, Edouard, *La France juive*, 92
Dualism, 208
Duggan, Jeremiah, 207–208
Dugin, Aleksandr, 87
Duke, David, 181
Dyer, Charles H., 200

Eckart, Dietrich: apocalyptic paranoia of, 116–117, 118, 126, 129*n*19–20; as mentor to Hitler, 114, 126, 130*n*33. *See also Bolshevism from Moses to Lenin: Dialogue between Hitler and Me* (Eckart)
Eco, Umberto, 79, 87
Eisenmenger, Johann Andreas, 54
Eisner, Kurt, 112
Eisner, Will, 79
El-Amin, Mustafa, 201
Emanuel, Rahm, 180
endism, 41
Enlightenment, 102, 103
Esterhazy, Ferdinand, 9, 97–98
evangelicals. *See* conspiracy theories
Evans, Michael D., 200
Exodus, 121–122

fanaticism: medieval roots of, 107–108; modern, 10, 101–103, 104, 108. *See also* conspiracy theories
Farrakhan, Louis, 16, 180
Federal Council of Churches of Christ in America, 174
Feder, Gottfried, 114
Ferguson, Walter K., 49
Ficino, Marsilio, 52–53
Florenskii, Pavel, 83
Ford, Henry: anti-Semitic newspaper columns, 15, 173–177; apology for columns, 152, 176, 184*n*19; embrace and dissemination of *Protocols,* 173–174, 176; as Freemason, 178; *The International Jew,* 176, 179; libel suit by Aaron Shapiro, 176–177
France: anti-Semitism of, 92. *See also* Dreyfus Affair; French Revolution
Frank, Hans, 114
Freemasons, 178, 184*n*5, 188, *195, 196,* 201, 203

French Revolution: as ideological betrayal, 4, 27, 106; Jewish manipulation of, 122; triumph of Restoration over, 31
Freud, Sigmund, on paranoia, 35, 37–38
Friedman, Thomas, 13
Fromm, Erich, 4, 31
Fuhrmann, Horst, 56
fundamentalism/fundamentalists: apocalyptic paranoia of, 35, 39–40, 43; conspiracy theories of, 199–200, 205, 206–207
Furet, Francois, 106

Gadamer, Hans-Georg, 101
Gautier de Coinci, 68
genocide, 14, 41. *See also* Holocaust; *Warrant for Genocide* (Cohn)
German Worker's Party, 113–114
Germany: early aristocracy, 24; fanaticism, 102, 104; nihilism, 104; post-World War I, 102, 104, 112–114, 117, 221. *See also* Nazism/Nazis; Thule Society of Ariosophists
Gibson, Mel, 18, 183
Glaber, Rodulf, 65, 71
Glazunov, Ilia, 86
Gnosticism, 17, 105, 110*n*21
Godwin, Joscelyn, 167
Goebbels, Joseph, 87
Goedsche, Hermann. *See Biarritz* (Goedsche)
Goldstein, Paul, 143, 150*n*44
Golovinsky, Mathieu, 92
Goodman, David, 12–13, 135–151
Goodrick-Clarke, Nicholas, 167
Gorenberg, Gershom, 200
Gougenot des Mousseaux, Henri, 95, 108
Graus, František, 71
Greenspan, Alan, 180
Gregory, Dick, 200
Grenier, Jean, 108
Griffin, David Ray, 206
Griffin, G. Edward, 199
Gritz, Bo, 204
Guérin, Jules, 94
Guillaume de Nangis, 64, 65

Japan: apocalyptic paranoia of, 137–138, 147, 149*n*15; embrace of *Protocols,* 12–13, 135–137, 140, 141, 142–147, 148*n*3–4; gift of *Protocols* to Hebrew University, 27, 33*n*18; millenarian beliefs, 138–140, 143, 147; philo-Semitic views, 12–13, 141–142, 151*n*50. *See also* Aum Shinrikyō
Jaspers, Karl, 104
Jenkins, Jerry B., 200
Jesus Sananda, 166
Jews/Judaism: belief in discipline of power, 24, 32*n*2; demonization in early modern era, 6–7, 54; equating with Nazis, 2, 229, 230, 244*n*2–4, 245*n*6; risk of reducing to innocuousness, 95–96, 239; self-criticism by, 232–237, 241–243, 245*n*10, 247*n*28; sincerity in facing modern world, 241, 242; success in modernity, 30–31, 239–241; true vs. false, 164, 165. *See also* anti-Semitism; Christian anti-Judaism; conspiracy stories; conspiracy theories; Israel; Judeophobia; Qabbalah; rabbinic literature; stereotypes of Jews; Talmud
Joachim of Fiore, 41
John Birch Society (JBS), 198–199, 203
John de Oxenedes, 62
John of Kronstadt, 80, 85
John of Patmos, 41
Joly, Maurice, 9, 92, 94. See also *Dialogue in Hell between Machiavelli and Montesquieu*
Jones, James, 41
Joshua 6, 122, 130*n*36
Judaism. *See* Jews/Judaism
Judeophobia: neo-Nazi, 187, 190–191, 197, 203; ongoing spread of, 238; Russian, 81–82
Juenger, Ernst, 221
Jung, Carl, 44*n*10

Kafka, Franz, 223
Kant, Immanuel, 103
Kartashev, Anton, 89*n*13
katéchon, 8, 83, 89*n*15
Katz, Jacob, 54
Katz, Steven T., 1–20, 89*n*20, 92
Keller, Catherine, 40–41

Kelly, Michael, 196, 203
Khazar Jews, 165
King, Dennis, 192
Kiš, Danilo, 79
Kita Ikka, 140
Klein, Naomi, 206
Koestler, Arthur, 102, 108, 165
Kohn, Hans, 102
Kreis, August, III, 190
Kuniaiev, Stanislav, 86

LaHaye, Tim, 200
Landes, Richard, 1–20, 19, 23–33, 51, 71, 229–250
Lane, Mark, 201
Langmuir, Gavin, 64, 107
Lanz von Liebenfels, 113, 129*n*24
La Penca bombing case, 201–202, 204
LaRouche, Lyndon: distribution of conspiracy literature, 182, 192–193, 203, 204; fraud trial, 143
LaRouche network, 192–193, 203, 204, 207–208
Lazare, Bernard, 96
the Left, criticism of Israel, 230–232, 242–243, 245*n*10, 248*n*40
Left Behind book series, 40, 91*n*31, 200
Le Goff, J., 50
Levin, Marc, 3
Levi-Strauss, Claude, 108
Levy-Bruhl, Lucien, 101
Liberation Theologians, 40
Liberty Lobby, 143, 150*n*40, 203, 204
Libya, 234
Lifton, Robert Jay: on nuclearism, 42; on paranoia, 6, 17, 35, 39, 43*n*7; on thought reform, 45*n*23
Lindsey, Hal, 143, 207
Lipstadt, Deborah, 16, 18, 172–185, 181–182
List, Guido von, 113
Lorentzen, Lois Ann, 40
Losev, Aleksei, 89*n*21
Lotter, Michael, 113
Lukacs, G., 108
Luther, 53
Luther, Martin, 145

nihilism, 101, 104

Nilus, Sergei: apocalyptic interpretation of *Protocols,* 7–8, 80–85, 87, 89*n*13, 89*n*17, 108, 115; belief in ultimate salvation of Jews, 83–84, 87; bio, 79–80, 84; on Jewish star, 129*n*27; on *Protocols* as forgery, 8, 96, 97, 98; recent Russian rediscovery of, 84–85; rejection of modernity, 115; and Serafim of Sarov, 80, 115; writings, 80–81, 86, 89*n*17, 108, 115

North Korea, 42

nuclearism, 42

nuclear weapons, 41–43

Nuremberg pogram of 1349, 63

Obama, Barack, conspiracy theories about, 186, 196, 198, 199

Ohta Ryu, 144–146

Olcott, Henry Steel, 166

Otto of Freising, 71

Ōhashi Totsuan, 137–138, 149*n*15

Palamarchuk, Petr, 86

Palestine Liberation Organization (PLO), 12

Palestinians/Palestinian Authority: anti-Semitic political cartoons, 157–159; anti-Semitism among academics, 153–157; demonization of Israel, 19, 230, 236, 237, 248*n*32; embrace of *Protocols,* 13–14, 152, 153, 154–157, 160; genocidal hatred toward Jews, 13, 14; oppressiveness toward own people, 230, 236; Oslo Peace Process, 14, 237. *See also* Israeli-Palestinian conflict

paranoia/paranoid mindset: as adaptive, 36, 43; characteristics of, 5–6, 35–36; historical crisis as trigger, 35; links with intelligence, 5, 36; moving from passive to apocalyptic, 29–31; and "paranoid imperative," 4, 25, 230; as projection of one's inner sense of evil, 25, 36–38, 44*n*10; suffering of, 38–39; treatment of, 35, 36, 37–39; and victimhood, 6, 39; violence of, 38–39. *See also* apocalyptic paranoia

Passion of the Christ (film), 18, 183

Patriot Movement, 199

Paul (apostle), 82, 83

Paulus Christianus, 52

Peñaforte, Raymond da, 51

Pfefferkorn, Johannes, 53

Pico della Mirandola, Giovanni, 52–53

Picquart, Lieutenant-Colonel, 9, 97

Pierce, William, 190

Pipes, Daniel, 13, 29

Pipp, Edwin G., 176

Plato: critique by Karl Popper, 32*n*15; on democracy, 4; on justice, 26, 32*n*6; on noble lies, 8; *The Republic,* 26, 32*n*6

Platonov, Oleg, 86

PLO (Palestine Liberation Organization), 12

The Plot: The Secret Story of the Protocols of the Elders of Zion (Eisner), 79

Poland, 108–109

Poliakov, Leon, *History of Anti-Semitism,* 101

political religion, 10, 105. *See also* secular religion

Popper, Karl, 32*n*15, 101

Post, Jerrold, 35

postmodernism, 229

The Project, 29

Protocols of the Elders of Zion: authorship of, 87*n*1, 92; English translation, 10, 128*n*10, 190; as forgery, 1, 8, 9, 26, 96, 114, 164, 168, 187; on Internet, 209*n*8; Jews portrayed as demopaths in, 4, 25–28, 34, 51, 87*n*1, 93, 115, 190–195; as justification for genocide of Jews, 1, 28–29, 34, 92, 127, 208; medieval roots of, 7, 49–54, 56, 66, 72, 107–108, 109; modern revival and spread, 2–3, 109, 114, 128*n*10, 147, 232–239; origins of, 87*n*1; plagiarized sources for, 4, 92–95, 114–115; post-World War II banishment of, 1–2; publication of, 87*n*1; as response to modernity, 10, 49, 100–109; as stigmatized knowledge, 15, 168–170. *See also* apocalyptic paranoia; conspiracy theories; *Protocols* in America; *Warrant for Genocide* (Cohn)

Lightning Source UK Ltd.
Milton Keynes UK
UKHW010040130521
383642UK00007B/310